THE DIFFICULT PATIENT
IN GROUP

THE DIFFICULT PATIENT
IN GROUP

Group Psychotherapy with Borderline and Narcissistic Disorders

edited by

BENNETT E. ROTH, Ph.D.,
WALTER N. STONE, M.D.,
and
HOWARD D. KIBEL, M.D.

Monograph 6
AMERICAN GROUP PSYCHOTHERAPY ASSOCIATION
MONOGRAPH SERIES
Series Consulting Editor:
Walter N. Stone, M.D.

INTERNATIONAL UNIVERSITIES PRESS, INC.

Madison   Connecticut

Library of Congress Cataloging in Publication Data

The difficult patient in group : group psychotherapy with borderline and narcissistic disorders / edited by Bennett E. Roth, Walter N. Stone, and Howard D. Kibel.
     p.   cm.—(Monograph series / American Group Psychotherapy Association: monograph 6)
  Includes bibliographical references.
  ISBN 0-8236-1286-4
  1. Borderline personality disorder—Treatment. 2. Narcissism—Treatment. 3. Group psychotherapy. I. Roth, Bennett E.
II. Stone, Walter N. III. Kibel, Howard D. IV. Series: Monograph series (American Group Psychotherapy Association): monograph 6.
  [DNLM: 1. Narcissism. 2. Personality Disorders—therapy.
3. Psychotherapy, Group. W1 M0559PU monograph 6 / WM 430 D569]
RC553.N36D54   1990
616.85'85—dc20
DNLM/DLC
for Library of Congress   89-24407
                                             CIP

Manufactured in the United States of America

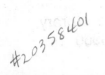

Contents

Contributors

Howard A. Bacal, M.D., F.R.C.P.(C), is a training analyst at the Toronto Institute of Psychoanalysis, and Associate Professor in the Department of Psychiatry, University of Toronto, Toronto, Ontario, Canada.

Serena-Lynn Brown, M.D., Ph.D., is Assistant Professor in the Department of Psychiatry, Albert Einstein College of Medicine, and Director, Psychopharmacology Clinic, Albert Einstein College of Medicine/Bronx Municipal Hospital Center, Bronx, New York.

Eugenio Gaburri, M.D., Ph.D., is a training psychoanalyst at the Italian Institute of Psychoanalysis, Milan, Italy.

Susan Hannah Hull, Ph.D., is in private practice in El Paso, Texas.

David E. K. Hunter, Ph.D., A.C.S.W., is Assistant Clinical Professor in the Department of Psychiatry, Yale University School of Medicine, New Haven, Connecticut, and Director, Inpatient and Partial Hospitalization Division, Greater Bridgeport Mental Health Center, Bridgeport, Connecticut.

Sigmund W. Karterud, M.D., is Clinical Director, Psychiatric Department B, Ulleval University Hospital, Oslo, Norway.

Howard D. Kibel, M.D., is Associate Professor of Clinical Psychiatry at Cornell University Medical College, and Coordinator of Group Psychotherapy at the New York Hospital–Cornell Medical Center, Westchester Division, in White Plains, New York.

Robert H. Klein, Ph.D., is Associate Professor in the Department of Psychiatry, Yale University School of Medicine, New Haven, Connecticut, and Director, Adult Individual and Group Psychotherapy, West Haven Mental Health Clinic, West Haven, Connecticut.

Jerome W. Kosseff, Ph.D., is a training analyst in the Group and Adult Departments, Postgraduate Center for Mental Health, New York, New York, and Adjunct Professor of Clinical Psychology at Teachers College of Columbia University, New York, New York.

Beatrice Liebenberg, M.S.W., is in private practice in Washington, D.C.

Andrew P. Morrison, M.D., is Assistant Clinical Professor of Psychiatry at Harvard Medical School, Boston, Massachusetts.

Malcolm Pines, D.P.M., is a member of the Group-Analytic Practice and the Institute of Group Analysis, and is a former consultant psychotherapist at Tavistock Clinic, London, England.

William E. Powles, M.D., is Emeritus Professor of Psychiatry at Queen's University, Kingston, Ontario, Canada.

Bennett E. Roth, Ph.D., is in private practice in New York City, New York.

Walter N. Stone, M.D., is Professor in the Department of Psychiatry at the University of Cincinnati College of Medicine, Cincinnati, Ohio.

Saul Tuttman, M.D., Ph.D., is Clinical Associate Professor of Psychiatry at the New York University School of Medicine, and is a training and supervising analyst and faculty member at the Division of Psychoanalytic Training, New York Medical College, New York, New York.

Isaac Zeke Youcha, C.S.W., is senior supervisor and training analyst, Group Therapy, at the Postgraduate Center for Mental Health, New York, and is Assistant Clinical Professor of Psychiatry at Albert Einstein College of Medicine, New York, New York.

Foreword

When the history of the recent analytic concern with borderline and narcissistic disorders is written, two salient aspects will likely be noted: the first is our lack of phenomenological understanding of these ego deviations and their developmental origin; the second is our theoretical grappling with the causes of the psychic turbulence they produce.

Group psychotherapy, as a distinct therapeutic modality, comprises many different theories. No comprehensive theory has yet emerged. Currently there are theories of group leadership, of interpretation, of group cohesion, of the individual in the group, of the group as a dynamic psychic entity, of group regression, and of the development of groups in society.

This volume appears at a stage in the development of group theory that must accommodate this plethora of theoretical perspectives. It therefore presents a range of thinking that stretches across the landscape of group-oriented treatments. These chapters, contributed by senior clinicians addressing different theoretical aspects of group treatment, may best be treated as a "good group" collection. Such a collection is not necessarily constructed to be read from start to finish. The sequence of chapters is determined by the editors, who make no claim that the book could not be ordered otherwise. This kind of book will appeal to the good reader, one willing to pick it up and sift through the various theoretical viewpoints, the descriptions of different kinds of groups conducted in various settings, to find what is most helpful. To aid this reader, each section has its own introduction.

Another way to approach this collection is to start with the table of contents and read the chapter that is most attractive. Finish it or not, then read another, read the one before or after. It can be read however one wishes. The reader who comes to value this book shares with its various authors a concern for the treatment and understanding of these patients. Some of what is written here may already have been learned from patients. Some of it, because it appears wrongheaded, soft, overly structured, or right on the mark, may challenge the reader to new formulations. That is what this collection is all about. We all light our own candle in the darkness of ignorance and that small light leads us toward understanding.

In these pages are to be found many worthwhile ideas, discoveries, and shared perspectives and experiences. We are particularly pleased that this book contains contributions from European colleagues working with similar patients, but from different theoretical perspectives. Whenever we work with these difficult patients in groups, it is comforting to know that there are like-minded group therapists over there who are struggling to comprehend and convey to us the same thorny issues in all their complexity.

Bennett E. Roth, Ph.D.
Walter N. Stone, M.D.
Howard D. Kibel, M.D.

Part I
Theory

Introduction

The most influential contributors to the theory of borderline and narcissistic disorders are Kohut and Kernberg. The integration of these theoretical perspectives and those of their followers into a comprehensive model applicable to the understanding of patient "behavior" in group psychotherapy is continuing to evolve. The diversity of available models only underscores the obvious—we have no theory that provides a complete explanation of the observable phenomena. The very nature of this pathology, which is thought to arise both from basic genetic givens and from interactions between the growing child and the milieu, particularly the mother, in the early months of life up to several years of age, is filled with complexities and with questions that have not been answered. The chapters in this section have been chosen because they contribute to a basic theoretical understanding of group dynamics. The seminal works of Freud and Bion are cited continually as fundamental building blocks and provide a foundation for a group theory that integrates with our knowledge of individual dynamics.

Tuttman (Chapter 1) begins the section with a review of psychoanalytic contributions to the understanding of group processes. Following a brief historical overview of the development of group psychotherapy, he examines the contributions of Freud and Bion. Tuttman observes that Freud's contributions focus primarily on oedipal and superego dynamics as these pertain to members' relationships with the leader. In this regard, Freud's emphasis was on a particular sector of group dynamics. By contrast, Bion, who wrote from a Kleinian perspective, examined also the question of attitudes

3

among members and to the group as a whole. More recent advances in ego psychology and object relations are reflected in hypotheses regarding the impact of group membership. It activates early object relations but also provides important stabilizing and reassuring influences. Within such a frame, regressions provide an opportunity to reexperience very early merger and union fantasies, while at later developmental levels the group is experienced as a transitional object and provides an opportunity to play (the latter notion is addressed more extensively in the chapter by Kosseff).

With this as a background, Tuttman reviews the theoretical positions of Kernberg and Kohut as regards the evolution of narcissistic and borderline pathology. In treatment, followers of Kernberg adopt a neutral interpretive stance with the goal of modifying partial self- and object representations that are unconscious, primitive, and dissociated. Followers of Kohut adopt an empathic stance and allow idealization and mirroring needs to emerge in the group setting. Through the inevitable frustrations of the group and through the patient's own restitutive efforts, the experience offers the opportunity to develop a more cohesive self. These contrasting positions are well drawn by Tuttman and provide an excellent backdrop for the entire volume.

In Chapter 2, Pines takes a theoretical position, in essence that of Foulkes, to the effect that the borderline's experiential world differs from that of the ordinary person, who has a deep sense of safety and is not constantly threatened with fragmentation or loss of cohesion as regards the self. Recognition of this deficit leads Pines to emphasize the importance of both internal and external boundaries in creating a sense of safety and an opportunity to grow. The group leader needs to establish clear boundaries between the group and the outer world as a critical step in establishing safety. Borderlines themselves are unable to contribute to boundary development, but can use it and will test it. In this model, rage may temporarily plug gaps in group boundaries but does not repair the inner emptiness of the individual.

Of equal significance in understanding these patients is the fact that their internal world is not differentiated—it lacks inner boundaries—and is experienced as blurred and confusing. Pines analogizes this lack of structural organization to the situation of a ship without bulkheads—a leak in one area is not contained and may flood the entire vessel. The development of inner boundaries is associated with the capacity to symbolize. The group comes to symbolize wholeness and the functions of containment. The group matrix, as represented by its culture, patterns of communication, and meaningful understandings, is the entity from which the borderline patient can internalize boundaries.

According to Karterud (Chapter 3), Bion's formulations of basic assumptions were a consequence of his ideas regarding members' perceptions of part object relationships and primitive fantasies about the content of the mother's body as embodied in the therapist and/or the group entity. In his studies with hospitalized and day hospital patient groups, in which he examined contemporaneous associations among basic assumptions, Karterud found that the fight-flight and pairing basic assumptions are significantly associated with one another, whereas fight-flight and dependency are inversely related. He suggests that Bion's theories are insufficient to explain these findings, which, according to Karterud, are concordant with the theoretical views of Chasseguet-Smirgel.

Karterud believes that Kohut's theories provide the best explanation of the data. Specifically, disappointment with a selfobject leader (the pairing basic assumption) is followed by restitutive efforts on the members' part as expressed in the fight-flight basic assumption. Self psychology explains prominent dependency behaviors as the expression of a wish to merge with the idealized leader or group.

In Chapter 4, Powles traces the history of the borderline concept and concludes that in many instances a definitive diagnosis may not be possible until the patient is engaged in the treatment process. His approach is based on the classical Freudian drive model as modified by the group focal conflict theory of Whitaker and Lieberman. This theory posits a disturbing motive (wish) that is countered by a reactive fear (anxiety) resulting in a compromise solution (defense). Powles illustrates the application of this theory with a vignette of a borderline patient's participation in a group. He concludes that the theory attempts to "make something simple, clear, manageable, and logical out of the complexities and ambiguities of borderline personalities and group psychotherapy, as against the horrifying fear that it can never be so, that all is flux and uncertainty!" The clinical example will doubtless evoke further discussion of group focal conflict theory.

Finally, in Chapter 5, Kosseff examines some of the elements involved in the induction of therapeutic change. Using a pithy automotive metaphor, Kosseff discusses two kinds of change, one similar to depressing the accelerator, the other to shifting gears.

Shifting, an order of change qualitatively different from mere acceleration, is accomplished through a mode of activity Kosseff describes as play. This type of relating and interacting, he argues, has been traditionally undervalued, ignored, or feared, and proves to be an important vehicle for internal change. Patients in a group gradually gain an understanding of their play and come to appreciate that objects in the group are both real and not real. For play to occur, the group must become a safe place in which to experiment, a development that takes time. Once this is achieved, play, as expressed in humor, wry remarks, and group metaphors carrying poignant messages, seems to arise spontaneously.

Kosseff adds that change is facilitated by pairings that arise from congruences between patients with similar developmental experiences and defensive operations. Together with play, these congruences serve as powerful stimulants to change; they go beyond insight and the interpretation of transferences. Kosseff's theory is sensitively illustrated with an extended clinical example linked to a clear exposition of the place of play in personality development and personal fulfillment. This overlooked dimension of human interaction may become a significant element in effecting change through the group therapy experience.

1

Principles of Psychoanalytic Group Therapy Applied to the Treatment of Borderline and Narcissistic Disorders

SAUL TUTTMAN, M.D., Ph.D.

The goal of this chapter is twofold: (1) to survey, in a historical context, the major concepts of psychoanalytic theory which may enhance the therapeutic effectiveness of group therapy as a treatment method; and (2) to consider the applicability of the psychoanalytic group therapy milieu in treating patients who suffer emotional developmental disorders (including borderline and narcissistic personalities).

A BRIEF EARLY HISTORY OF GROUP TREATMENT

The human species probably could not have survived its early beginnings were it not for cooperative group behavior. And yet some group activities (for example, war) have almost succeeded—and might yet—in obliterating it. Group dynamics and interactions have been influential throughout history. Ancient Greek drama (including the chorus), medieval morality plays and pilgrimages, eighteenth-century mesmerism, and innumerable social traditions and institutions (family, school, work) all involve varying degrees of group activity, much of it of a therapeutic nature.

The first practical use of groups in the United States involved imparting information to large groups of patients who during the first quarter of this century were coping with widespread tuberculosis. This method appeared to be more practical than addressing each patient singly. Pratt (1917) and Lazell (1921) decided independently that persuasion, reeducation, inspiring hope, and overcoming isolation could be accomplished by means of group activity. Meanwhile, in Europe, Jacob Moreno (1911) devised his "theater of spontaneity," which led eventually to psychodrama, a form of psychodynamic group therapy. In like manner, influenced by psychoanalytic insights, group analysis and psychoanalytic group psychotherapy emerged (Slavson, 1950; Wolf, 1950; Foulkes, 1964).

As psychoanalysis began to spread in this country, a small number of independent psychoanalysts and sociologists, among them Trigant Burrow (1927), Paul Schilder (1939), Leo Berman (1950), and David Rapaport (1959), expressed dissatisfaction with the psychoanalytic tradition of focusing almost solely upon the individual, in a manner that excluded social reality. One advantage of the group milieu is that the psychoanalyst who is experienced in groups has a better opportunity to understand the reality relationships of the patients the therapist treats individually (Berman, 1954). The group permits the study of psychoanalytic social psychology, as the private session facilitates the study of individual or intrapsychic dynamics. Rapaport (1959) concluded that when an exclusive blank screen model or countertransference conception of the therapist's role is overemphasized, analysts foreclose the development of a psychoanalytic theory of reality relations. Further, the analyst can be misled when relying solely on the patient's communications about the important events and persons in the course of reconstructing early history. These group-oriented analysts valued the group as a research medium much in the manner of Powdermaker and Frank (1953), who saw the group as an opportunity to conduct research and exploit processes of interaction among patients while the personal content unfolded in the group relationships.

Traditionally, psychoanalysts have conceived of action mainly in terms of "acting out." Berman (1949) considered it unfortunate that this moralistic connotation resulted in the neglect of studying and understanding "action" proper. Rapaport, Berman, and a few others in the 1950s tried to

> bridge the gap between the internal dynamics of the person which are revealed by psychoanalytic investigation and everyday actions in social reality which are directly observed. Since both of them seemed . . . accessible to observation in

the psychoanalytic group therapy situation, . . . [Berman] strove to demonstrate that psychoanalytic work with groups is the method by which this gap can be bridged and a psychoanalytic group psychology be built [Rapaport, 1959, p. 338].

In England, the Kleinian psychoanalyst Wilfred Bion was one of the first since Freud to offer new psychodynamic concepts relating to group dynamics. Bion (1959) was impressed by the fact that "the psychoanalytic approach, through the individual and through the group, is dealing with different facets of the same phenomena. The two methods provide the practitioner with a rudimentary binocular vision" (p. 8).

Early on, psychoanalytically inclined group therapists in the United States did not focus on or exploit group dynamics. They did find the group a potentially facilitating environment that encouraged catharsis. For example, Slavson (1950) believed a permissive group climate stimulates a benign regression in which early-life conflict can be relived in a stable, accepting environment. Although many today would agree with this notion, group factors afforded by the group situation—cohesiveness, for example—are considered of great potential advantage. Wolf (1950) began to practice psychoanalysis in groups quite effectively, *but not by treating the group.* For him, the group was a re-creation of the family in which the patient has an opportunity to "work through" unresolved problems. He still doubts the usefulness of group dynamics, but values the group as an atmosphere that catalyzes more profound analytic searching than is likely in individual treatment because the "group ego" offers support and facilitates deeper exploration. Each group member becomes a source of support and an experienced ancillary therapist.

PSYCHOANALYTIC THEORY IN RELATION TO GROUP THERAPY

Freud's one paper on group psychology (1921) contains many important formulations, although not one that *directly* addresses the therapeutic use of groups. Nevertheless, it has many implications for group therapy that are worthy of consideration. Influenced by Le Bon (1895) and McDougall (1920), Freud noted how group situations evoke a powerful emotional bond, and that the very structure of a group enhances the expression of previously repressed, unconscious, and primitive patterns. As a member of a psychological group, the individual acts differently from what would be expected in a state of isolation. A sort of group mind takes over which Le Bon characterizes as a sense of invincible collective power. This allows the group members to yield to instincts that would be under restraint were they not in a group; in a sense, each person becomes anonymous and nonresponsible. Further, this spirit is characteristically contagious and the members become highly suggestible. Le Bon thus described the group (for him, actually, the crowd) as an unstructured, spontaneous, and violent creature lacking critical faculties, in which feelings are very simple and exaggerated.

Freud recognized that these characteristics are similar to the affective life of children and neurotics, and to the qualities of dream productions. There is a predominance of fantasies and illusions born of unfulfilled wishes and an intensification of every emotional expression. These qualities of group behavior are pathognomonic of regressive unconscious phenomena. Le Bon had concluded that groups manifest a collective inhibition of intellectual functioning. Freud agreed that this may apply to groups of a short-lived character, such as a crowd, or to hasty conglomerates composed of various sorts of individuals. Nevertheless, he added, the group is often capable of creative genius, making profound use of unconscious forces (for example, those expressed in folklore, in music, and in language itself). He did not specify the conditions under which such higher-level manifestations occur.

Freud examined specialized groups (such as the church and the army) and concluded that the underlying group power is *libido*. All group members become bound by love of common ideals or of one another. Rage is externalized. They love the leader-father (Freud, 1913) and he in turn loves them like a father. The leader comes to replace each member's ego ideal. Should this idealized object be lost, panic and chaos ensue. Since at this time he was primarily concerned with developing structural concepts, Freud preferred to concentrate on the ego ideal and the process of identification rather than on problems regarding group psychology and its implications for psychotherapy.

Like Freud, most psychoanalysts have not pursued these matters, particularly not from the vantage point of their applicability to group treatment. Balint (1968), for one, expresses despair and consternation at this fact and considers that both psychoanalytic theory and group therapy have suffered as a consequence.

An examination of the literature on group therapy reveals how the neo-Freudian cultural and interpersonal schools and the various action-oriented group methods (T-groups, encounter groups, EST) have focused on the potential for treatment in the group modality, whereas until quite recently this treatment possibility was ignored, if not actually denigrated, by those primarily concerned with intrapsychic processes and structural change. Fortunately there are important exceptions, some of which will be reviewed below.

Bion (1959) studied the behavior, both manifest and latent, that may be observed in group situations. Using intuitions developed in psychoanalytic training and applying Kleinian hypotheses, he examined attitudes of the group toward him or another group member, as well as the attitudes of members toward the group itself. He noted a series of recurrent themes and episodes that have led to his propositions concerning group dynamics. First, every group meets to *do* something. The group is thus geared to a task in some way related to reality and attempts to use rational methods and cooperation. This aspect he called the "work group." Its characteristics are similar to those attributed by Freud to the ego, and Bion agreed with Freud and McDougall that under certain conditions work can be accomplished by the group: "When patients meet for group therapy sessions, some mental activity is directed to the solution of the problems for which the individuals seek help" (p. 144). But this work group activity is often obstructed or diverted by unconscious mental activities present in all participants. These powerful emotional drives and resistances spring from the unconscious basic assumptions Bion found to be prevalent in all groups.

In a therapeutic group, the analyst is automatically the work group leader (Bion, 1959). The emotional backing he can muster is subject to such factors as his skill in coping with the basic assumption at work in the group at a given time, as well as his ability to lead a work group. Interpretation serves the analyst-leader's purposes here. All group members instinctively participate in unconscious basic assumption activity, whereas work group functioning is not at all automatic. Realistic work in the group situation requires cooperation and reality testing. Bion concluded that psychoanalysis, or some extension of it, is essential to the exploration and interpretation of the underlying fantasies and basic assumptions. Since these unconscious assumptions provide both the fuel for group vitality and the resistance to work, they must be appreciated and harnessed by the working group. It is the purpose of the work group to translate needs, feelings, and thoughts into realistic behavior. Regarding the *psychoanalytic* work group, here the purpose is the psychoanalytic goal, that is, promoting growth via understanding and relating internal and external realities. The work group and the analyst-leader interact in terms of a therapeutic alliance, enhancing the observing egos' monitoring of archaic assumptions and eventually facilitating exploration of the underlying primitive sources at work.

Bion (1959) noted that all human beings are frightened of unconscious, primitive, part-object fantasy remnants that persist from the distorted perceptions of early life. Chaotic and extreme impulses and mental representations related to these archaic perceptions remain deeply buried in our psyches. In addition to these problems, people often find thinking and questioning painful and anxiety-provoking. Contemplating the unknown and questioning forces beyond our control which are outside our narcissistic sphere of influence arouses tension, apprehension, and dread. Bion concluded that group situations bring out the human psyche's difficulty in realistically comprehending and perceiving ourselves and others. Ever present themes deal with the archaic images of father, mother, or infant; with oedipal rivalry; and with the enigmatic, questioning Sphinx from whom disaster emanates. Whichever defensive assumptions become activated, they are reflective of deeply repressed fantasies of these early anxieties.

Whereas Freud (1921) related group functioning to family ties (and oedipal issues), Bion (1959) stressed preoedipal fantasies involving paranoid, schizoid, and depressive "Kleinian" features. He stated that the conscious experiencing of the emotions and fantasies underlying the basic assumptions is the greatest therapeutic opportunity the group affords. A healthy group or society may resemble Freud's oedipal group structure. But the more disturbed it is, the less the group can be understood on the basis of family patterns or neurotic behavior. "This does not mean I consider my descriptions apply only to sick groups. On the contrary, I very much doubt if any real therapy could result unless these psychotic patterns were laid bare with no-matter-what-group" (Bion, 1959, p. 144).

The primitive mechanisms of splitting and projective identification operate in group behavior. Analyzing and understanding these dynamics provides an opportunity for a profound "working through" of personality patterns that leads to meaningful therapeutic resolution. Bion used a Kleinian treatment method that stresses the exposing of primitive unconscious material without holding back strategically in terms of technical, structural considerations relating to defenses and resistances. Perhaps this orientation permitted him to enter a field which more reticent orthodox analysts avoided. Therapeutic interaction with groups often involves eruptive potential. It is an almost universal observation that group situations evoke regressive, primitive manifestations.

While Bion had worked with the archaic within the framework of unstructured small *therapy* groups, the majority of classical psychoanalysts who have studied group phenomena psychoanalytically have concentrated on group psychology as it relates to social institutions or violent mobs and crowds. Psychoanalytic concepts are used to better understand social phenomena or to illustrate the psychic mechanisms at work in them.

In recent years, with the greater focus on psychological developmental issues, "Freudian" analysts have become more concerned with the earliest preoedipal features. Emphasizing structural and developmental considerations, their current reports regarding group behavior stress primitive self-object relationships and early mechanisms underlying group dynamics. The contributions of Greenacre (1972) and Peto (1975) on the psychoanalytic study of crowds and their violent behavior present penetrating hypotheses regarding early psychic processes manifested in certain group situations.

"In understanding this process," writes Greenacre, "we must realize that the introjective-projective reaction leading ultimately to individuation, characteristic of the early stages of life, is never lost and may be revived with special strength in any situation of stress sufficient to cause a feeling of helplessness . . ." (pp. 143–144). She comments on Freud's concern about the

> relations of the leader to individual members of the group in terms of libido theory, with the emphasis on oedipal relationship involved. It was a period in which ego psychology in the terms in which we now know it had not yet been enunciated. A number of his footnotes, however, make suggestions regarding the processes going on in individual members of large groups in terms of early identifications

essentially belonging to the period of separation and individuation, but then referred to simply as characteristic of the
oral phase [p. 154].

In her analysis of crowds and crisis, Greenacre applies psychoanalytic
insights, much as Freud had fifty years earlier, to illustrate the
powerful emotional influence of group behavior on individual psychological states. In addition, Greenacre makes use of Freud's later
structural concepts and ego psychological constructs. She contem-
plates sociological aspects and political possibilities, but nowhere in
her interesting study does she pursue the issue of implications for
treatment.

In 1975, Andrew Peto, focusing on group behavior during crowd
violence, explored the nature of regression in relation to body image
and the archaic superego. He described the dissolution of ego
boundaries and the self, the regression of ego and superego in certain
group situations. In other articles, Peto (1960, 1967) refers to the
therapeutic potential of fragmentation, the experience and reintegration of archaic manifestations; as for group function, however, he
emphasizes (as do Greenacre and Freud) an interest in the further
understanding of social psychology and of particular dynamic developmental and regressive processes, while voicing no concern with the
therapeutic potentials or implications for group treatment.

The more recent writings of Freudian analysts interested in
group phenomena (Saravay, 1975; Kernberg, 1976) refer to group
therapeutic process in terms of transference reactions, modifications
in intrapsychic organization, interpersonal relationships, and object
relations.

I have observed (Tuttman, 1984a, 1985) and others (Anthony,
1972; Rutan and Stone, 1984) have reported that the dyadic therapeutic process may be dramatically accelerated when group therapy
sessions are part of the treatment program. One pragmatic application of analytic treatment in conjunction with group therapy is
suggested by Kernberg (1983), who puts forward the hypothesis that
individual treatment activates object relations at the "higher level" of
the transference neurosis, whereas group interaction tends to arouse
regression to "primitive level," preoedipal object relations; further,
the more unstructured the group, the more likely the emergence of
primitive fantasies. I wish to add an additional observation—that the
group often provides structure, support, encouragement, and feed-

back conducive to growth. A cohesive working group situation offers not only a "regressive pull" but also a progressive potential. I consider Kernberg's hypothesis both useful and limiting. Although the group situation can activate primitive, unconscious "basic assumptions" (Bion, 1959) that are agitating though therapeutically useful, it also provides important stabilizing and reassuring influences. Among these are the group's holding or facilitating environment and its provision of transitional experiences and objects, emotional play, realistic feedback, exposure to the clash of inner worlds, and confrontations in a safe and structured matrix.

Comparing the probable impact of different therapeutic conditions permits us to enlarge our repertoire of helpful strategies and to select appropriate modalities to deal with different levels of psychic conflict according to the nature of the individual's pathology and relevant issues of phase specificity and fixations. The recent work of Durkin (1983), Horwitz (1983, 1984), and Stein and Kibel (1984) lend further credibility to this viewpoint.

Fried (1954, 1982) and Glatzer (1960, 1962, 1975) illustrate, by case examples, the therapeutic potential of psychoanalytic group therapy. Durkin (1964) and Scheidlinger (1968) recognized rather early on that in group therapy the "group-as-a-whole" focus and an individual analytic focus are complementary rather than contradictory.

Scheidlinger (1980), in his extensive writings on identification in small groups and regression in group therapy, has described both contemporary-dynamic and genetic-regressive levels. The first level, he proposed, pertains to conscious needs and ego-adaptive patterns, group roles, and the network of attractions and repulsions, as well as to group structure. On this level, the group is viewed by the member as a means of belonging, learning, and gaining personal satisfactions. The genetic-regressive level, by contrast, involves unconscious and preconscious motivations, defensive patterns and conflicts, and phenomena such as transference, countertransference, resistance, identification, and projection. This level will more likely emerge under regressive conditions, which tend to lift repression and expose deeper needs and emotions. Scheidlinger (1974) suggested that on an archaic symbolic level the group represents the nurturing mother. He has hypothesized (1980) that the universal human need to belong, to establish a state of psychological unity with others, represents a covert wish to restore an earlier state of unconflicted well-being inherent in the exclusive union with the mother. Long ago he observed that group therapy patients whose early deprivations have resulted in ego disturbance and identity diffusion often perceive a supportive group in a manner that enhances their opportunities for ego repair; the group may serve as a bridge to reality and to more mature object relationships (Scheidlinger, 1955).

Applying Winnicott's concepts (1951) and Greenacre's focus on ego psychology (1971), Kosseff (1975) suggests that the group situation, since if offers some of the functions of a "transitional object," may at times be "a tangible symbol of a relationship undergoing change" (p. 352); emancipatory possibilities are present as well as the ongoing availability of support. "By its very plasticity the transitional object allows a multidirectional bridge to extend to objects which may provide further appropriately random playful activity. . . . Play, which then gains the value of primitive experiment and reality testing, leading to knowledge . . . seems to precede each new maturational achievement" (pp. 344–345).

I recognize (Tuttman, 1980) the "transitional object" or "phenomena" aspects of the group situation; however, I consider the differences between the "transitional object" and the group to be worthy of consideration. Winnicott's original formulation (1951) refers to the soft, moldable quality of transitional objects, which the child relates to as part "me" and part "not me." The group situation often has such soft aspects. (For example, a group patient recently stated, "Where else can I share so freely with others my very personal feelings and have them accepted?") Yet at other times there appears the open clash of inner worlds. When a group member needs another member to be his "selfobject" and to accommodate completely, there frequently ensues a tug-of-war between conflicting needs. A power struggle and fight for control may develop. I consider such interactions to be "hard" rather than "soft" phenomena. Either eventuality may be helpful or traumatic, depending on phase specificity and other dynamic factors. Although there may be a painful clash, traumatic consequences are often muted by the relatively protected environment of the group therapy situation, which offers group members the opportunity for trial and error behavior and practicing.

Winnicott's concept of "play" and a "space between" (1971) are applicable to group therapy. The group may offer a "good enough facilitating environment," which is partly a transitional extension of the analyst and partly an autonomous venturing into areas which some patients can utilize on behalf of growth.

In recent years, an increasing number of psychoanalytically oriented group practitioners have discovered such therapeutic opportunities in the group therapy modality. Among them are James (1982) and Schlachet (1984), who recognize, as have Kosseff (1975) and myself (Tuttman, 1980), that a therapeutic opportunity is available to the patient in group that can provide growth-conducive conditions as understood by Winnicott. This can be particularly useful as the patient works through separation problems (along the symbiosis-individuation continuum) in relation to the analyst with whom he has worked both individually and in group.

Another benefit that psychoanalytic group therapists appreciate is specific to the treatment of difficult patients suffering serious developmental character pathology. The intensity of the "split-off" rage in borderline and narcissistic patients and their consequent tendency to develop negative therapeutic reactions have been observed in individual treatment (Tuttman, 1980, 1985). Group therapy as a supplement to individual sessions can operate as one means of "working through" such problems. For example,

> when patient P experiences the "neutral" analyst's interpretations about P's rage as though the analyst was a "bad object" assaulting P and "accusing" P of badness, aggression, etc., the analyst's objective may have been constructively intended and theoretically clear, but P either fights off the interpretation, experiencing it as denigrating, or incorporates the subjectively experienced "sadistic assault." He may "exploit" it masochistically against himself. In such a predicament, the group situation permits a variety of alternative "scenarios." For example, in a therapeutic group, the negative transference is often "split" and may be displaced from the analyst onto one or more group "siblings," permitting an ongoing therapeutic alliance with the analyst. The rage displaced onto others will induce a counterreaction in group members. As the pattern is repeated (and it usually is), the group responses provide feelings, interpretations and feedback. The analyst is able to maintain a more effective, neutral analytic stance, acknowledging the perceptions of each participant and bringing perspective to the patient's struggle.

Thus, P's behavior is understood in dynamic and historical terms and a "working through" is facilitated. At the same time, a negative therapeutic reaction is avoided and often the individual sessions can proceed more classically without impediment or stalemate [Tuttman, 1980, pp. 227–228].

In a related way, the group becomes an excellent arena for working out problems created by the mechanism of projective identification, so frequently utilized by the borderline patient.

A further advantage offered by the group situation is the opportunity for consensual validation and mirroring. The reactions of other group members are often very valuable to a patient in gaining understanding and perspective. Further, the group therapist is afforded a chance to observe the patient's interaction with others. This provides a kind of data different from the patient's subjective reports and introspections. (For a more thorough elaboration of the ways in which psychoanalytic concepts are applied therapeutically in the group milieu, see Tuttman, 1985, 1986.)

TREATING BORDERLINE AND NARCISSISTIC PATIENTS BY PSYCHOANALYTIC GROUP THERAPY

The psychodynamic theories of two noted psychoanalysts have increasingly been used in individual, modified psychoanalytic therapy and in psychoanalytic group treatment. The theories of Otto Kernberg (1975, 1976) focus on borderline conditions; those of Heinz Kohut (1968, 1971, 1977) on narcissistic pathology. In the recent past (Tuttman, 1978, 1984b), these theories of character pathology have been conceptualized, compared, and categorized in terms of the treatment stances they imply. Kernberg's treatment approach stresses the neutral interpretive stance of the analyst (encouraging insight and awareness), whereas Kohut stresses the empathic stance (encouraging a shared subjective view in a facilitating atmosphere).

KERNBERG'S TREATMENT OF BORDERLINE PATIENTS AND THE ROLE OF GROUP THERAPY

Based mainly on the theories of Anna Freud, Edith Jacobson, Melanie Klein, and Margaret Mahler, Kernberg proposed that in the course of normal development each individual goes through an early undifferentiated stage during which there is as yet no perception of internal psychological boundaries or of distinctions between self and others; that is, there are no delineated self- or object representations. The earliest mental distinctions are said to be made with respect to psychophysiological affect-laden engrams of the "all good" or the "all bad"; tension-reducing pleasures connected with a libidinal "all-good" core are set over against the "all-bad" core resulting from frustrating, traumatic, and aggressively toned states and reactions.

Under conditions of healthy emotional development the "all-good" and the "all-bad" cores become less polarized. The distinction of "self" and the appreciation of "other" as *separate* gradually become mentally differentiated. In time, the child comes to experience a stable, separate self-representation and a representation of others. Further, with maturity the qualities of the self and of others come to be sensed more realistically, as both good and bad.

Kernberg views the borderline patient as someone who has not been able to achieve these crucial internal psychological distinctions. It is the task of the analyst, he believes, to strive toward structural change in these patients. The goal of treatment is to help them internalize a more stable and delineated sense of self and a realistic, less polarized view of others.

For the dyadic treatment situation, Kernberg advocates a focus on the interpretation of transferences and resistances from a neutral position. (Underlying these resistances are repressed fantasies intimately related to primitive internalized representations of self and objects.) Kernberg contends that treatment can often modify the patient's personality, which has been dominated by internalized archaic self- and part-object representations. He concentrates on the patient's split-off aggressive components, especially projections and projective identifications that displace repressed rage.

The specific fixation point in the borderline personality is conceived as involving that early stage of psychic development when self- and object representations have been partly differentiated within the all-good core: hence "good self" and "good object" representations. Thus there is experienced, in one sense, a definite differentiation of the "good self" from the "good nonself." As a result, these patients can maintain a stable (if naive and unrealistic) sense of self that protects them from a chaotic, undifferentiated, psychotic state. However, such patients have not been able to differentiate the self from the archaic, fused "bad-self-and-object" representation. Consequently, such persons have no choice but to use primitive intrapsychic mechanisms in an attempt to externalize and get rid of the all-bad core. Often one finds in such patients an idealization of the "early" mother and the good self, in an effort to preserve the need for a good object, along with an expelling of the bad "selfobject" core via the mechanisms of splitting and projection. This is an attempt to rid the psyche of hate and aggression.

In this manner, the negatives have been "deported," but at a high price: an integrated sense of self is lacking, as is a balanced, empathic, unpolarized view of others. Such deficits interfere with a realistic "human"[1] conception of people, including oneself. The capacity for empathy and reality-oriented self-esteem regulation is severely limited, since the active dissociation of polar opposites results in a pathological split leading to extreme idealized and persecutory images. The projections and internalization of overwhelming hate can further sabotage healthy development. Paranoid distortions and subsequent reinforcement of bad self- and object images ensue, leading to ego weakness, identity diffusion, and faulty superego development.

In this approach to pathology and treatment, the task becomes to modify self- and object representations that are unconscious, primitive, dissociated, and partial. This requires great patience and skill. Negative therapeutic reactions frequently develop with these disturbed patients, as do stalemates in treatment.

Despite the patient's provocations, accusations, misperceptions, and projections, a sense of proportion of a therapeutic nature becomes more possible for the therapist who understands the dynamics involved here. Countertransference is more readily moderated when the pathological roots of the patient's "acting out" and distortions are appreciated. Of course, a great deal depends on the personality of the therapist; nevertheless, an understanding of the stereotypic "idealized" extremes that imprison the patient's mental life can help the therapist monitor the interactions and interpret therapeutically.

Since Kernberg's formulations (1975, 1976) for the individual treatment of borderline patients with psychoanalytically oriented therapy, dynamically inclined group therapists have extended his concepts to group situations, if only to better comprehend the

---

[1]"Human" in the sense of an appreciation of the subtle range of impulses and affects all human beings are heir to, in contrast to the naively extreme and polarized "all-good" heroes or "all-bad" villains of the old melodramas, in which there are "good guys and bad guys," "cops and robbers," "cowboys and Indians."

mechanisms involved in dealing with borderline group members, who are inclined to be provocative and "acting-out." Kernberg's perspective can be helpful regarding both countertransferential elements and technical interventions. An appreciation of recent contributions to the understanding of early self and object relationships and the pathology arising from them has expanded the group therapist's repertoire of working hypotheses and treatment strategies. Regarding group treatment directly, Kernberg (1983) has summarized his position in a recent article on group process. Implicit in his view of group therapy is a theory of treatment that combines individual and group methods in dealing with different levels of intrapsychic conflict. Bellak (1980), Porter (1980), Tuttman (1980, 1985), Wong (1980), and others have recognized the value of such combined treatment. For example, Grobman (1980) has reported the successful treatment of borderline pathology in groups for patients who were unable to be treated effectively in a one-to-one setting because of the "intimacy, intensity and primitive nature of the transference" (p. 299).

Bion (1959), the first psychoanalyst to apply Kleinian concepts (Segal, 1964) to group therapy, focused on archaic fantasy reactivation within the group-as-a-whole. His interpretations about group basic assumptions directed to the group-as-a-whole have been powerful and effective in delving into the primitive, unconscious, psychotic-like fantasies that erupt in the course of unstructured group interaction. Kernberg (1976, 1980), also very much influenced by Klein, has highlighted the archaic part-object representations of self and others, tinged with primitive libido and aggression that are ever present in borderline patients. He has demonstrated the typical mechanisms of splitting and projective identification that are used defensively by these patients.

This perspective can enable the group therapist to better monitor the defensive projections and underlying impulses and affects projected by one patient in the group onto other members and the leader. The intrapsychic world of each participant can be seen to "emigrate" across borders and thus become part of the interpersonal world. Sometimes one member's unconscious part-object mental representations clash and interact vividly with the projections of another. Here we have a veritable

Pandora's box—the externalization of a bedlam of chaotic, unrealistic, conflict-laden primitive worlds of intense love and hate which may burst forth in the treatment room like *Worlds in Collision*. On the other hand, meaningful growth may result when a gifted, experienced group leader can respond to those eruptions therapeutically: (1) by maintaining enough of a working alliance and exploring systematically with the group the rich and powerful forces at play [in the context of a neutral interpretive stance]; (2) by tracing back to developmental origins the intimate, intense needs and feelings; (3) by struggling together to communicate experiences and gain perspectives and insight into these archaic projections [Tuttman, 1984a, p. 44].

The more effectively the group leader can relate intimately to archaic material calmly and proportionately without overinterpreting or acting out, the greater the chance for a therapeutic modification of the patient's dynamics.

It is crucial that the group therapist appreciate the psychological dilemmas of the borderline patient including the need for the specific defensive maneuvers. It is helpful when the group therapist understands the developmental pathways of self and object delineation and the developmental vicissitudes of aggressive and libidinal drives as well as object seeking (Fairbairn, 1954). Such understanding fortifies the convictions and sensitivities of the group therapist which, in turn, facilitates opportunities in the group milieu for ventilation, channelization, interpretation, insight and meaningful growth [Tuttman, 1984a, pp. 44–45].

It is quite possible that the very structure of the group situation offers specific advantages for treating the borderline patient. Despite Kernberg's efforts (1975, 1976) to establish an alliance and interpret the patient's split-off rage in individual treatment in the hope of generating growth, his method often evokes resentment, guilt, and defensiveness. It is clear from his treatment reports that some of his patients experience the interpreting analyst as critical and accusatory. "The patient will hear, too often: 'Patient, you are bad. The hate is in you!' Thus a nonproductive and vicious cycle ensues, leaving the patient projecting hate, envy and rage—attributing it to the analyst—while the therapist interprets and appears to deposit hate, envy and rage into the patient" (Tuttman, 1984a, p. 45). The group situation provides an excellent alternative or complementary modality to individual treatment as a means of avoiding such nonproductive stalemates and negative therapeutic effects.

In the group treatment situation, group members sometimes experience another member's split-off rage and will offer interpretations. In such instances, the group leader need not be the bearer of narcissistically injurious or accusatory interpretations. Sometimes the therapist can acknowledge the value of the group's perceptions of a patient, by empathizing with his feelings and his history and exploring the possible sources of frustration and underlying rage.

Such interactions can help sensitize group members to themselves and each other and open the path toward deeper exploration of conflict-leader repressed material.

A sensitive group leader and an effective working group can enhance awareness among participants. A sense of cohesiveness gradually increases and the cauldron of overreactions and blind, split-off rage gradually becomes an alliance of more aware individuals.

In such ways, group therapy offers an opportunity to the therapist treating borderline states to apply psychodynamic theory productively.

KOHUT'S THEORY OF TREATING NARCISSISTIC PATHOLOGY AND THE ROLE OF GROUP THERAPY

Kohut's theory of narcissistic pathology and its treatment (1971, 1977) has influenced group therapy theory and practice. His psychoanalytic self psychology for treating narcissistic pathology differs dramatically from Kernberg's approach, though it should be noted that the two deal with different patient populations. Ferenczi, Balint, Sechehaye, Winnicott, Guntrip, and Jacobson had taken up the issues that interested Kohut, but he did not integrate his ideas with their contributions. Instead he developed systematically a singular, direct method for dealing with a very important psychological issue—namely, the need for each person to develop a cohesive sense of self and a healthy self-esteem. Although much of what he proposed is to be found in the work of others (a fact he did not acknowledge), his concepts are presented succinctly and eloquently, with clarity and rich applicability.

> Kohut contends that all human beings require an experience during early childhood where the caretaker serves as a "self-object"—that is, a phase during which the child is completely dependent upon someone who continually provides the experience that this ever-available object exists solely to satisfy the child's needs. If this has not been provided, narcissistic pathology results. Kohut's major proposal is: Narcissism has a separate line of development and the "self-object" phase is the crucial initial step followed by a series of essential experiential stages leading to mature and healthy narcissism.
>
> As the child matures beyond the need for a self-object, the stage of idealization ensues during which time the grandiose self emerges. Following this, a mirroring stage occurs. Finally mature, narcissistic health is possible as reflected by a sense of cohesiveness and self-esteem [Tuttman, 1984a, p. 46].

If a youngster felt the security of having adequately experienced a self-object; if there was sufficient opportunity to idealize a parent figure and to internalize a viable source of identification so as to feel like the "grandiose self" for an adequate period; if empathy has provided enough sensitive mirroring of the child's needs and feelings—then narcissistic maturation will evolve naturally over time. According to Kohut, treatment can make up for deficiencies in the evolution of the self. The function of the therapist is to provide empathically the longed-for responses, the deprivation of which has stalemated narcissistic development of the self. In good enough treatment, patients are offered the opportunity to experience idealizing and mirroring transferences. The analyst's function is not to interpret resistances or to explain behavior. Rather, it is to provide understanding and empathy.[2]

---

[2]One countertransference factor that can interfere with effective treatment occurs when the analyst's unresolved issues about grandiosity result in analyst discomfort; this leads to premature analysis of the patient's idealizing need, rather than working through at a pace in accord with the patient's needs.

Unlike Kernberg, who focuses upon the patient's aggression as an important factor in psychopathology, Kohut considers aggression to be a disintegration product of frustration and deprivation rather than a drive that creates conflicts and symptoms. Kohut contends that the main therapeutic thrust results from identification with the empathic analyst, which leads to transmuting internalizations and personality change.

Stone and Whitman (1977), Kosseff (1980), Tuttman (1980, 1984a), Harwood (1983), and Bacal (see Chapter 8) have reported that group therapy can be helpful to narcissistic patients. I feel some hesitation in recommending group therapy for self pathology until after the patient has experienced idealizing and mirroring transferences in dyadic treatment. When a therapeutic alliance exists with the individual analyst, I believe it can prove advantageous to work, preferably with the same therapist, in group treatment. Otherwise, those who were deprived of needed attention and support in early life, often

> find it difficult to utilize a group therapeutically given the shared attention and frequent clash of needs. A group therapist who understands Kohut's concerns may facilitate the introduction of a narcissistic patient into group treatment. Narcissistic injuries are so easily aroused in the group! This can be bearable, indeed productive, when the leader has the capacity to encourage the availability of self-objects (in the person of the leader or the entire group of compatible members), when there is potential for an idealizing transference, and when the capacity to tolerate manifestations of a grandiose self and opportunities for mirroring are available [Tuttman, 1984a, p. 47].

Despite the possibility of added tension and anxieties for the narcissistic patient in group therapy, the very situation provides a "natural" medium for supplying support and mirroring. Over the course of working together in a group, members come to appreciate each other's histories, language, symbols, patterns of behavior, philosophies, and sensitivities. Respect, understanding, and reciprocity often develop with time. Since narcissistic patients have often experienced isolation and preoccupations that "close" them off from the inner worlds of others, the group can open lines of exchange and

commun-
ication. Since this can prove frightening as well as exhilarating, the
leader's skill and availability for support and insight and for transla-
tion of needs and feelings can be important and facilitating.

CONCLUSIONS

Group psychotherapy has become increasingly effective as a
therapeutic method, as the understanding of group dynamics and
psychoanalytic theories of early developmental processes have been
applied to treatment in groups. Opportunities and advantages inherent in the group milieu can aid the therapist who works with patients
suffering difficult-to-treat, tenacious developmental character pathology, including narcissistic and borderline conditions.

REFERENCES

Anthony, E. J. (1972), The history of group psychotherapy. In: *The Evolution
of Group Therapy*, Vol. 2, ed. H. I. Kaplan & B. J. Sadock. New York:
Aronson, pp. 1–26.
Balint, M. (1968), *The Basic Fault*. London: Tavistock.
Bellak, L. (1980), On some limitations of dyadic psychotherapy and the role
of group modalities. *Internat. J. Group Psychother.*, 1:7–22.
Berman, L. (1949), Countertransference and attitudes of the analyst in the
therapeutic process. *Psychiat.*, 12:159–166.
————(1950), Psychoanalysis and group psychotherapy. *Psychoanal. Rev.*,
37:156–163.
————(1954), Psychoanalysis and the group. *Amer. J. Orthopsychiat.*, 24:421–
425.
Bion, W. (1959), *Experiences in Groups*. New York: Basic Books.
Burrow, T. (1927), The group method of analysis. *Psychoanal. Rev.*, 14:268–
280.
Durkin, H. (1964), *The Group in Depth*. New York: International Universities
Press.
————(1983), Developmental levels: Their therapeutic implications for analytic group psychotherapy. *Group*, 7:3–10.
Fairbairn, W. R. D. (1954), *An Object-Relations Theory of the Personality*. New
York: Basic Books.
Foulkes, S. H. (1964), *Therapeutic Group Analysis*. New York: International
Universities Press.
Freud, S. (1913), *Totem and Taboo*. London: Hogarth Press, 1950.
————(1921), Group psychology and the analysis of the ego. *Standard Edition*,
18:69–143. London: Hogarth Press, 1955.
Fried, E. (1954), The effect of combined therapy on the productivity of
patients. *Internat. J. Group Psychother.*, 4:42–55.
————(1982), Building psychic structures as a prerequisite for change.
Internat. J. Group Psychother., 32:417–430.

Glatzer, H. (1960), Discussion of symposium on combined individual and group psychotherapy. *Amer. J. Orthopsychiat.*, 30:243–246.

———(1962), Narcissistic problems in group psychotherapy. *Internat. J. Group Psychother.*, 12:448–455.

———(1975), The leader as supervisor and supervisee. In: *The Leader in the Group*, ed. Z. Liff. New York: Aronson, pp. 138–145.

Greenacre, P. (1971), *Emotional Growth*. New York: International Universities Press.

———(1972), Crowds and crisis: Psychoanalytic considerations. *The Psychoanalytic Study of the Child*, 27:136–155.

Grobman, J. (1980), The borderline patient in group psychotherapy: A case report. *Internat. J. Group Psychother.*, 30:299–318.

Harwood, I. (1983), The application of self-psychology concepts to group psychotherapy. *Internat. J. Group Psychother.*, 33:469–487.

Horwitz, L. (1983), Projective identification in dyads and groups. *Internat. J. Group Psychother.*, 33:259–279.

———(1984), The self in groups. *Internat. J. Group Psychother.*, 34:519–540.

James, D. C. (1982), Transitional phenomena and the matrix in group psychotherapy. In: *The Individual and the Group: Boundaries and Interrelations*, Vol. 1, ed. M. Pines & L. Rafaelson. New York: Plenum, pp. 645–661.

Kernberg, O. F. (1975), *Borderline Conditions and Pathological Narcissism*. New York: Aronson.

———(1976), *Object Relations Theory and Clinical Psychoanalysis*. New York: Aronson.

———(1980), *Internal World and External Reality*. New York: Aronson.

———(1983), Psychoanalytic studies of group processes: Theory and applications. In: *Psychiatry Update*, Vol. 2, ed. L. Grinspoon. Washington, DC: American Psychiatric Press, pp. 21–36.

Kohut, H. (1968), The psychoanalytic treatment of narcissistic personality disorder. *The Psychoanalytic Study of the Child*, 23:86–113.

———(1971), *The Analysis of the Self*. New York: International Universities Press.

———(1977), *The Restoration of the Self*. New York: International Universities Press.

Kosseff, J. (1975), The leader using object relations theory. In: *The Leader in the Group*, ed. Z. Liff. New York: Aronson, pp. 212–242.

———(1980), Symposium: The unanchored self. *Internat. J. Group Psychother.*, 4:387–446.

Lazell, E. W. (1921), The group treatment of dementia praecox. *Psychoanal. Rev.*, 8:168–179.

Le Bon, G. (1895), *The Crowd: A Study of the Popular Mind*. London: Fisher, Unwin, 1920.

McDougall, W. (1920), *The Group Mind*. Cambridge: Cambridge University Press.

Moreno, J. (1911), *Die Gottheit Als Komediart*. Vienna: Aszengurber Verlag.

Peto, A. (1960), On the transient disintegrative effect of interpretations. *Internat. J. Psycho-Anal.*, 41:413–417.

———(1967), Dedifferentiations and fragmentations during analysis. *J. Amer. Psychoanal. Assn.*, 15:534–550.

———(1975), On crowd violence: The role of archaic superego and body image. *Internat. Rev. Psycho-Anal.*, 2:449–466.

Porter, K. (1980), Combined individual and group psychotherapy: A review of the literature, 1965–1978. *Internat. J. Group Psychother.*, 1:107–114.

Powdermaker, F., & Frank, G. A. (1953), *Group Psychotherapy.* Cambridge, MA: Harvard University Press.

Pratt, J. H. (1917), The tuberculosis class: An experiment in home treatment. *Proceedings*, New York Conference on Hospital Social Services, 4:49–68.

Rapaport, D. (1959), *The Structure of Psychoanalytic Theory: A Systematizing Attempt.* Psychological Issues Monograph 6. New York: International Universities Press.

Rutan, J. S., & Stone, W. N. (1984), *Psychodynamic Group Psychotherapy.* Lexington, MA: Collamore.

Saravay, S. (1975), Group psychology and structural theory. *J. Amer. Psychoanal. Assn.*, 23:69–89.

Scheidlinger, S. (1955), The concept of identification in group psychotherapy. *Amer. J. Psychother.*, 9:661–672.

———(1968), Therapeutic group approaches in community mental health. *Social Work*, 13:87–95.

———(1974), On the concept of the "mother group." *Internat. J. Group Psychother.*, 24:417–428.

———(1980), *Psychoanalytic Group Dynamics: Basic Readings.* New York: International Universities Press.

Schilder, P. (1939), Results and problems of group psychotherapy in severe neurosis. *Mental Hygiene*, 23:87–98.

Schlachet, P. (1984), Paper presented at AGPA Annual Meeting, Dallas.

Segal, H. (1964), *Introduction to the Work of Melanie Klein.* New York: Basic Books.

Slavson, S. R. (1950), *Analytic Group Psychotherapy.* New York: Columbia University Press.

Stein, A., & Kibel, H. D. (1984), A group dynamic peer interaction approach to group psychotherapy. *Internat. J. Group Psychother.*, 34:315–334.

Stone, W., & Whitman, R. (1977), Contributions of the psychotherapy of self to group process and group therapy. *Internat. J. Group Psychother.*, 3:343–360.

Tuttman, S. (1978), Kohut symposium: "The Restoration of the Self." *Psychoanal. Rev.*, 65:624–629.

———(1980), The question of group therapy: From a psychoanalytic viewpoint. *J. Amer. Acad. Psychoanal.*, 8:217–234.

———(1984a), The applications of object relations theory and self-psychology in current group therapy. *Group*, 8(4):41–48.

———(1984b), The impact of psychoanalytic theories of conflict upon treatment. *J. Amer. Acad. Psychoanal.*, 12:491–509.

———(1985), *The Unique Opportunities Offered by Group Psychotherapy.* Group Therapy Monograph 12. New York: Washington Square Institute for Psychotherapy and Mental Heath.

———(1986), Theoretical and technical elements which characterize the American approaches to psychoanalytic group psychotherapy. *Internat. J. Group Psychother.*, 36:499–515.

Winnicott, D. W. (1951), Transitional objects and transitional phenomena. In: *Collected Papers.* New York: Basic Books, 1957, pp. 97–100.

————(1971), *Playing and Reality.* New York: Basic Books.

Wolf, A. (1950), The psychoanalysis of groups. *Amer. J. Psychother.,* 1:525–558.

Wong, N. (1980), Combined group and individual treatment of group borderline and narcissistic patients. *Internat. J. Group Psychother.,* 4:389–404.

2

Group Analytic Psychotherapy and the Borderline Patient

MALCOLM PINES, D.P.M.

My frame of reference for understanding the nature of the borderline syndrome includes four predominant aspects: (1) the threat of loss of cohesion of the self-representation and self-organization, which places the syndrome on the continuum of self organization proposed by Kohut (1971); (2) the organization of the underlying personality structure, the nature of which has been considerably elucidated by Kernberg (1975); (3) the model of the inner world, the internal representation of self and other (Jacobson, 1965); and (4) the realm of narcissistic development and psychopathology (Akhtar and Thompson, 1982).

My perspective as to the etiology and meaning of the syndrome is that there is a structural deficit in personality development that arises from disturbed interpersonal processes at an early developmental stage. This disturbance has led to a structural deficit in the personality and to an arrest in the evolution of the separation-individuation process (Mahler, Pine, and Bergman, 1975), a process that, when it proceeds normally, leads to the capacity for full autonomy of the individual and for emergence from childhood into adulthood with the capacity for self-containment, for stability in time and space, and for volition and relatively mature mental functioning. These attributes of the self are matched by a recognition that they are to be expected and respected in others and that there are certain types of exchanges that are possible between independent entities in the world. There are clearly defined boundaries to individuals, interpersonal space exists between them, and they can leave, separate, be lost,

and return to the field of interaction of the self and others. Affects
that are aroused by these experiences are admitted to consciousness,
recognized, and, even if painful, allowed to remain in consciousness
until the natural processes of affect change have occurred.

According to the interactional model exemplified in the work of
Margaret Mahler (Mahler, Pine, and Bergman, 1975) and in the
theoretical schema proposed by Hans Loewald (1973), individuals
emerge from the matrix of the mother-child relationship, itself placed
in the context of the family and of culture, as autonomous entities,
persons who have internalized the capacities that will enable them to
carry out functions of the self for which previously they were
dependent on the environment. This capacity for self-organization
goes profoundly into the depths of the personality, organizing even
what otherwise might be regarded as basic instinctual drives. These
drives are themselves fashioned and formed from the start, even
before birth, by the actions, attitudes, and capacities of the family
situation into which the individual is born (Foulkes, 1948; Erikson,
1950; Loewald, 1980). This is not to say that I subscribe to the
approach that attributes the etiology of the borderline syndrome to
innate qualities, such as a heightened oral-sadistic phase or the
constitutional envy of the neonate, notions I regard as a contemporary version of the doctrine of original sin.

Experience has led me more and more to try to understand the
phenomenological world of the borderline patient. I have been led to
this both by my own experience and by the growing literature that
emphasizes the need for understanding the "state of mind" of the
other. The experiential world of the borderline patient, of the
narcissistic patient, is, like that of the psychotic patient, significantly
different from that of the "ordinary" neurotic patient or of the
"ordinary" normal person. By this I mean that the person who lives in
a world in which the background of experience includes a deep sense
of safety, in which fragmentation or loss of cohesion of the self is not
a constant threat, will find it difficult to empathize with the experience of the borderline patient. We find it difficult to identify with the
desperate efforts to maintain the integrity of the self against attacks
from without and within that the borderline patient experiences, and
more than difficult to sympathize, let alone empathize, with the
narcissistic defenses of arrogance, contempt, and attacks on others
that we see so frequently, or to follow the patient into the agonizing
depths of helplessness, hopelessness, and self-abandonment. Nor do

we find it easy to follow the oscillations of feeling states so character-istic of these patients—elation quickly followed by despair, friendli-ness by rage, warmth by destructive coldness. The only key that we have, I believe, to maintaining a relatedness with the patient is through a deep understanding of the dynamics of the personality structure. This understanding enables us to maintain the necessary distance from the patient, to maintain an interpersonal space and a capacity for relating and reflection that are constantly under attack but that are essential if any therapeutic gains are to be made.

Let us return for a moment to the realm of narcissism and to the concept of the narcissistic relationship. Freud (1914) held that object relationship can be of two types, the anaclitic and the narcissistic. In the narcissistic object relationship we relate to the other primarily through those qualities which represent aspects of our own selves. We relate to the other as who we were, as who we are, or as who we would like to be. Though narcissistic elements must enter into many aspects of our personal relationships, there is a clear distinction between persons who have a sense of being in their own right, and who can relate to others as separate centers of autonomy and volition, and those whose relation to others is based primarily on a narcissistic need. Kohut (1971) has assigned the term "selfobject" to the type of relationship whereby the other is needed to maintain the coherence and cohesion of the self and is invested with narcissistic rather than object libido. It is as if the object is needed to fill a gap, to plug a hole in the self-organization, and that without it vital energies and re-sources will simply flow out of the self into the world, leaving the self to collapse and disintegrate unable to maintain its integrity. In fact this aspect of being false, of being pseudo, permeates the life of the narcissistic or borderline patient. There is a pseudo-self, a pseudo-cohesion, a pseudo–object relationship type pattern, and often a sense of pseudo-vitality and initiative.

Now, we know that within the realm of narcissism we will always find grandiosity and idealization, qualities that may be attributed either to the self-representation or to the object representation. We know too that their opposite, destructive narcissism, will annihilate the recognition of good qualities, whether in the other or in the self. Thus both the positive and the negative narcissistic forces can be essentially sterile and maladaptive. No progress and no change can occur in these states in which narcissistic self- and object relationship processes and fantasies are constantly being churned over, externalized, and reinternalized. Real change can come about only through the "metabolization" of the self as real self and the other as real other. Aliment, nutriment of bodily and of psychic nature, must come from without the self and must enter through the external boundary of the self. I propose now to turn to considerations that relate to boundary functioning, external and internal, of the borderline and narcissistic personalities.

The function of an external boundary of a living system is to maintain the differentiation of that system from the outside world and to allow for the exchange of vital supplies and the products of metabolism, that permeability so essential for the life and growth of the organism. But the external boundary when defended by narcissistic fantasies, as it were by a narcissistic "boundary object" (Grotstein, 1980), is in fact a barrier rather than a boundary. Because the person needs to maintain the self structure and because, as we shall see later, there is such a vast failure of internal structure to maintain the integrity and cohesiveness of the self, enormous efforts are made to guard the external boundary. It represents a Berlin Wall, a Spartan shield, to contain and to defend an unhealthy internal system that cannot allow free exchange with the outside world. This barrier is manned and guarded by the narcissistic defenses of grandiosity, contempt, and arrogance—by dragon's teeth. What little exchange with the outside world there is is organized with paranoid scrutiny of what emerges and what enters through the barrier of the self into the internal space. It is as if access to the vulnerable self is guarded by heightened levels of defensive aggression, as if all the psychic orifices based on the bodily openings are armed with teeth. There is a greatly heightened attention cathexis at the boundary, with close scrutiny of what goes in and out, desperate attempts to guard against intrusion and invasion and also to protect the external world from destruction by dangerous inner contents. Because so little exchange occurs with the outside world there is an inner sense of starvation and of profound emptiness and discontent that erupts periodically in rage and profound experiences of envy of those who seem to possess the missing qualities of the self. The person is inordinately sensitive to impingements in unwanted and unexpected ways onto the boundary of the self, and desperate attempts at healing are made by the mobilization of primitive countercathectic forces. The white cells, the psychic phagocytes of narcissistic rage, rush to the breach in the stimulus barrier to plug the gap and to counterattack by invasion of the other. This is a regular sequence, as the immediate response to hurt in the self is to try to force, to hurl, through massive projective identification, one's bleeding, wounded experience into the mind of the other.

An alternative response is to withdraw from any contact with the world of others, including their inner representations, and to try to fill the empty self with substances or experiences that will restore some sense of cohesion and of fullness. In females this can lead to bulimia or less episodic forms of overeating. Typically this consists of food, drink, drugs, excitement, sexuality, forms of sensorimotor stimulation which at their most primitive level will take such forms as self-mutilation, pathological forms of masturbation, rocking, and head banging. Often the precipitants of these responses are, as already noted, the impingement of the other in a painful way upon the self. It is characteristic of patients whose psychic economy is based on narcissism that they cannot bear the sense of loss of admiration, love, attention, or approval. They need these narcissistic supplies to maintain the false inflationary narcissistic economy whereby the psychic supply is constantly increasing and thereby losing its value. Another great loss to the patient is with regard to mirroring (Pines, 1980; Zinkin, 1983), a process whereby others are significant only insofar as they reflect back those images to which the individual is addicted for the maintenance of a desired self-image. There are clear links here to Lacan's mirror stage of development (1977).

I turn now to a consideration of the internal boundary. As the infant grows, so gradually does his inner world become more complex and more differentiated. This notion is inherent to the psychoanalytic structural model and is beautifully illustrated by Kurt Lewin's model of the lifespace (Schellenberg, 1978), in which he shows experimentally how in the course of development the inner world of a child comes more and more to be differentiated and filled with representations, both of the self and of the other. Increasing complexity and internal differentiation lead to the capacity for specialized functions and for the taking over by the child of functions previously performed by significant others, principally the mother, but within the context of the economic unit of the family, typically supported by the father. Within this inner space, through the process Kohut has aptly named "transmuting internalization," the growing organism acquires self-maintaining and adaptive capacities (Tolpin, 1971). We know that there are crisis points in this development, well illustrated in Mahler's separation-individuation schema and in Erikson's epigenetic schema (1959), in both of which there occurs a sudden, as it were, quantum leap from one stage to another. The child who becomes the toddler, who can explore space, who can experience separateness from the mother physically and begin to grasp the separateness of self from other in the inner map of the mind, is in a position enormously different from that of the infant, whose self-concept has not yet been differentiated, clearly and stably, from its concept of the mother. Such achievements as object constancy, stability of internal representations, and development of the symbolic function are clearly crucial here.

In the inner world of the borderline patient is found the experience of a failure to clearly differentiate the self-representation from that of the object; there is a state of blurring, of fusion and confusion. The threat of separation brings about a "separation anguish" that threatens the whole sense of stability and the existence of the individual. But the consequences of this failure of structural organization and differentiation go much further. My image of the person who is psychically built like this is that of a ship without bulkheads, without watertight compartments to keep the vessel buoyant even when one compartment is breached and flooded. Without such compartments the entire vessel is quickly flooded and goes under. There is the danger also of internal catastrophe: an explosion or fire will spread rapidly through the vessel and destroy it. The inner state of these patients is similar; affect storms flood the entire personality, which quickly sinks beneath the waves. Damage to the self, and to self-esteem, is reacted to by the whole organism, which does not contain its own capacities to heal, to soothe, or to control the damage. The level of experience of this hurt, and the consequent rage or despair, is very primitive. At a fantasy level it resembles the primitive contents of the body of the infant and of the mother. Higher levels of soothing, patience, comfort, distraction, reparation, rejoicing, and rejoining scarcely exist.

The borderline patient has not developed certain higher-level structures and functions of the mind. One of these functions that is essential for psychic growth is what Schafer (1968) has called the reflective self-representation, by means of which we know we are the thinkers of our own thoughts (Bach, 1980). When this is established we have the capacity to objectivize thought and to know that a thought is a thought; we are in a position to know and to say "I think, I believe, I feel, I remember, I see, etc. . . ." If this capacity for reflective self-representation is suspended or unavailable, the thinker vanishes but the thought remains. The thought is now a thing, an event, a concrete external reality, for there is no thinker to know it for what it is. This self-representational function can be temporarily suspended, as in the daydream, which allows for the gratification of tension. We are constantly moving in and out of higher levels of consciousness, but this is something of which we can be aware; we know the difference between one and the other. Our borderline patients, however, do not always know the difference between the daydream and higher levels of consciousness, do not know the difference between thoughts they are thinking and thoughts that come at them, as it were, out of inner or outer space.

We can also relate the psychic experience of the borderline patient to a failure in symbolic functioning. The etymology of the word "symbol" shows that it is a construction of two Greek roots— "sym" (together with) and "bollon" (that which has been thrown). Thus "symbol" conveys the idea of things which have been put together in what is now a container of meaning. Implicit in this is the concept of putting together what has been torn apart or lost. Thus, reparation, putting together, and finding of the lost object are implicit in the concept of symbolization. This has been linked to the capacity to achieve the depressive position (Segal, 1957)—that is, to experience separation, frustration, and reparation. The lost object is replaced by the symbol. The development of the symbolic function also enables the infant to experience itself as a being in the world, as one part of a process that needs another part to bring it to completion. This is clearly linked to the capacity for reflective self-representation, to see oneself as the "I" in a world in which there is also a "you" and therefore, taking them together symbolically, a "we."

By contrast to the proper development of the symbolic function, in the narcissistic personality there is no real other, and therefore only pseudosymbolization, a pseudorelationship, and a pseudosymbol of the other, who in fact represents only an extension of the self.

Reverting to the concept that when reflective self-representation is missing the thought is experienced concretely as a thing that may emerge from either inner or outer space, we can speak of diabolic functioning rather than symbolic functioning. The word "diabol" as opposed to "symbol" refers to something which has been thrown across ("dia") or jumbled up rather than having been brought together to make a coherent and meaningful whole. Thus what appears "diabolically" may appear on the surface to be like a symbol but in fact is not conducive to object formation or object use. It can be experienced only in terms of violence, of accusation either from the self against the other or from the other against the self, and represents an improper projection, an excessive projection, rather than one that is part of a normal projective and introjective process. These important distinctions have been made by Gemma Fiumara (1977).

I wish now to turn to the theory of treatment and to try to show something of the place of group analytic psychotherapy in the treatment of the borderline and narcissistic personalities. As far as individual psychotherapy goes there is a spectrum of opinions ranging from despair to optimism. It is clear that if the theoretical etiology is a solely intrapsychic one based on instinct theory, as in the Kleinian approach, individual psychotherapy in the standard setting, with great emphasis of the maintenance of boundaries and of the ground rules of psychotherapy, is indicated. Despite this theoretical assumption, I think there are very few even among the Kleinian school who would affirm that individual psychoanalysis with the more disturbed of these patients can be carried out with the standard technique. It is possible to have a different approach to a solely intrapsychic view of etiology; there can be a modification of technique with the prime aim of containment and holding of the patient so that the metabolism of primitive affects, fantasies, and ideation become possible through the transference relationship and the effect of mutative interpretations. Here the relationship aspect comes to the fore, as opposed to the more purely interpretive approach.

THE GROUP ANALYTIC VIEW OF TREATMENT

It is not possible to treat a group made up entirely of borderline patients. A group must have the capacity to operate at higher levels of functioning, lacking in borderline patients but available to the neurotic, to the normal person, and to the therapist. A group of borderline patients will scarcely represent the norm of society from which each is a deviant, which for Foulkes (1948) was the basic law of group dynamics. Foulkes seemed to be thinking not so much of a group of psychotics or borderline patients as of a group composed of neurotic personalities. It is perfectly possible, using our model, to include in a group one or two persons functioning at a much more primitive level than the others, for the capacity of the group to maintain higher-level functioning would be well established and indeed there are considerable advantages to the group as a whole if there are persons in it who are determined to bring the group into contact with the powerful and primitive forces of the psyche. A growing amount of written evidence, however, shows that the attempt to run completely borderline groups is doomed to disaster.

Kutter (1982), working in Germany, described his group of borderline patients as having progressed to self-destruction as a group. The group was very active, chaotic, and frightened; destructiveness and premature self-revelation were characteristic. Cohesion was never long-lasting and was often broken up by destructive attacks. Primitive mechanisms, predominantly splitting and other mechanisms consequent on it, characterized both the individuals in the group and much of the group dynamics. Members would come to the session as if to a place of security which they tried to make good, and yet each time split-off destructive parts projected into the others prevented the establishment of good relationships and mutual understanding. Whenever a problem was brought in by one member, the others felt that this was too demanding; everyone had pressing problems. The group as a whole, unable to stand up to this enormous internal pressure, gradually began to disintegrate; its remnants seemed to the therapist to resemble a dismembered torso. Both the therapist and the group were progressively devalued, and the former was constantly seen as cold, rejecting, dogmatic, and repressive. Dreams of concentration camps, and of frightening and destructive bodily and sexual fantasies, recurred; through associations it was possible to see that the members felt that the group, personified in the therapist, resembled a weak father kept under control by a powerful mother; the father was seen as a complete failure, unable to protect his children from the devouring destructive mother. The group felt like unwanted, abandoned, and rejected children. After ninety-eight sessions, the group dissolved.

In retrospect the therapist saw the patients as regressed to an oral stage of drive organization and as unable to deal with their emotions in a constructive manner. From the beginning they split off unintegrated destructive forces and projected them onto the group. There was no mutual empathy, and ruthless questioning about each other's vulnerabilities took its place. The group increasingly became for its members a frightening destructive object, a perilous hole into which they might fall; the therapist was seen as weak, disappointing, unreliable, and irresponsible. As they did not feel that there was any protection by authority, the members could experience each other only as mutually exploiting objects. Eventually they had to protect themselves from these experiences by leaving the group and projecting the damaging parts of the self onto it. Kutter saw them as operating at a level on which they wanted to destroy everything because of their envy of the therapist, an envy that led to the fear of abandonment and of retaliatory rage by the rejecting mother.

On the basis of this report and my own a priori theoretical position, I strongly advocate the creation by the therapist of a standard group analytic setting. Here the group circle stands as a symbol of containment and of wholeness. Its external boundary, which is created by the therapist in that he offers the space and the time and the situation for persons to become members of the group as a living boundary is maintained by the therapist's therapeutic functions and by the collaboration of the group members. They maintain the boundary by their presence, their reliability, their punctuality, and, where the group is run by a therapist in private practice, their payment of fees. The patients contribute their labor and their money, and the therapist contributes his skill in exchange for this. Thus a mutual system, not of exploitation but of division of labor, begins to build up. Continuing with this mode, within the group processes of exchange, support and acceptance go on between the peer members of the group, who themselves begin to create the group matrix (Roberts, 1982; Van der Kleij, 1982).

The concept of the matrix is basic to the group analytic model. It represents the growth of culture, of patterns of communication and meaningful understanding which have been established in the group and which can be drawn on by all the members because they themselves have had a part in its creation. It is as if there is an opportunity for therapist and patients together to create this new entity, the group, which has never existed before; it therefore becomes "their" group, the subjective object, the "environmental mother" of Winnicott (1965). Winnicott proposed that for the infant there is an environmental mother before there is an object mother— that is, before the mother is represented in the child's mind and objectified out of the infant's subjective experiences. If we recall the defects in boundary functioning that I described earlier, the failure of healthy maintenance of separation and individuation from the outside world by a boundary that allows relatively free exchange across it, the borderline patient is unable in many ways to contribute to the establishment of this healthy boundary functioning in the group but is also able gradually to accept and to internalize the boundary functioning created by the healthier members of the group. The borderline patient will characteristically test out this boundary again and again for its strength, its acceptance, and its reliability, as he will distrust and fear the group as a potentially bad maternal situation, the black hole into which the individual will fall endlessly, to use Kutter's model. What he has to find out is that he can gradually exchange this "diabol" for a true "symbol" of caring, patience, understanding, and holding.

The borderline patient functions much of the time at the level of projection and introjection, in primitive forms of externalization, which in the narcissistic mode of existence leads to no exchange and therefore to no change. What becomes available in the group is that these processes of projection and introjection are raised to a higher level because the other members of the group are able to maintain this higher level, to offer understanding and support, and then to metabolize these processes in a mutative exchange of psychic products. Naturally this is difficult to achieve in the face of the enormous and destructive attacks of the frightened patient. Here the therapist's function is extremely important. Often he has to act as the container of these enormous tensions and to act as a negotiator, a person who mediates between the opponents in these destructive relationships. But the therapist, too, has basically to trust to the capacity of the group to maintain high levels of psychic functioning such as love, caring, the search for truth, and the maintenance of integrity.

A basic feature of therapy and in particular of group therapy replicates an essential maternal function; the infant relates to the mother solely as a part object to begin with, but the mother, the good loving caring mother, relates to that infant as a whole person, a whole object, with love, respect, and understanding, from the first and indeed from before the first, when the infant is still but a fantasy, a symbol in her mind. Thus there is a constant process of transformation of part-object processes into whole-object responses. It is very important, therefore, that the therapist relate to the group as to a whole entity, sees it as a whole, and is able to tolerate and understand its growth while at the same time seeing its individual members as whole persons in their own right, though carrying roles in the group that represent part-person activities. If a person appears to be acting as a focus in the group for, say, feelings of envy, rage, jealousy, and so on, the therapist must be able to see that that person is being used by the group as a focus of communication for these affects and fantasies, it is the therapist's function to help free the person from being used in this way—i.e., as a focus of destructive activities rather than as a nodal point in a communications network (Pines, 1983).

Thus, the therapist constantly relates to the individuals in the group as to whole persons, trying to show them their place in the pattern of the group as a whole. This is not possible if the therapist is devoted to transference-based interpretations at the part-object level, interpretations which have as their basis the group's relation to the therapist. The therapist who does this, wittingly or not, inevitably fragments the group's efforts to become a whole and to relate to each other as whole persons. I have heard therapists describe sessions in which severely disturbed patients seem desperately trying to create a living entity out of the group and have to fight off the therapist's demands, which seem to me narcissistically based, that they pay attention to him, to his function, and to his interpretations. The therapist needs constantly to listen to his patients, to follow, to care, and to be interested in their efforts to grow, to understand, and to create a viable group. When this ongoing group process takes place then we have both matrix, a basic maternal function, and pattern, a basic paternal function as demonstrated by Cortesao (1971).

Earlier I mentioned the extreme oscillations to which borderline patients with their lack of inner structuration, are prone. These patients will constantly bring their states of despair and emptiness to the group, and it is remarkable how a well-functioning group can bring them back to a higher level of functioning and establish meaning for them in what seems a meaningless state of despair. Gradually the wild oscillations begin to cease, as the patient can begin to use the group as a structure and the process of "transmuting internalization," which has failed in these patients, begins to develop.

We must not neglect the opposite process; for any change in psychic structure to take place there must be a dedifferentiation of the existing structure. This is a process whereby parts of each individual are given up to form a group mixture. Out of this predominantly benign mix a redifferentiation can take place, with each member now containing something new from the intercourse of the group. Here again it must be a genuine intercourse, a real meeting of feelings, thoughts, and fantasies, and not solely a contest between therapist and patient.

Other deficiencies in the patient that can be remedied include a weak capacity for reflective self-representation, for in the group there is a constant demand for reflection and an offer by other members of the group to act as mirrors for each other (Pines, 1980). Time and again one hears members saying to each other that they now see something of themselves in the other they had not seen previously. On the basis of this understanding they are able to improve not only their relationship with the other but also their relationship to the self; they can now see at a distance something of themselves to which previously they had been blind. This allows for introjection and reintegration of split-off, repressed, and unconscious parts of the self.

In a properly conducted analytic group the patients will make reasonable demands on each other for reciprocity and for exchange. The group demonstrates, over time, capacities for altruistic caring, for nonpossessive love, and for healthy confrontation, all of which have been absent or seriously defective in the childhood of borderline patients. But these patients are not simply the passive recipients of this bounty; they are also active contributors in the processes that bestow it.

REFERENCES

Akhtar, S., & Thompson, J. A. (1982), Overview: Narcissistic personality disorders. *Amer. J. Psychiat.*, 139:1–20.

Bach, S. (1980), Self-love and object-love: Some problems of self and object constancy. In: *Rapprochement: The Critical Subphase of Separation-Individuation*, ed. R. Lax, S. Bach, & J. Burland. New York: Aronson, pp. 171–197.

Cortesao, E. (1971), On interpretation in group analysis. *Group Analysis*, 4:39–53.

Erikson, E. (1959), *Identity and the Life Cycle*. Psychological Issues Monograph 1. New York: International Universities Press.

———(1950), *Childhood and Society*. Rev. ed. New York: Norton, 1963.

Fiumara, G. (1977), The symbolic function, transference and psychic reality. *Internat. Rev. Psycho-Anal.*, 4:171–180.

Foulkes, S. H. (1948), *Introduction to Group Analytic Psychotherapy*. London: Heinemann. Maresfield Reprint, 1984.

Freud, S. (1914), On narcissism. *Standard Edition*, 14:67–102. London: Hogarth Press, 1957.

Grotstein, J. (1980), A proposed revision of the psychoanalytic concept of primitive mental states. *Contemp. Psychoanal.*, 16:479–546.

Jacobson, E. (1965), *The Self and the Object World*. London: Hogarth Press.

Kernberg, O. F. (1975), *Borderline Conditions and Pathological Narcissism.* New York: Aronson.

Kohut, H. (1971), *The Analysis of the Self.* London: Hogarth Press.

Kutter, P. (1982), *Basic Aspects of Psychoanalytic Group Therapy.* London: Routledge & Kegan Paul.

Lacan, J. (1977), The mirror stage as formative of the I as revealed in psychoanalytic experience. In: *Ecrits.* London: Tavistock.

Loewald, H. W. (1973), On internalization. *Internat. J. Psycho-Anal.,* 54:9–17.

———(1980), *Papers on Psychoanalysis.* New Haven, CT: Yale University Press.

Mahler, M. S. Pine, F., & Bergman, A. (1975), *The Psychological Birth of the Human Infant.* London: Hutchinson.

McDevitt, J. D., & Settledge, C. F., eds. (1971), *Separation-Individuation: Essays in Honor of Margaret S. Mahler.* New York: International Universities Press.

Pines, M. (1980), Reflections on mirroring. *Internat. Rev. Psycho-Anal.,* 11:27–42.

———(1983), *Evolution of Group Analysis.* London: Routledge & Kegan Paul.

Roberts, J. P. (1982), Foulkes' concept of the matrix. *Group Analysis,* 15:111–126.

Schafer, R. (1968), *Aspects of Internalization.* New York: International Universities Press.

Schellenberg, J. A. (1978), *Masters of Social Psychology.* New York: Oxford University Press.

Segal, H. (1957), Notes on symbol formation. *Internat. J. Psycho-Anal.,* 38:391–397.

Tolpin, M. (1971), On the beginnings of a cohesive self. *The Psychoanalytic Study of the Child,* 26:316–352.

Van der Kleij, G. (1982), About the matrix. *Group Analysis,* 15:219–234.

Winnicott, D. W. (1965), The development of the capacity for concern. In: *Maturational Processes and the Facilitating Environment.* London: Hogarth Press.

Zinkin, L. (1983), Malignant mirroring. *Group Analysis,* 16:113–125.

3

Bion or Kohut: Two Paradigms of Group Dynamics

SIGMUND W. KARTERUD, M.D.

In recent years several authors (Stone and Whitman, 1977; Gustafson and Hartmann, 1978; Pines, 1982; Harwood, 1983; and Horwitz, 1984; see also Chapter 8) have been concerned with self psychology and groups. In general, their main focus of interest has been how to apply the concepts of self psychology within the context of group psychotherapy. Battegay (1976) and Løfgren (1983) are among those who have been preoccupied with group dynamics. Løfgren has pointed to the similarities between the dependency group (Bion, 1961) and the collective projection of the idealized parental imago (Kohut, 1971). Battegay (1976) has used the term "narcissistic group-self" which he defines as a collective manifestation of grandiosity, a position it is possible to avoid. Bion's theory has still an unchallenged hegemonic position within psychoanalytic group dynamics. No author has yet presented a comprehensive self psychological reinterpretation of Bion's observations on group dynamics. Such a reinterpretation is the aim of this chapter.

I will first discuss the shortcomings of Bion's group theory, after which I will present research material that further challenges that theory. I will then discuss the alternative perspective presented by Chasseguet-Smirgel (1985) and finally outline a self psychological alternative based on the theories of Kohut.

Work on this chapter was supported by the Norwegian Research Council of Science and the Humanities (NAVF).

45

BION'S BASIC ASSUMPTIONS THEORY

The psychoanalytic metapsychology of group dynamics was initiated by Freud (1921) in "Group Psychology and the Analysis of the Ego." Here Freud presented his classic definition of a group: "a number of individuals who have put one and the same object in the place of their ego ideal and have consequently identified themselves with one another in their ego" (p. 116). In this paper Freud was preoccupied with the problem of narcissism and regarded the ego ideal, which was projected onto the leader of the group, as of narcissistic origin. He had not yet completed the structural theory, and the ego ideal concept he used in this paper included phenomena he would later attribute to the superego.

Bion presented his theory of group dynamics in a series of papers published between 1948 and 1952. Here the nature of groups was formulated in Kleinian object relation terminology. Melanie Klein and her followers have not been much preoccupied with narcissism, as they regard the ego as existing from birth. The child is from birth thought to be in relation to an object, although early on this relationship is primitive and fragmentary. For Klein there could be no stage of primary narcissism. Accordingly, Bion did not even mention narcissism in his pioneering *Experiences in Groups* (1961).

The key concepts in this work were the so-called basic assumptions of fight-flight, dependency, and pairing. These were described as collective group phenomena threatening the goals of the "work group." Bion was somewhat ambiguous concerning the nature of the basic assumptions. Initially he conceived them as manifestations of a "protomental" layer in man. The members were linked to each other in that specific way due to their "valence." Later he used the terminology of Melanie Klein. It was crucial for Bion to demonstrate that groups are much more influenced by psychotic anxieties than Freud supposed. Freud held that the family group provided the basic pattern for all groups. Against this, Bion took the position that the basic assumptions were "formations secondary to an extremely early primal scene worked out on a level of part objects, and associated with psychotic anxiety and mechanisms of splitting and projective identification such as Melanie Klein described as characteristic of the paranoid-schizoid and depressive positions" (p. 164). He elaborated:

the basic assumption phenomenon appears far more to have the characteristics of defensive reactions to psychotic anxiety, and to be not so much at variance with Freud's views as supplementary to them. In my view, it is necessary to work through both the stresses that appertain to family patterns and the still more primitive anxieties of part-object relationships. In fact I consider the latter to contain the ultimate sources of all group behaviour [p. 189].

What were the arguments for the group activating fantasies related to "an extremely early primal scene" that makes necessary the collective defensive reactions of basic assumptions? Bion argued that

the group approximates too closely, in the minds of the individuals composing it, to very primitive fantasies about the contents of the mother's body. The attempt to make a rational investigation of the dynamics of the group is therefore perturbed by fears, and mechanisms for dealing with them, that are characteristic of the paranoid-schizoid position. The investigation cannot be carried out without the stimulation and activation of these levels [p. 162].

In this line of argument—the group representing the mother's body, the investigation of the group thus activating fantasies of an early primal scene, the basic assumptions as defenses against these fantasies—the basic assumptions become consequences of *the self-study activity* of the group. However, Bion claimed that his theory of group dynamics was valid for all types of groups, irrespective of task, be it therapy, self-study, leisure activity, or material production. This highlights the speculative nature of these arguments. It is not at all self-evident that activity groups, which also are hampered by basic assumptions, should be afflicted by the fantasies of a primal scene.

Bion was fond of terms derived from the natural sciences, devoid of any previous psychoanalytic meaning—"protomental," "valence," "alpha-functions," and so on. He hoped this openness would be constructive in the long run. However, the "neutral" concept of "valence" is still, thirty years after its inception, without any meaningful substance. When Bion turned to Kleinian terminology, he did not develop his valence theory and thus obscured the crucial question of what unites members in a group on a level deeper than the cooperative efforts of the work group. Surprisingly enough, Bion seems to equate "libido" with almost overt sexual investment. The obvious sexual element in the pairing group made him state that "the bond between individuals is libidinous" in the pairing group: "I regard Freud's use of the term libido as correct only for one phase, though an important one, and feel the need for some more neutral term that will describe the tie on all basic assumption levels" (p. 176). However, what preoccupied Freud in 1921 was not sexual object libido so much as the vicissitudes of narcissistic libido. According to Freud, it was the narcissistic quality of the ego ideal that accounted for the perfection imputed to the group leader. In Freud's classic formulation, the members identify with each other through the common investment of the ego ideal upon the group leader. When Bion concluded by saying that the nature of the bond in the pairing group is libidinous, he was speaking of a bond between individuals, not between individuals and the leader. Later he argued that the bond between individual members and the leader in the fight-flight or dependency group was that of projective identification, but left other members aside. He was never to return to the search for that "more neutral term that will describe the tie on all basic assumption levels."

So we are left with a rather confusing picture. The basic assumptions are secondary formations, defensive reactions due to the group's approaching itself as to the mother's body. The bonds between the members in the pairing group are of a libidinous nature, while the relation to the leader is highly unclear. The bonds to the leader in the dependency group and the fight-flight group are those of projective identification, while those between the members are highly unclear. It seems to me that what Bion presented were very sophisticated observations and formulations put together in something that resembles a coherent theory but that upon closer scrutiny appears highly fragmentary. I have already pointed to the fact that this theory can hardly account for basic assumption functioning in groups formed for purposes other than self-study. There should be no difficulty in demonstrating the libidinous component in the dependency group, the common libidinous investment in the wished-for good leader. But what constitutes the bond in the fight-flight group? Why do its members continue to meet? What do they hope for? An outlet of sadism, a fusion of libidinous and aggressive drives?

In the next section I will present research data that cannot be accounted for by Bion's theoretical position.

RESEARCH DATA

The basic assumptions are widely accepted as clinical realities by group psychotherapists. However, as has recently been pointed out by Armelius and Armelius (1985), the research on them has been meager. Most studies have obvious shortcomings: unsuitable populations (mostly students rather than patients), diluted occurrences of basic assumptions, short duration of observation, a limit number of observational situations, inadequate methods, indirect measures, and lack of adequate reliability testing. Recently I completed a study on Bion's basic assumption groups (Karterud, in press) that was based on rigorous observation with reliable methods (Karterud and Foss, in press; Karterud, 1988) on seventy-five small group sessions with six different inpatient groups. The presence of basic assumptions was abundant in the material gathered. The extreme fight-flight groups were of a kind which no scientist would dare provoke experimentally and which are seldom experienced in outpatient groups, private practice, or Tavistock conferences. These groups produced life-threatening situations, several suicide attempts, and one actual suicide. The dependency group in this research material was less extreme, and the pairing groups more closely resembled Tavistock experiences. One drawback with this material was a preponderance of fight-flight groups over the other two types.

Nothing in Bion's theory suggests any special affinities or antagonisms between one basic assumption and another. However, the data revealed an antagonistic tendency between fight-flight and dependency groups and a curvilinear relation between fight-flight and pairing groups. The occurrence of fight-flight and dependency on the group session level ($n = 75$) was negatively correlated ($- .20, p = .04$), while fight-flight and pairing were negatively correlated at extreme fight and pairing occurrences, but positively correlated at medium levels. The extent to which fight or dependency was "allowed," the fight/dependency ratio—separated groups as well as group sessions and individuals in ways that were highly significant statistically. Statistical analysis confirmed the connection to the paranoid-schizoid and depressive positions: schizophrenia and "rejecting" personality disorders (schizotypal, narcissistic, antisocial) had a high valence for fight-flight, while major affective disorders and neuroses had a high valence for dependency. Borderline personality disorders had a high level for both fight-flight and dependency. Differences concerning pairing behavior were not statistically significant for the diagnostic subgroups of DSM-III, but were significant for distinguishing psychoses versus nonpsychoses. This last finding suggests that pairing is a phenomenon of higher level psychic functioning. The difference between the most extreme, best consolidated fight-flight group and the dependency group, as regards pairing, was statistically highly significant ($p < .01$). The fight-flight group showed a high pairing frequency, while the dependency group did not. Qualitative analysis of this material revealed that pairing played a significant role for the consolidation of the fight-flight group. On the overt or subconscious level, the reason for fight-flight group reactions was not the hatred activated by approaching the primal scene, but the narcissistic rage activated by disappointment in the wished-for good (or idealized) leaders. This hatred led to a fragmentation of the group (which was sometimes observed) were it not for some other possibilities: rapprochement with the idealized leader or the declaration of the group as self-sufficient, seemingly needing no leader except for the group itself, which would care for the members. The group thus exhibited pairing and declared its love and care toward the inside, while directing its hostility to the outside—or to the inside if members did not live up to the all-good group's requirements.

Figure 1 shows these dynamics. The frequency of fight and pairing statements are plotted in five-minute intervals during an inpatient group session of forty-five minutes duration. In the first fifteen minutes a fellow patient is being attacked for not doing her duty for the group. This is a fight-flight segment. In the next fifteen minutes, a pairing sequence, the members express their care and love for each other. In the last fifteen minutes they fight against the staff who will not send a rescue expedition to a suicidal day-patient who has not turned up at the ward and whom the patients want to save by making her an inpatient and thus a member of the *real* caring group, not an outsider day-patient. The three phases in this group are extremely well delineated. No fight statement appears in the pairing phase and vice versa. Although these phases are distinctly separated, they are dynamically linked.

These observations confirm the views put forward by Hartmann

Figure 1

Graph of a fight-flight
and pairing group

Fight ——— and
pairing ----- statements

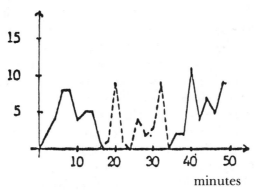

minutes

Total interaction: 456
Fight statements: 73
Pairing: 29
Dependency: 12
Flight: 35

and Gibbard (1974) that "pairing and messianic fantasies occur at those times when the group is most in danger of ending and dissolving (p. 334; see also Slater, 1966).

THE GROUP AND THE EGO IDEAL

Chasseguet-Smirgel (1985) has extensively explored the close relation between utopian illusions and hostility in groups that I have found in my own research. She points to the fact that Freud's work on groups preceded his elaboration of the superego concept and thus his concept of the ego ideal contained both the ego ideal in the narcissistic sense (the heir to primary narcissism) and the superego in the moral sense (the heir to the oedipal conflict). The classic formulation of Freud (1921), that group members identify with each other by replacing their individual ego ideals with one and the same object, the leader, refers, according to Chasseguet-Smirgel, mainly to the superego in the moral sense. The ego ideal has a "male quality" representing the predominantly male-established incest taboo. The group leader for Freud was thus seen to be molded according to a father mythos. The superego quality of the leader (favoring a dissolution of the individual superego) was used as an argument for the loss of individuality and moral responsibility so commonly observed in members in a wide range of groups. Members are thus tempted to perform acts that would otherwise violate their individual consciences. Chasseguet-Smirgel, however, emphasizes the narcissistic part of the combined ego ideal/superego notion of Freud and points to its maternal origin and the ego's striving for fusion with this still existing (not having been dissolved into the superego) ego ideal. Citing Anzieu (1971), she writes: "The ideal ego seeks to realize a fusion with the omnipotent mother and the introjective restoration of the lost primary love object. The group becomes, for the members, the substitute for this lost object" (p. 81). The group then becomes one of the most important societal vehicles for the restoration of the "illusion." "The group illusion is then a realization of the wish to heal one's narcissistic injuries and to identify oneself with the good breast (or with the omnipotent mother)" (p. 82). The leader

> cannot, to my mind, be equated with the father. . . . the leader is the person who activates the primitive wish for the union of ego and ego ideal. He is the promoter of illusion, he who makes it shimmer before men's dazzled eyes, he who will bring it to fusion. Times will be changed, the Great Day (or the Great Eve) will arrive, a heavenly Jerusalem will offer itself to our astonished gaze, our needs will be met, the Arians will conquer the world, the day will dawn, the future yield its promise, etc. The group thirsts less for a leader than for illusions. And it will choose as leader whomsoever promises it the union of ego and ego ideal [p. 82].

The group wants to deny the "law of the father," the sex and generational differences, the incest taboo and thus the necessity to wait, grow, develop, and gain knowledge. The linkage between the exalted euphoria of the fusion (pairing) and aggression is elaborated in this way:

> Now, since the goal of the Illusion is the idealization of the ego, and there can be no idealization of the ego without

projection, the objects receiving the projections must be hunted down and annihilated. I do not think it sufficient to say that the murder is then committed in the name of the superego and hence it becomes legitimate. I think that it is undertaken above all in the name of the ideal, as in the case of the Infidels murdered by the Crusaders on the road to Jerusalem. Any reactivation of the illusion is thus ineluctably followed by a bloodbath, provided only that the group has the means to match its violence [p. 84].

Is this schema valid for all types of groups? Chasseguet-Smirgel:

It goes without saying that the structure of the collective groupings that I am attempting to describe . . . is particularly regressive, and is a structure that is not found in those groups that do not depend upon an ideology. I would not include as an ideology those systems of thought that do not promise fulfillment of the Illusion. A group of ideas (a government policy for example, a program having limited objectives) does not, in this perspective, constitute an ideology of the full sense of that term. Thus, in other groups, the leader may have the role of a father, as in the Freudian schema. . . .

    . . . . I would propose a classification that took account of their relationship to the Illusion. One could in this way make an essential distinction between ideological groups and others, the latter retaining to a greater or lesser degree the oedipal dimensions of the psyche, whilst the former tend towards primary narcissism and hence to an eclipsing of that which has been in the course of development [pp. 91–92].

What Chasseguet-Smirgel elaborates in her book fits very well with the fight-flight groups observed in my own research: the inwardly self-sufficient illusionary group so hostile to dissenters and outside enemies. The classification she proposes represents the fused fight-flight/pairing group (the group of ideology, illusion, and maternal fusion) on the one hand, and the work group in Bion's sense (or the father-dominated superego group of Freud, obeying the reality principle) on the other. But what of the dependency group, a well-described clinical and societal reality as regressed (but not so malign) as the fused fight-flight/pairing group of Chasseguet-Smirgel? It is not a work group in Bion's sense, being incapable of the intricate societal work expected of "parliamentary committee" with integrated superego. The deficiency in accounting for the regressed dependency group, where hostility is feared and forbidden, seems due to the classical notion of narcissism as a unipolar phenomenon, a notion adhered to by Chasseguet-Smirgel.

THE GROUP AND SELF PSYCHOLOGY

So far I have demonstrated that Bion's theory cannot account for the close relationship between pairing and fight-flight, a relationship convincingly elaborated by Chasseguet-Smirgel, who cannot, however, account for the dependency group. I will now proceed to demonstrate that the concepts of Kohut can account for both, thus demonstrating as well the superior explanatory power of self psychology as compared either to the group theory of Bion or to the theory of Chasseguet-Smirgel, who reestablished the link to Freud which Bion broke by neglecting the relevance of narcissism to group dynamics.

Readers acquainted with the concepts of self psychology might at this point realize, in light of my remarks concerning the group and the ego ideal, that I am about to posit two principal group configurations—the grandiose group and the idealizing group—these configurations being manifestations of a group self tied together by identifications based on a shared selfobject (transference) relationship to the leader.

THE GROUP SELF

Kohut's later interest in group psychology (1985) was not an interest in group psychotherapy but in applied psychoanalysis. In "Creativeness, Charisma, Group Psychology," Kohut (1976) suggested the term "group self":

> It will have become obvious to those who are familiar with my recent work that I am suggesting, as a potentially fruitful approach to a complex problem, that we posit the existence of a certain psychological configuration with regard to the group—let us call it the "group self"—which is analogous to

the self of the individual. We are then in a position to observe the group self as it is formed, as it is held together, as it oscillates between fragmentation and reintegration, as it shows regressive behavior when it moves toward fragmentation, etc.—all in analogy to phenomena of individual psychology to which we have comparatively easy access in the clinical (psychoanalytic) situation [p. 837].

This group self should not be equated with members' conscious or preconscious notions about their identity. "The psychoanalytic concept of a self, however—whether it refers to the self of an individual or to the self of a person as a member of a group or, as a 'group self,' to the self of a stable association of people—concerns a structure that dips into the deepest reaches of the psyche" (p. 837). Kohut did not further define the concept of group self. However, there is no reason now to follow the psychoanalytic tradition and define the group self as constituted by members identifying with each other (in their selves) through a shared relation to a selfobject leader.

Does this imply an entity separate from the members, an independently thinking and acting group self? Certainly not, but it implies something more than the mere sum of the individual selves. The individual self has loosened its boundaries both "horizontally" (by identification with fellow members, thus giving up parts of its own individuality) and "vertically" (by merger with a selfobject). This two-axis loosening of self-boundaries accounts for the potential for oceanic feelings and euphoria so often described as group phenomena. Obviously, an individual brain and a concrete body are necessary in order to speak and act. However, unconscious identification and sharing vis-à-vis selfobjects give ample opportunity for action or speech on behalf of the group. This extension of the self to the group is well demonstrated by the common reaction when members experience a group trauma (e.g., humiliation) as equivalent to an individual trauma, thus activating narcissistic rage.

According to Kohut (1984), the individual self is a precarious structure in need of lifelong sustenance by nurturing selfobjects. Prone to disintegration, it will undertake consolidating efforts and compensatory acts in an effort of self-restoration. Kohut argues against the traditional psychoanalytic view that narcissism is developmentally transcended once and for all, and also against the view of Chasseguet-Smirgel, who holds that the ultimate goal of psychoanal-

ysis (and of the mature human being) is the complete fusion of the
ego ideal and the superego, whereby the superego takes on the
self-nurturing role and whereby social existence is characterized by
whole object relations.

Group experiences provide perhaps the most ample evidence of
the validity of Kohut's theories. For example, whenever apparently
well-integrated persons in leading positions congregate at Tavistock
conferences, they immediately regress to archaic self positions. Deprived of work, familial, and leisure selfobjects, they engage in
frenetic activity to restore the self through new selfobject relations.
Their rage and pairing activity flourishes when the conductor rejects
the role of idealized selfobject.

The group self, even more than the individual self, is a vulnerable structure. The group, however, has the possibility for a life
transcending that of the individual; granted firm group structures, it
may last for centuries. The regulation of these transcendent groups is
carefully monitored by a priesthood, be it the church elders, the
psychoanalytic association, or the juridical faculty, who protect group
scripture and traditions, and claim a formidable devotion on the part
of initiates. Lacking such structures, however, groups come and go as
summer flies. Many of them suffer fragmentation and ultimate
dissolution. Excessive frustrations or demands due to reality represent serious threats to the life of groups with a loose group self. But
a loose group self should not be equated with an archaic group self.
Archaic groups can be very well consolidated, as attested by the
grandiose ideology groups described by Chasseguet-Smirgel.

Some of the inherent frustrations of a psychotherapy group are
linked to the interventions of the group therapist, which hamper its
"natural" development into an ideology group. An ideology group is
an attempt to consolidate the self through an organized group self, be
it a grandiose group, an idealizing group, or a mixture of both.
However, it must be emphasized that the presumably optimal and
"natural" course for therapy groups is one of modest idealizing. This
has partly to do with selection. Most people applying for group
therapy do so because of symptoms, feelings of helplessness, and a
wish for help. Grandiose patients are usually in the minority. They
will tend to "cure" themselves through the merging and illusionary
aspects of ideology or work groups (Kriegman and Solomon, 1985).
Borderline patients stay midway between these grandiose patients
and the majority. Their defensive splitting, consequent suffering, and

chaotic social experience bring them to therapy, where they oscillate between grandiose and dependent positions.

Therapy groups only gradually move to establish a firm group self. The group therapist's emphasis on self-reflection prevents any premature closure of the group self, with its inevitable denial and projecting of conflicting aspects of the self and related object representations. For example, a strong alter ego transference will deny the existence of greed, envy, and jealousy. Most consolidated groups with an ideology of equality contain this denial. In their utopian society, every man is generous and shares freely and equally with his fellow beings. The consolidated idealizing group has to ward off the grandiose self and continually defend itself against the wish to be the center of the universe, with its related exhibitionism and possible perversions, the wish for self-sufficiency and the narcissistic rage due to insufficient mirroring. The grandiose group has to ward off experiences of helplessness and longing for merger with an idealized selfobject who magically will lift the burden from the members' shoulders and take responsibility for their lives. Since people in therapy groups are expected to work through all these areas, the group self should not be over consolidated; optimally, it should be only semistable and somewhat vulnerable. As Chasseguet-Smirgel has pointed out, the essence of a closed and invulnerable archaic group self is a defensive denial of the demands of reality, of sexual and generational differences, and of the necessity to grow and learn.

This notion of a group self does not lead to the either-or presented by Chasseguet-Smirgel. Instead it allows for the explanation of group existence on all maturational levels. From this perspective, Nazi groups, women's liberation groups, and creative workshops may all function at the level of the grandiose group, though at different maturational levels. The group self must not be conceived as a unipolar entity. As in individual psychology, we must conceive of it as bipolar or even tripolar (Kohut, 1984). This contrasts with the orthodox analytic position that views narcissism solely in terms of phenomena linked to the grandiose self, as in the DSM-III definition of narcissistic personality disorder. The idealized parental imago is not included in this concept, whereby narcissism is regarded as object-related and mediated through the superego as heir to the Oedipus complex. The religious group, the group of true believers, the helpless patients waiting for the magic cure of the therapist— these are not regarded as "narcissistic" by Chasseguet-Smirgel. However, as Kohut has convincingly demonstrated (1971, 1977), the idealizing transference has the same basic features as the mirroring transference. A weak and vulnerable self experiences diffuse psychic and somatic distress and dysphoric mood when cut off from consolidating selfobjects; symptoms which fairly rapidly decline when the transference is established. Merging with the therapist manifested as lack of concern for the therapist, who is treated as an extension of the self, and despair that follows when this merger is threatened by disappointment in the therapist's presumed omnipotence and complete understanding. When in the idealizing transference limitless wisdom is seen to reside within the idealized selfobject, the fragmentation-prone self is consolidated through a fantasy of merger. In religious groups, as miracles seldom occur, inevitable disappointment and rage, which are regarded as sin and weakness of faith, must be dealt with by prayers and penance.

Chasseguet-Smirgel uses the concept of idealization in another way. She does not speak of the idealization of a selfobject, the projected ego ideal, but of the "idealization of the self," as in the ideology group, which makes an ideal of the utopian illusion. However, within Kohut's terminology this is not, properly speaking, an idealization. Rather, it is a confounding of grandiosity and idealization. Ideology groups will rationalize or give their grandiose strivings a particular form, maintaining, for example, that homosexuality is superior to heterosexuality, communism to capitalism, Germans to Jews, English football to Belgian, and so on. The confounding will stem from the fact that, contrary to the unitary notion of Chasseguet-Smirgel, the group self is polarized. Each group will be characterized by a unique and specific relationship between the grandiose and the idealizing group self. One of the poles will be dominant, which implies complex relations to the subordinated pole. The healthy, well-integrated group self will be characterized by oscillations between the idealizing and the grandiose poles according to temporary needs and challenges. In groups organized around primitive wishes, one of the poles will be repressed and produce symptoms. In some groups fairly archaic selfobjects of both kinds may operate almost simultaneously. Maoist groups in Europe around 1970 present illustrative examples of both grandiose and idealizing transferences. The relation to Mao Tse-tung and his thought was humble, submissive, almost religious, and his sayings were studied and repeated ritualistically. Everyone was small and weak in relation to Mao, the great leader. But

Chairman Mao said: "The masses are the *real* heroes." And the masses had as their mission making Maoism a worldwide movement. Missionary appeal can thus be seen to activate the grandiose self. This may also be looked at the other way around: the activated grandiose self, due to specific historical circumstances, reaches out to a form, a content, and a rationale and chooses what is suitable for the time being.

When things occur on such a grand scale as the worldwide student riots of 1968–1970 we must assume a dialectic. The activated grandiose self searches for ideals to rationalize its efforts, and the ideas of Marcuse, Sartre, Reich, Marx, Mao, etc., activate the grandiose self. In any case, submissiveness to the idealized selfobject contrasted with the grandiosity of the subsequent mission: the self-righteousness, the arrogance, the devaluation of other views, the refusal of dialogue, the internal declaration of love and brotherhood, the internal pairing and marriages, and the potential violence when frustrated. Obviously the danger to society comes not from cultivated forms of idealizing and grandiose groups like the peaceful, humble group of devoted religious, or the grandiose group of artistic or adventurous explorers, but from the mixture (and fusion?) of archaic grandiosity and archaic idealization within a single group.

In individual psychoanalysis the vicissitudes of one of the main selfobject transferences will take precedence. Temporary shifts in the working through of an idealizing transference will allow for the emergence of a mirroring transference previously warded off due to shame, fear of self fragmentation and loss, or oedipal anxieties. There is a tendency for psychoanalytic theorists to transpose experiences in individual psychoanalysis to group situations and to ignore the fact that concurrent multiple transferences develop in groups. Because of a plurality of therapists, psychiatric wards particularly favor multiple transferences. A psychiatric ward that allows for positive transferences to develop, such as a therapeutic community with an intermediate or long-term stay, can properly be described as a "multiple selfobject milieu" (Karterud, 1986). A typical picture is the evolution of, and resistances to, an idealizing transference to the medical director or individual therapist, simultaneous with a mirroring transference to the milieu therapists and an alter ego transference to one or more fellow patients. One should be careful in interpreting such occurrences as merely defensive reactions.

In particular, a staff with unresolved envy and rivalry may all too easily define idealization as a manifestation of splitting and therefore counteract a needed unfolding of the idealizing transference. If such a multiple positive transference situation is established, and the symptoms consequently reduced due to the consolidating effects of these selfobject relations, the further course of therapy will depend on the vulnerability, defenses, and frustrations linked to these multiple transferences and their relation to each other. A staff that is empathically attuned to multiple selfobject needs is crucial to the working through. In my opinion, much of the turmoil at psychiatric wards is the result of empathic failures regarding these complex transference manifestations.

GROUP PHENOMENOLOGY

The concepts of group self, group selfobject, group object, and group-as-a-whole may be confusing, and particularly if one invests these concepts with meanings from other phenomenological realms. According to the phenomenological terminology of Sartre (1968), the group self must be conceived as a prereflexive being, as "the group-for-me." A prereflexive ("spontaneous") being cannot be grasped from outside in any other way than through a "vicarious empathic introspection" of the observer. In the "content" group-selfobject relationship, the group self is extended to include the selfobject (or leader), which is experienced as part of the self. The selfobject is then not a matter of concern. The group (or group self) will be preoccupied with other matters which will be their group object, cathected with narcissistic or object libido or aggressive drive energy. These may be outer tasks, the problems of a member, or whatever. The selfobject will be an object for the group only in a state of disequilibrium or frustration, or in need of refueling or reassurance because of disappointments that will be experienced as a threat to the group self.

When the group starts to take *itself* as object, things become complicated, both for the theoretician and the group member. The group then reflects on itself (the now objectivated prereflexive being) from the position of "the group-for-the-other," i.e., with the eyes of a stranger. Since these acts are not performed by "the group" but by individuals with different self-reflective capacities and different positions with regard to the group self, they obviously will not agree on what they see. They will encounter a mess of self- and object representations invested with narcissistic or object libido and aggressive drive energy. And by this very act of self reflection, the group self (the prereflexive being) will change. For example, the therapist will say, "The group avoids exploring its relationship with me because it fears the prevalent solution to the group's problem will then be pulverized, and that the consequences will be exposure to unknown anxieties." The individual then has to reexamine his role in the group: Is this true? Am I participating in a group that does such and such? If so, why? Do I want to be a member of such a group? and so on. Through group-as-a-whole interpretations, the group self and the individuals are thrown into perpetual existential dilemmas. These dilemmas are more similar to those described by Turquet (1975) in his "Threat to Identity in the Large Group" than to the anxieties due to a primal scene hypothesized by Bion.

THE LEADER AND THE SELFOBJECT

In the idealizing group, the selfobject is not difficult to identify. If not an actual person, his remnants will do, be it the Bible, the Koran, the thoughts of Mao Tse-tung, the collected works of Sigmund Freud, and so on. A faculty of priests can act as deputies of the remote selfobject, which thereby will be counted as present, embodied in persons acting on its behalf. This is a bit more difficult in the grandiose group because this modality has so many different manifestations, ranging from almost pure fight-flight groups to benign creative groups. These will parallel the enormous variance in individuals, from the archaic grandiose self to the healthy and creative grandiose self. However, the leader in the grandiose group will be *the mirroring agent*. In the psychoanalytic situation the patient will mainly be mirrored through a projected mirroring agent and an experience of being deeply understood, rather than by praise and declarations of love from the side of the psychoanalyst. In real life, mirroring is to a large extent a reciprocal situation, much like falling in love. The mirroring is mutual. The admiring glance will most likely produce a similar response. There is a deep truth in the saying that one can fall in love with falling in love. But who is then the leader or the mirroring agent? During the exhibitionistic Nazi parades, Hitler mirrored the masses, just as the masses mirrored Hitler. The supremacy of Hitler was nevertheless clear to the masses. The authoritarian but admired leader is a frequent phenomenon in grandiose groups, but not a necessity. In more benign pairing groups, the members obviously mirror each other. This is the ideal for many women's liberation and gay groups: a flat, nonhierarchical organization and mutual mirroring. When such groups become organized, they most likely will develop authoritarian leaders in a traditional sense, although the structure will remain informal.

A SEPARATE ALTER EGO GROUP?

In his latest book, Kohut (1984) proposed a tripolar self. The search for an alter ego selfobject relation, which earlier was conceived as a species of the mirroring transference, was given an independent position parallel to the grandiose and idealizing self. Contrary to the grandiose self that searches for admiration of its supremacy, and to the idealizing self that admires the wise selfobject, the alter ego self searches to merge with something or somebody equal to itself, a twin. Kohut reckoned this pole to be the unconscious substrate for intimate friendship and for group and national identity. He illustrated this by citing the relaxed feeling experienced by travelers returning from abroad. In an alter ego relation there is no need for explaining everything. One knows, or believes one knows, that other people share the same basic experience of the world.

Will there be a specific group modality dominated by this twinship transference? I suggest that twinship transferences are an undercurrent in many different groups, but perhaps occur most frequently in the grandiose groups to which Kohut originally attributed them. In my own research, alter ego transferences rationalized by the group ideology were seen within the grandiose groups. Twinship, I believe, should not be equated to egalitarian ideology per se. All groups require that their members be equal in some respects. This equality may very well refer to submission to a strong group morale and thus differs from the deep experience of being basically the same. In therapy groups one can observe twinship transferences between two members that are the result of their individual psychopathology rather than a feature of the group as a whole. This is an area in need of further exploration and clarification.

THE GRANDIOSE GROUP, PAIRING AND COLLECTIVE NARCISSISTIC RAGE

I began this chapter by asserting that Bion could not account for the apparent close connection between sexual love and hate in groups and argued that the sexual love and hate group should be conceived of as belonging to one particular group modality. The societal counterpart ("the specialized work groups") to sexual love and hate groups in Bion's schemata is the aristocracy and the army. The aristocracy was believed to represent an organized pairing group because of its preoccupation with breeding. However, to most people the grandiosity of the aristocracy will be more apparent than their breeding activity: the declaration of their supremacy; their devaluation of common people; their arrogance; their preoccupation with costumes, celebration, and beauty; and their violent fight for the preservation of their power and privileges. The preoccupation with pairing in the aristocracy seems mainly a means of preserving the exclusivity of their grandiose position. Be it the breeding of racehorses or of the aristocracy itself. The blood must not be contaminated with inferiority.

The fight group spectrum of the grandiose group should be conceived as collective narcissistic rage reactions. A fight group as reaction to a group trauma cannot be regarded as a "group" in the way Bion describes it, since cohesive forces will be established *prior* to the fight reaction and the group will, it is hoped, survive *in spite of* the rage. In the *organized* hostile grandiose group, recurring outlets of rage are due less to excessive group trauma than to the individual infantile traumas of its members. These groups are best conceived of as organized outlets for chronic narcissistic rage. This rage, however, is mobilized not so much in the name of sadism as in the interest of avoiding self-fragmentation. The process of externalizing rage through projective identification will purify the self and restore its supremacy. It safeguards the "good self." The question of fragmentation of the self leads us to consider sexuality as a source of internal disruption. Kohut regarded cathected part objects as partly products of self-fragmentation and partly attempts at restoration. The child turns to fetish activities not because of strong inherent drives whereby transitional objects become cathected with oral, anal, or genital libido, but in order to counteract further disintegration due to insufficient mirroring. Oversexualization of objects can be regarded as a restorative activity, something frequently observed in the analysis of narcissistic and borderline personality disorders. Løfgren (1983) has pointed to the sexual elements in pairing groups as possibly a first line of defense of this sort. However, sexuality is also linked to the so-called hypercathexis of the grandiose self. The lively, creative, hopeful, joking, and euphoric group abundant with sexual metaphors, whereby the group resembles a party, has all the signs of this hypercathected grandiose self.

CONCLUSION

I have tried to outline here a self psychological theory of group dynamics. The metapsychological definition of groups is close to the original definition proposed by Freud. The ties that hold the group together are defined as identifications and selfobject relations. This theory has greater explanatory power than that of Bion. This is particularly true for the phenomenon of the grandiose group, which Bion divided into fight-flight and pairing groups. This theory has therapeutic implications different from those of the object relations theory of Bion and Melanie Klein. In accordance with Kohut, the self psychologically oriented therapist will have a more profound empathic understanding of the individual's need for selfobject relations, with both individuals and groups.

REFERENCES

Anzieu, D. (1971), L'illusion groupale. *Nouvelle Rev. Psychanal.*, 4:73–93.

Armelius, K., & Armelius, B. A. (1985), Group personality, task and group culture. In: *Bion and Group Psychotherapy*, ed. M. Pines. London: Routledge & Kegan Paul, pp. 255–273.

Battegay, R. (1976), Three central factors of group psychotherapy: Oedipal complex, rivalry conflict, narcissistic group-self. In: *Group Therapy 1976*, ed. R. Wolberg. New York: Stratton International.

Bion, W. R. (1961), *Experiences in Groups*. London: Tavistock.

Chasseguet-Smirgel, J. (1985), *The Ego Ideal*. London: Free Association.

Freud, S. (1921), Group psychology and analysis of the ego. *Standard Edition*, 18:69–143. London: Hogarth Press.

Gustafson, J. P., & Hartmann, J. J. (1978), Self-esteem in group therapy. *Contemp. Psychoanal.*, 2:311–329.

Hartmann, J. J., & Gibbard, G. S. (1974), A note on fantasy themes in the evolution of group culture. In: *Analysis of Groups*, ed. G. S. Gibbard, J. J. Hartmann, & R. D. Mann. San Francisco: Jossey-Bass.

Harwood, I. H. (1983), The application of self-psychological concepts to group psychotherapy. *Internat. J. Group Psychother.*, 33:469–487.

Horwitz, L. (1984), The self in groups. *Internat. J. Group Psychother.*, 34:519–538.

Karterud, S. (1986), Consolidation of the self through inpatient group psychotherapy. Paper presented at Ninth International Congress of Group Psychotherapy, Zagreb.

—— (1988), A reliability study of a hermeneutic method: Group focal conflict analysis. *Group Analysis*, 21:333–346.

—— (in press), A study of Bion's basic assumption groups. *Human Relations*.

—— Foss, T. (in press), Group emotionality rating system. *Small Group Behav.*

Kohut, H. (1971), *The Analysis of the Self*. New York: International Universities Press.

—— (1976), Creativeness, charisma, group psychology. In: *The Search for the Self: Selected Writings of Heinz Kohut, 1950–1978*, ed. P. H. Ornstein. New York: International Universities Press, 1978, pp. 793–843.

—— (1977), *The Restoration of the Self*. New York: International Universities Press.

—— (1984), *How Does Analysis Cure?* Chicago: University of Chicago Press.

—— (1985), *Self Psychology and the Humanities*. New York: Norton.

Kriegman, D., & Solomon, L. (1985), Cult groups and the narcissistic personality: The offer to heal defects in the self. *Internat. J. Group Psychother.*, 35:239–261.

Løfgren, L. (1983), The self in a small group: A comparison of the theories of Bion and Kohut. In: *Kohut's Legacy*, ed. P. Stepansky & A. Goldberg. Hillsdale, NJ: Analytic Press, pp. 203–214.

Pines, M. (1982), Reflections on mirroring. *Group Analysis*, 15:2–26.

Sartre, J. P. (1968), *Being and Nothingness*. New York: Washington Square Press.

Slater, P. E. (1966), *Microcosm: Structural, Psychological and Religious Evolution in Groups*. New York: Wiley.

Stone, W., & Whitman, R. M. (1977), Contributions of the psychology of the self to group process and group therapy. *Internat. J. Group Psychother.*, 27:343–359.

Turquet, P. (1975), Threats to identity in the large group. In: *The Large Group: Dynamics and Therapy*, ed. L. Kreeger. London: Constable, pp. 87–144.

4

Problems in Diagnosis and Group Treatment Design with Borderline Personalities: Can Focal Conflict Theory Help?

WILLIAM E. POWLES, M.D.

ROOTS OF THE CONSTRUCT "BORDERLINE"

The construct of "Borderline Personality Disorder" (DSM-III) has emerged from a somewhat muddy brew whose ferment commenced in the late 1930s. American psychoanalysts of that period began to recognize ambulatory patients presenting as neurotic but whose thinking, motivation, and emotionality turned out on deeper acquaintance to be more like what was encountered in psychotics: a hidden primitiveness or "schizophrenia" was found in persons who were relatively well adapted socially, and who never moved into a patently psychotic diagnosis. A host of labels were proposed for this finding, terms like "latent," "as if," "narcissistic," "ambulatory," and "pseudoneurotic." Stern (1938) seems the first in the literature to have used the term "Border Line." Bleuler's classical monograph on the schizophrenias (1911) had repeatedly, if briefly, alluded to a "latent schizophrenia" as very common but rarely presenting for treatment; his usage was followed by authors such as Federn (1947). By the 1950s a clinical consensus had emerged that the diagnosis "borderline" should be a caution signal calling for specific treatment strategies (Eisenstein, 1951). Grinker, Werble, and Drye (1968) published the first and apparently the only systematic nosological study. Perry and Klerman (1978) have issued a clarion call, so far seemingly unheard, to drop the proliferation of descriptive and clinical studies and get

While I assume full responsibility for the shortcomings of this chapter, I am most grateful to Dr. Dorothy Stock Whitaker for discussion and comments on its contents.

67

down to some serious testing of hypotheses. As psychotherapists tend to be particularly slovenly nosologists, and because borderlines are their special concern, the diagnosis may well be said to be "riding off madly in all directions."

A good capsule discussion, including names for many precursors of the terms "narcissistic personality disorder" and "borderline personality organization," is Stanton's (in Nicholi, 1978, pp. 288–289). Links (1982) reviews a number of studies attempting to validate the construct. Gunderson and Singer's review (1975) is definitive. They find six relatively operational criteria for the "borderline patient" (their term) for which some consensus exists: (1) intense affect, usually hostile, often depressive; (2) impulsive behavior, often self-destructive; (3) possession of skills in social adaptation; (4) brief psychotic experiences, usually paranoid; (5) primitive, bizarre projective test responses, and (6) personal relationships polarizing between transient/superficial and dependent/demanding. We might add to these some features of a more metapsychological kind which have become popular in statements on the subject: impaired object relations (both external and internal); defective or regressive reality testing; the development of "instantaneous" and "psychotic" transferences; "pan-anxiety"; "pan-sexuality"; and developmental problems at all levels.

PROBLEMS IN MAKING THE DIAGNOSIS

The many valiant attempts to make of "borderline" a formal *clinical diagnosis* with operational criteria, cannot, I believe, ever be successful. DSM-III offers an Axis II template narrow enough in specificity to exclude many patients you or I might consider borderline. There are simply too many kinds of borderline people with too many presenting pictures (see Roth, 1982) to force them into any one clinical state. In view of the many possibilities for utter chaos, then, let us recall that "diagnosis" means "understanding" or "thorough knowing": *diagnosis is process*, not label. Some of us who taught at Cincinnati in the 1950s and 1960s use with affection the diagnostic schema recommended by the late Maurice Levine. The sequential process consisted of several steps, paraphrased as follows:

1. *Clinical diagnosis:* finding the "best fit" between the patient's presenting state and templates in a standard classification of disorders.

2. *Dynamic diagnosis:* laying out the strengths of various psychic structures and forces, the interactions between them, the mental mechanisms involved, and the amount of regression present—*in the present.*

3. *Genetic diagnosis:* discerning the patient's developmental line, tasks and levels achieved, fixations and vulnerabilities—*in the past.*

4. *Transference diagnosis:* what the patient does with the professional relationship, and what that indicates.

5. *Countertransference diagnosis:* intuiting the patient's makeup from the clinician's subjective "gut" reactions.

6. *Treatment planning:* tactics for immediate, restorative help, strategies for longer-term reconstructive assistance (the patient's ability to participate intelligently in treatment planning and to contract realistically might be included here as well as under "transference diagnosis").

If "borderline," then, cannot be a *clinical diagnosis,* it can be a shorthand statement of *dynamic, genetic, transference, and countertransference diagnosis* and therefore is highly relevant for treatment planning: a kind of red sticker that says "Fragile: Handle with Care" and that we attach to the regular manifest of contents.

But how does a watchful clinician really begin to think of "borderline" early in the assessment process?

Perhaps the patient makes us more uncomfortable than the clinical diagnosis warrants; despite persistent efforts we realize we are not getting a coherent history; the history as obtained is far more horrendous than the clinical diagnosis would suggest; the patient seems to be expecting far more from us than we realistically can provide; we receive shocks and disappointments in the patient's ability to comprehend and to contract; the patient erupts with strong feelings that are disavowed and that we do not comprehend. If all goes well and we are on our toes, we begin to piece together the diagnostic picture, using Levine's axes, and arrive at the image of a person with social skills and a social facade, with relatively normal or neurotic functioning, but with significant inferred ego weaknesses, uncompleted developmental tasks or problems "at all levels," fear pervading all transactions ("pan-anxiety"), and potentials for serious distortion and disruption of the therapeutic relationship. We attach the appropriate diagnosis—Paranoid Personality Disorder, Schizoid, Histrionic, etc., or perhaps Dysthymic Disorder, Anxiety Disorder, etc.—*but with the important rider* "borderline" to warn us of potential booby traps and the necessity for special strategic considerations in treatment.

Thus we need eternal vigilance and a "high index of suspicion" for the presence of borderline organizations. But, conversely, we must not abuse the label by finding a borderline under every bed and lurking in every closet. Such abuse, most often for what might be termed countertransference reasons, is dealt with by Reiser and Levenson (1984). The following case would, I believe, be considered reasonably typical of the genus under discussion.

CLINICAL ILLUSTRATION

Mr. T.N., now 38, is a blond, bright-eyed man with a gruffly friendly manner and a soup-strainer mustache; he works conscientiously in a job well below his potential in a drug company warehouse and is well esteemed by his superiors and coworkers. He referred himself with indolent but painful depression. I have hospitalized him four times for refuge, reassessment, and trials of antidepressant and antipsychotic drugs, which simply made him ill without any benefit. The initial clinical diagnoses were Dysthymic Disorder and Obsessive-Compulsive Neurosis, with the rider of borderline with paranoid coloring; when he is not depressed, one would think of him as a pretty solid Axis II Paranoid Personality Disorder.

A *first* warning was the intensity, yet vagueness, of a central complaint: when despondent he experiences a horrifying feeling of being corroded or polluted by some unknown poisonous substance on his clothes or skin, with discomfort in the lower abdomen and aching in the genitalia, which is unrelieved by washing his clothing repeatedly. At the best of times he has trouble acquiring new clothing: he puts off shopping, then washes any new clothing a dozen times or more before uneasily putting it on. When suffering from this complex he feels totally cut off from human contact; the feeling comes on invariably after masturbation, though this is not the only trigger. He enjoys casual sexual intercourse.

A *second* warning was that we never got a comprehensive history; I still know little of his life before the age of 12, and much of what I know is reconstructed from psychotherapy sessions.

He is an articulate but cold and lonely man who conceals strong loyalties and antipathies; probably the high point of his life was living with a rather harsh girl for two years and begetting a child who, they decided, had to be aborted. He has an annual grief reaction at the time the child would have been born. His most fervent fantasy is that a mature, warm, and loving woman will come into his world, marry him, give him children, and make life right for him. His actual heterosexual relations are either casualfeelingless nights in bed or tenuous, evanescent friendships which dissolve rapidly, with feelings of abandonment and bitterness.

T.'s parents married very young, and he was their firstborn; a younger sister, from what I understand, is surprisingly normal, a successful nurse happily married with children who are fond of their uncle. His father he depicts as a huge man who works at a skilled trade, always drank too much, and was consistently cruel and abusive to T. By early adolescence this abuse reached the level of physical violence. After being hurled downstairs at age 16, T. decided that he would kill his father, if necessary, but would never again submit to his aggression. He acquired a reputation as a potentially dangerous fellow, not to be fooled with, yet he managed to have a couple of close buddies, with whom he still has distant contact. His mother seems to have been a nervous, diffident, eccentric woman who developed a paranoid type of psychosis during T.'s early adolescence: she rummaged in his dresser drawers for evidence that he was masturbating, and accused him of impregnating girls and being in the drug traffic with the Mafia.

T. has always firmly believed that his puberty was delayed abnormally and that he has a permanent defect of some vague kind in his genital system and his brain. No medical evidence exists for this: he is a muscular, athletic, healthy male. However, he seems to have suffered a very distinct obsessive neurosis at puberty, conflicted about sex and washing clothes and linen endlessly, without relief, after masturbation.

We will return to his case later.

IMAGES AND REFLECTIONS

Why has the word "borderline" been adopted as shorthand for the kind of people with whom we are dealing here? On what analogy or model is the word based, and what images does it conjure up? Clearly, the borderline lives, more or less permanently, hovering over, or stuck or impaled upon, a border between somewhere and somewhere: "neurotic" and "psychotic" (or "schizophrenic") are the names or qualities of these somewheres. But he never comes down solidly to dwell in either one as a definitive citizen or landed immigrant. If he did, the diagnosis would no longer be "borderline" but classically "neurotic" or "psychotic." And that is exactly what the "borderline patient" does not do.

The borderline patient, then, lives hovering in suspended animation in a kind of other-world. He is a stubborn, tenacious fence sitter who never, or only momentarily, falls off. Have you ever tried sitting over a long time atop a fence, trying not to fall off on either side, with a slimy morass on one side and a menacing bull grazing on the other? Whether the fence is of plain or barbed wire, hard-edged planking or mossy rail, it is not easy to keep safe amid such disequilibrium and discomfort. To get to safety you would have to become a tightrope walker, teetering and gyrating along, trying not to be noticed, panicked, harassed, despairing, expecting destruction at any moment. Or maybe you have walked a railroad track in the country. There seems no very good way of doing this. The ties do not fit your stride. You try to walk along a rail, swaying, flailing, frustrated as you fall off again every few steps. The best way to get somewhere is to have a partner; each of you walk one rail, holding hands or both grasping a long stick. That way you help each other balance for long distances. If you come to a bridge, keep going, look ahead, do not look down through the terrifying gaps in the ties. If you come to a tunnel, do the same. Do not quit, because a train may come thundering along: if bridge or tunnel are long enough you will be provided with resting places where you can step aside for a train. Then you heave a great sigh of relief when you reach the end or the other side.

Borderline patient and therapist, or borderline patient and group, are of course that dyad walking the rails, balancing each other, headed in an agreed-upon direction, traversing frightening stretches, maintaining the best distance between them, not too far, not too near, but always in contact. Recent presentations of the principles of treatment for the borderline mirror but do not greatly improve upon what was recommended in the early days (see Eisenstein, 1951): the monitoring and maintenance of a working alliance, the need to maintain optimal distance, the avoidance and resolution of stormy transference developments, and the injection of support and sympathy (has this become a bad word?), along with incisive interventions, consistency, and careful contracting in which one does not promise more than can be delivered.

Among this complex array of patients, dare we say out loud that some should not be treated? It is of course difficult to be sure who these are, but the torment of a relationship meant to be therapeutic may bedevil and imperil rather than assist their lonely pilgrim's progress. Many are helped best by infrequent and minimal therapeutic contact, the value of which we should never derogate. Of the ones who can be helped by systematic or intensive psychotherapy—and again I am not sure how we can discern these clearly, short of a trial of therapy from which patient and therapist may have trouble extricating themselves—most clinicians would agree that they need a face-to-face, clearly structured approach, with a clear contract and clear limits. Group psychotherapy is just such an approach—face-to-face, contracted, and lacking some of the transference traps of individual work.

A TREATMENT DESIGN DECISION TREE

The following clinical decision tree is also a set of hypotheses that need to be tested by controlled observation and analysis. Neither clinical experience nor research have to date provided us anything more solid.

1. *Is this patient "borderline"?* An affirmative answer to this diagnostic question can be inferred from dynamic, genetic, transference, and countertransference material, regardless of the manifest clinical diagnosis. The most harrowing and difficult psychotherapy case of my career started out with my neglecting this question. Fortunately, this person is alive and reasonably happy twenty years later.

Another case of missed diagnosis and its consequences was that of Mrs. U. W., age 36. Referred by a colleague for a trial of group psychotherapy because of general dysphoria and marital dissatisfactions, she felt isolated and affect-starved with her academic, undemonstrative husband in a rural farm home. Likable, creative, somewhat flamboyant, and gregarious in temperament, she fitted a diagnostic template of Mild Dysthymic Disorder in a Histrionic Personality. She accepted my instructions for the group and validated a contract for a trial of eight sessions.

U. burst into our group like a tornado, scattering flabbergasted peers and group mores in all directions. She demanded changes of procedure at every session. Once she suggested doing away with chairs and coffee table and sitting on the floor; the group responded with embarrassed passive rejection. She baited the therapist frequently; he tried to support her but had trouble with his own feelings of dismay. The group accomplished little save trying to understand and accept this wild creature and the wild part of all of us.

Her eighth session she dominated with a raucous barrage of criticisms of the group and rather personal insults toward the therapist; she stomped out dramatically just before time was up, never to be seen again.

I had failed to consider the possibility of borderline pathology in the beginning; perhaps even then I might not have spotted her failure to understand our contract, or predicted the stormy "instant" transference to the group as unsatisfactory mother and to the therapist as unconcerned oedipal father. But I might have questioned her eligibility for an analytic group.

2. *Do I treat this patient at all?* This question should be asked once one has made the diagnosis and attached the "borderline" caveat. Even a protracted diagnostic process may enmesh patient and clinician in a sticky relationship or "instant transference," difficult to resolve and potentially harmful. We must courageously tell the patient what course of action, or inaction, is best recommended for the present, and deal with our own anxieties and uncertainties on our own, or with the help of a trusted consultant. Strategically limited psychotherapy, including no treatment at all, is best contracted at the beginning, for positive reasons; then we must stick to the contract.

3. *Is systematic, intensive psychotherapy desirable for this patient?* If so, what form should it take: individual? group? combined? sequential? If you start with individual treatment, you are stuck with that for some time, with all the transference vicissitudes to be expected and resolved; a cardinal safety rule is never to transfer a patient from individual to group because things are going badly transference-wise. If you opt for combined or simultaneous individual and group treatment, you will find many borderlines never "cathecting" the group, because of intense dyadic needs. Starting the patient in a group seems to me to run minimal risks, particularly if the contract is clear and includes an agreed-upon trial period and clearly stated treatment goals. Borderlines need a clear structure and boundaries to help with continuing anxiety over the inherent ambiguities of psychotherapy.

4. *What kind of group psychotherapy is indicated?* The basic choices are three in number: actional psychotherapy; problem-centered "group guidance"; and group psychotherapy proper (Slavson, 1960; Powles, 1983). By *actional psychotherapy* I mean psychodrama and its several derivatives (see Sacks, 1976). I still wonder if Mrs. U. W. would have had a more therapeutic outcome in an actional group. She needed to *do* something; words, feelings, and thoughts she found maddening. By *group guidance* I mean the kind of group with a problem focus, a clear task, and a relatively homogeneous patient population related to that problem and task; here solidarity develops by virtue of the members being in the same boat, and problem solving and interpersonal skills are rehearsed and enhanced. Such a group (designed, for example, around women's issues, depression prone-ness, or self-esteem and self-assertion) can well provide the kind of structure borderlines need, the security of an agreed-upon agenda, the chance to experiment within structured limits with closeness, an appreciation and sharing of whatever social skills they possess, the chance to learn new interpersonal skills and techniques for better assertion and need-satisfaction, better reality testing through consid-ering a range of interpretations and options, and the real opportunity of shifting internal images and balances in the process. By *group psychotherapy proper* I mean the range of psychoanalytically derived techniques of fostering, and using interpretively, free-floating discus-sion in a group. Here agenda and task are seen as resistance, and the sole formal aim is to foster communication as honest and spontaneous as possible, with the therapist being in a catalytic and conceptualizing role. Though a face-to-face situation with some clear boundaries, this would nonetheless be too frighteningly ambiguous for many border-lines. Indeed, we need considerably more information about which borderlines can be safely placed in free-floating group discussion therapy. Any further remarks of mine must be considered almost purely conjectural. But let me make them.

5. *If a borderline is placed in a psychoanalytically oriented group, should it be a heterogeneous group or a group designed for borderlines alone?* The latter I find a daunting proposition, suggesting all sorts of patholog-ical resonances, communication blocks and distortions, unanalyzable transferences, and unmanageable acting out. But no doubt coura-geous (or foolhardy) therapists somewhere are doing just this, and achieving perfectly good results in their innocence. My own experi-ence is of treating one or two borderlines in a heterogeneous group

and generally doing what therapeutic judgment and sensitivity dictate. The advisability of concurrent or sequential individual therapy is a question that arises again here. I know of no solid criteria for making this decision: "clinical judgment," what is practically available, and individual biases as to the relative merits of group and individual therapy are what guide us here.

6. *Is group-centered or leader-centered technique more likely to benefit the borderline patient?* Until relatively recently, "group-centered" technique has generally been rejected in North America. Instead of consistent attention to multiperson themes and group processes, and attempts to help patients help each other and the group to help the individual, our style has emphasized the therapist, working with individual problems in the group setting, as the main helper. Group-focused efforts, it has widely been believed, devaluate and denigrate the individual patient. Only one clear theory has originated in North America that provides a framework for analyzing the interpenetration of group and individual dynamics. Thus, the testing of an important and extremely difficult research question has to my knowledge not yet commenced: Are the impaired object relations, reality testing, and emotionality of the borderline patient in a group best remedied through guided peer interaction and the working through of interpersonal conflicts and attachments, or by the exploration of historical and intrapsychic matters more effectively carried out in individual therapy?

THEORIES OF GROUP MANAGEMENT: FOCAL
CONFLICT THEORY

As I suggest, we have not in North America a mainstream theory of *conducting groups* as opposed to *treating patients* (or clients or whatever else they might be called); of how to foster a cohesive group climate, keep channels of communication open, resolve conflicts and impasses, and conceive and interpret the thematic content of group transactions. The role of therapist as leader, facilitator, and helper *of the group*—as supporter, coach, and catalyst of the group's tasks *qua* group, as helping the group members to therapeutic benefit by their examining and helping each other—has been expounded mainly by our colleagues in other lands, prominent among them Foulkes (1965), who used the term "conductor" for the therapist. We may think here of the conductor of a train, or of a choir or orchestra. A generally

"British" approach has been particularly well expounded by Heath and Bacal (1968). Other well-known British theorists of group management include Bion, Rickman, and Ezriel. We are just beginning to understand what they have been trying to say, stimulated, I gather, by an interest in the British object relations movement so applicable to borderlines; we are almost entirely ignorant of South American and continental theorists of a similar orientation.

In a sense we now come back full circle. Psychoanalytic and North American in origin, the construct of "borderline" is our clinical concern. Psychoanalytic in ultimate derivation, and certainly North American in origin, even if its leading exponent has emigrated to England, is focal conflict theory. In two seminal papers (Whitman and Stock, 1958; Whitman, Lieberman, and Stock, 1960), two young psychologists (Stock and Lieberman) abetted by a psychoanalyst (Whitman) developed, from psychoanalytic foundations, a lucid and parsimonious way of summarizing and relating individual and group thematic phenomena. Whitaker (née Stock) and Lieberman (1964), then published a full-length volume of great sophistication, with the expressive title *Psychotherapy Through the Group Process*. Further expositions have come from Whitaker's pen in the same clear and elegant style (Whitaker, 1976, 1982).

Both the theory and its technical applications go under the name group focal conflict theory. Their original basis (Whitaker, 1982) was the work of Thomas French, a major psychoanalytic theoretician whose schema seemed applicable to the thematic aspects of group process. Human behavior can be most parsimoniously seen as the algebraic resultant, the solution to a conflict of motives. A *disturbing motive* (a drive, need, or impulse calling for expression and thus disturbing equilibrium) comes up against a *reactive motive* (a countervailing fear that prohibits or deflects its expression). The resultant compromise is a behavior that can be analyzed as containing elements of both sides of the conflict. Such algebraic resultants may include paralysis, inhibition, or silence as the behavior, and here there is little to indicate the nature of the conflict. Solutions can be seen to be more, or less, constructive: some block an adaptive outcome in what parallels the psychoanalytic notion of defensiveness; some open up possibilities for adaptive development, paralleling the psychoanalytic notion of sublimation. These polarities are termed "restrictive" and "enabling" solutions, respectively. In general, the aim of psychotherapy is to analyze conflicts so as to develop richer repertoires of enabling solutions.

Most persons harbor a collection of conflicts which run through their lives and are related to developmental business. Such longitudinal conflicts are termed *nuclear conflicts*. They give rise in day-to-day situations to derivative conflicts, dramatized in the here and now and therefore more immediately observable; these are the *focal conflicts* from which the theory takes its name.

Nuclear conflict is a construct inapplicable to therapy groups, which are ahistorical and, unlike individuals, contain no longitudinal, persistent characterological elements. However, in the transactions of therapy groups, in the complex thematic and associational chains of verbal and nonverbal behaviors, there is a rich opportunity for focal conflict analysis of the "gestalt," and this is offered as the central application of group focal conflict theory. Individual patients, reenacting aspects of their nuclear conflicts, both contribute to and are in turn influenced by the focal conflict of motives which can be seen to apply to the group. Thus, the therapist can technically apprehend both the unfolding of group focal conflicts and the part each individual may play in shaping them. Therapy, then, proceeds by a continuing series of focal conflict analyses.

This capsule review gives no idea of the many applications of group focal conflict theory. I must simply assert my impression of its great potential usefulness for group management and, if I am correct, for a group-centered type of therapy for borderlines. It can be used to achieve a focus on the essentials of a complex and apparently random group discussion, and of the complexities of the borderline character, thus interweaving the two. It is highly compatible with such psychoanalytic formulations as "transference," though this term is not used in focal conflict theory. Patients come to understand the frame of reference and to use it in their own way. Certain central precepts— e.g., the primacy of dealing with *reactive* motive—are guides to good psychotherapy in general. Its lucid formulations should permit good reliability among observers and the generation of useful research hypotheses.

CLINICAL ILLUSTRATION

Let us now attempt to apply the theory and method to our friend T. N. and his participation in two episodes in a therapy group. I shall try to formulate a relevant and plausible nuclear conflict running through T.'s life and to see, in focal conflict terms, how this interlocks with his relationships with the group.

T.'s complex development seems to have brought him into a relation with the world and with himself that can be simplified as the following nuclear conflict:

Disturbing Motive		*Reactive Motive*
Craving to be close, warm, and secure with others; more specifically, having his manhood affirmed by closeness to a loving and giving woman.	X	Fear of his own corrosive and poisonous rage (originally toward his violent father and intrusive, psychotic mother) as destroying others and all possibility for contact and love.

Solution

Warily and carefully monitor distance; experience his rage and desolation at the interface with others (skin and genitalia); direct his unattainable wishes toward an ideal and therefore unattainable woman.

T. N. was enrolled in once-weekly analytic group psychotherapy combined with once-weekly analytic individual therapy with the same therapist, on the assumption that this would provide good momentum and a "cushion" should either modality generate unanalyzable difficulties for him. He moved smoothly on from his trial period but shortly "bolted" therapy for the West Coast, from which he quickly returned, suicidal. He started back into therapy from the shelter of the hospital, then resumed work. His individual sessions (which we will arbitrarily neglect henceforth) tended to be dry recitations of present and past life events; perhaps the most "mutative" interpretation I ever offered was that he treated himself like a machine instead of a human being. In the group he became Mister Faithful in attendance and in upholding the group's tasks of free sharing and communication. Yet, as his peers repeatedly and gently commented, he was one of the least spontaneous members. The feeling which was most important for him, but about which he could not be free, was his chronic rage at the human race. He made good friends with both an older man and a younger (S.X.) and acted out mildly but frequently by fraternizing with them outside the group meetings; he became for a while a virtual member of the older man's family. The group (including therapists) intuited his need for closeness and did not set sharp limits for him.

Episode 1

A year after T.'s enrollment, S. X. reported that he had lost his temper in downtown traffic and had accidentally sideswiped a wealthy and influential citizen, who had charged him with a serious crime. He was terrified and defensive. There was collateral evidence that the group was struggling with envy toward the therapist at this time. Peers were ambivalent. Some sincerely supported S. and believed it was a true accident, some suspected uneasily that he had rammed the other car deliberately in his anger, knowing who the man was (a court later exonerated him of the charge). T. was angry and judgmental, insisting that S. was lying about the seriousness of the crime and his own motivation. They got into a real harangue, with loud voices and cursing; T. pounded the coffee table, and all, including the therapist, thought there would be a fistfight or wrestling match. It was the strongest and clearest feeling T. had ever shared in the group. S. stormed out of the room and never returned despite my efforts. Clearly, this was a restrictive rather than an enabling solution, but to what focal conflict?

For the group the conflict consisted of what to do with angry and threatening feelings of a transferential kind toward the therapist. Various members suppressed, denied, and (in the case of S.) displaced and acted out the group's disturbing motive. This might be formulated as follows:

Disturbing Motive		*Reactive Motive*
Fury at therapist for "having it made," being happy, prosperous, and powerful while members were powerless, unhappy, and frustrated.	X	Fear of retaliatory punishment or abandonment by powerful and needed therapist.

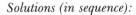

Solutions (in sequence):

1. Suppression, denial, and failure to express the conflict.
2. Displacement and acting out of the anger by a group member.
3. Punishment and extrusion of that member, through the agency of a more powerful T. N., the "conscience" of the group and now its policeman.

Now, what of T. N.? How does his nuclear conflict interweave with the group's current problem? He too is caught poignantly, needing to express anger at his terrible father, terrified that if he does he will lose the therapist, his best friend and lifeline (his own words some time later) and possibly be killed in the process. His solution includes obeying the group's injunction, of which he is the prime spokesman, to be feelingful and truthful, but in doing so to avoid his own dilemma by a judgmental wrath toward his younger and weaker friend, who at that moment becomes an enemy. His police action on behalf of the group ensures that the shared focal conflict remains submerged. His corrosive rage shows for a short time and once more proves destructive; however, he remains a member of the group and, he believes, the friend and ally of the therapist. He is greatly remorseful and tries, unsuccessfully, to bring his friend back into the group.

Episode 2

T. N. makes only slow headway over many months; his only visible gain is a spectacular (though relatively unreported and unobtrusive) improvement in his relation with his parents, whom he comes to enjoy—he believes this change comes from them rather than from himself! He finally terminates from the group under the following circumstances.

An older and a younger woman, both rather attractive, are being assimilated into the group; T. has been for some time covertly interested in a woman of his own age in the group, and may be having a secret liaison with her. The two newish members are lively and involved but tend conspicuously to be superficial, to fail to look inward, and to deny meaning to their life experiences and to events in the group; they are confronted gently and persistently with this, T. again being the group's most active spokesman. He clearly wants these women to like him and get closer to him, but he is judgmental of them. The group becomes polarized as to whether or not the new members are denying; E., an old-timer who still often uses denial, defends them, while T. might be said to be the prosecutor. We might state the focal conflict for the group as follows:

Disturbing Motive	*Reactive Motives*
Heterosexual curiosity and interest stimulated by entry of attractive new members.	1. Fear of disrupting group solidarity by rivalries and jealousies. 2. Fear of therapist's ridicule of these interests as juvenile (projected shame).

Solution

Please therapist and preserve group by polarizing and arguing about group mores being flouted by more recent comers.

T. asks leave to miss a meeting to go sailing with his father; it is agreed that this is important for him. He never returns. Privately he tells me he cannot stand so much denial, and that such a group cannot be of help to him. It is clear he has suffered a great loss in leaving the group, but my repeated suggestion that he not burn bridges to important human relationships do no good, nor do explorations and interpretations. He has been extruded now, or has withdrawn himself. He had taken part deeply in the group focal conflict; his role as conscience or policeman has this time, in his eyes, alienated him from the fellowship; he has shamed himself before the two new women, whom he really liked and who stirred his quest for the ideal woman; his old girlfriend in the group disapproves of him; he is outnumbered. Rather than disrupt the group, be ridiculed, and lose face, or let his anger come out again, he suicides, so to speak, from the life of the group. Over the next six months T. went steadily downhill until finally he was in continuous crisis, drinking heavily, putting off joining an alcoholism program, dogged by suicidal thinking, and almost constantly in his "contamination" complex. He entered the hospital briefly, and then his father took him home, where he began to rally. Then he met and rather quickly became engaged to a divorcee, five years his senior, with a ten-year-old son T. likes and who is apparently a surrogate for his aborted baby. Six months later still, he is happy and stable, has started up a small business with his fiancee, with whom he lives rather dependently in a faithful intimate relationship, and plans marriage as soon as her divorce is final. He remains the gruff, guarded man he always was, but has no complaints of depression, his "complex," or abuse of alcohol. We meet at long intervals and do no probing. He gives the group credit for many insights.

This brief exercise in focal conflict theory is, I suppose, my solution to a focal conflict: a disturbing motive to make something simple, clear, manageable, and logical out of the complexities and ambiguities of borderline personalities and group psychotherapy, as against the horrifying fear that it can never be so, that all is flux and uncertainty! I hope that it is an enabling rather than a restrictive solution, which may provoke thought, debate, and the reality testing of research. I hope too that others will give group focal conflict theory a serious trial.

REFERENCES

Bleuler, E. (1911), *Dementia Praecox or the Group of Schizophrenias*, trans. J. Zinkin. New York: International Universities Press, 1950.

Eisenstein, V. (1951), Differential psychotherapy of borderline states. *Psychiat. Quart.*, 25:379–401.

Federn, P. (1947), Principles of psychotherapy in latent schizophrenia. *Amer. J. Psychother.*, 1:129–144.

Foulkes, S. H. (1965), *Therapeutic Group Analysis*. New York: International Universities Press.

Grinker, R. R., Sr., Werble, B., & Drye, R. C. (1968), *The Borderline Syndrome*. New York: Basic Books.

Gunderson, J. G., & Singer, M. T. (1975), Defining borderline patients: An overview. *Amer. J. Psychiat.*, 132:1–10.

Heath, E. S., & Bacal, H. A. (1968), A method of group psychotherapy at the Travistock Clinic. *Internat. J. Group Psychother.*, 18:21–30.

Links, P. S. (1982), The existence of the borderline diagnosis: Studies on diagnostic validity. *Can. J. Psychiat.*, 27:585–592.

Nicholi, A. M., Jr., ed. (1978), *Harvard Guide to Modern Psychiatry*. Cambridge, MA: Harvard University Press.

Perry, J. C., & Klerman, G. L. (1978), The borderline patient: A comparative analysis of four sets of diagnostic criteria. *Arch. Gen. Psychiat.*, 35:141–150.

Powles, W. E. (1983), An overview of group methods. In: *Comprehensive Group Psychotherapy*, ed. H. I. Kaplan & B. J. Sadock, 2nd ed. Baltimore: Williams & Wilkins, pp. 71–73.

Rabin, H. M., & Rosenbaum, M., eds. (1976), *How To Begin a Psychotherapy Group: Six Approaches*. London: Gordon & Breach.

Reiser, D. E., & Levenson, H. (1984), Abuses of the borderline diagnosis: A clinical problem with teaching opportunities. *Amer. J. Psychiat.*, 141:1528–1532.

Roth, B. E. (1982), Six types of borderline and narcissistic patients: An initial typology. *Internat. J. Group Psychother.*, 32:9–27.

Sacks, J. M. (1976), The psychodrama group: Formations and beginnings. In: *How To Begin a Psychotherapy Group: Six Approaches*, ed. H. M. Rabin & M. Rosenbaum. London: Gordon & Breach, pp. 58–78.

Slavson, S. R. (1960), When is a therapy group not a therapy group? *Internat. J. Group Psychother.*, 10:3–21.

Stern, A. (1938), Psychoanalytic investigation of and therapy in the border line group of neuroses. *Psychoanal. Quart.*, 7:467–489.

Whitaker, D.S. (1976), A group centred approach. In: *How To Begin a Psychotherapy Group: Six Approaches*, ed. H. M. Rabin & M. Rosenbaum. London: Gordon & Breach, pp. 36–57.

———(1982), A nuclear conflict and group focal conflict model for integrating individual and group-level phenomena in psychotherapy groups. In: *The Individual and the Group: Boundaries and Interrelations*, Vol. 1, ed. M. Pines & L. Rafaelson. London: Plenum, pp. 321–338.

———Lieberman, M. A. (1964), *Psychotherapy Through the Group Process*. New York: Atherton.

Whitman, R. M., Lieberman, M. A., & Stock, D. (1960), The relation between individual and group conflicts in psychotherapy. *Internat. J. Group Psychother.*, 10:259–286.

———Stock, D. (1958), The group focal conflict. *Psychiat.*, 21:269–276.

5

Anchoring the Self through the Group: Congruences, Play, and the Potential for Change

JEROME W. KOSSEFF, Ph.D.

Before offering some ideas about changes in the self through group therapy, mostly those changes that tend toward anchoring the drifting self, first to the group and then to itself, I would first like to confront the perplexing issue of psychotherapeutic change. "Among the key concepts in psychoanalytic theory," writes Jackson (1968),

> are the assumptions that therapeutic change is caused by an increase in the patient's self-understanding and that transference is necessary if that self-understanding is to be sufficiently effective or "deep." . . . However, when both analyst and patient are included in the description of the analytic situation . . . it is possible to regard the analytic situation itself as largely responsible for a change in the patient . . . [p. 127].

Jackson puts it this way: the analyst tells the patient that he will be in charge of the treatment, but promptly proceeds to tell the patient what position to assume, how to speak (via free association) and generally directs his life in many ways, especially in placing the focus on feelings. The general framework is of the analyst as a benevolent helper, but the patient is punished by being labeled—if he does not conform to the analytic requirements—as "resisting." This paradoxical framework is at odds with the patient's experience; the patient is

87

forced out of his usual set and must change his ways, as cherished familiar ways no longer work. Both views, the efficacy of the analysis of transference and the paradoxical deployment of contradictory requirements, are valid ways of understanding change in this situation.

In other words, going to the analyst in the first place constitutes an effort at change. But it is change within an ongoing system. The patient is bound to continue in his symptomatic and dysphoric behavior because, despite his pain, the system is dear to him, the pain inextricably woven into the totality of his self. So we may regard his coming for treatment as first-order change, the seeking of change within a system that itself remains unchanged. Such first-order change always appears to be based on common sense: if the patient wants help, he goes where it appears it may be forthcoming. Or a more homely example: if we want our car to go faster up the hill, we simply give it more gas, more of the same. But if it is a steep hill, we may eventually have to shift gears as well in order to get up it. This is second-order change, a resort to another process, one outside the gas pedal system of acceleration alone. Thus, what is required to get up the hill is a discontinuity, a disjunctive jump from the gas pedal to the gear shift, from a change within the existing system to a change outside it, which will then influence the entire system of acceleration in any of several ways, e.g., we might then be able to ease up on the gas pedal, we might stall out, and so on.

Second-order change always seems discontinuous, disconcerting, or even illogical or weird. But it is the stuff out of which lasting change is made. Another example of this two-step concept of change: we have a couple who presumably began to encounter difficulties because of the routine nature of their sex life. Their frequency of intercourse decreased, they increasingly avoided each other; the ever decreasing frequency worried them and led them to engage in more of the same (i.e., more avoidance). One night, on vacation in the guest bedroom of a friend's house, the husband had to get out of bed, which was pushed against the wall. He started to climb over his wife and then, in his own words, "realized there was something of value there," and they had intercourse. This somehow broke the ice, and their sexual relations returned to an adequate frequency thereafter (Watzlawick, Weakland, and Fisch, 1974). This is second-order change.

In psychotherapy we must confound and neutralize the defensive disjunction we call resistance—or the loss of relatedness—by a counterdisjunction. Only by bringing in some counter to an accepted pattern of cognition, affect, and action can we prepare the patient for change (Schlesinger, 1981).

In talking about how the group prepares the patient for change, we are describing how the self gets a more secure footing for itself through the group. I shall deal with two of the preconditions for change in narcissistic and borderline patients that I deem essential. *Congruences* between group members is the first, and by this I mean those sufficient equivalences in the lives and selves of group members which make for feelings of kinship, as well as providing props for mirroring and projection. *Play* is the second central and unique precondition provided by the group, leading to both continuity and change in the self. The word should not be taken to imply that members regard the group as casual, only that there is a sense of security and comfortableness with each other that serves as a holding and facilitating environment for serious consideration of the self and others.

It is not easy, of course, to delineate with full vividness the feeling-tone in the group "at play." It is a mood evoked by many evanescent exchanges and fleeting nonverbal cues. Perhaps the quality of play can be overheard in the waiting room, in the soft exchanges of greeting, the laughter, the telling of quick anecdotes of the intervening week, even when admixed with anxiety. In the group, one senses play in the overall quality of pleased, slightly restless anticipation when sessions begin. Play is the result of the encouragement by the leader of easiness, trust, and a paradoxical kind of approach to affect-laden material (Schlesinger, 1981). Play employs a kind of joking use of phrases, fantasies, and metaphors that have become the idiomatic common property of the group, bearing emotional freight of the utmost significance. This kind of play gradually expands into a hardly perceptible but pervasive climate in the group which says to the members: We can all go into the Hall of Mirrors (Pines, 1981) and be a little scared by the distortions we see of our own bodies, our own selves, and each other, but we can at the same time laugh a bit at what we see, and this will make it just a bit easier to bear, because we are all in it together, and together we shall find our way out of it, perhaps a bit better off for this shared scary look at what we can do to our own selves when we have lost touch with true self-perspectives. Play is an essential precondition for true

psychotherapeutic change in the group. Through play, psychotherapeutic change can shift from threat to opportunity.

CLINICAL ILLUSTRATION

I shall present a synopsis of several months in the life of one
group, with a few micro-samples of congruences in the overall climate
of play I sought to foster, and how these two preconditions contributed to first- and second-order change in the selves of group
members. Of course, this group interaction does not take into account
the effects of individual therapy or other influences on the several
patients, but nevertheless, it can suggest the importance of congruences and play. The group I will describe was an ongoing one, in
existence about nine years, with ten members: Donald, Paul, Francine, Jim, Pamela, Janice, Cordelia, Norbert, Arlene, and Jacqueline.
The focus will be on special congruences that are apparent between
Donald and Paul, Jim and Pamela, Cordelia and Arlene, and Jacqueline and Pamela.

Donald, 50 years old, had been in conjoint therapy for almost
three years. He was a short, slightly heavy man of Jewish background
about which he was rather reticent, with a sister some eight years
younger. The group members were startled at accidentally finding
out that this sister was married. One member said that until now her
fantasy of the sister had been that she was a "dried-up prune."

Donald had come into group because of difficulties in establishing solid and enduring relationships. He had many nodding acquain-
tances among men, but feelings of rivalry and homosexual anxiety got
in the way of greater intimacy with them. While he had two women in
tow at the time he came into group, he was most concerned that he
not be "trapped" into continuing relationships with them, as had been
the case with his ex-wife. Early on, the group helped him to tell his
ex-wife that he was cutting down his alimony payments. He was most
surprised and gratified by this help, especially from the women of the
group, who seemingly accepted him almost at once as a full man
worthy of their interest.

After he had been in group about one year, Donald moved into
a somewhat larger apartment, with two bedrooms. This move, he said,
had stimulated the woman he had been dating to become "pushy," to
want to move in with him. She became hysterical one evening,
pounded him physically, and made such a racket that neighbors called

the police. Donald denied that he was upset at this, focusing instead on his relief that her actions had brought about the separation he had dreaded making himself. From time to time thereafter, one or another woman in the group laughingly offered to rent his spare bedroom, and while at first he seemed anxious at these offers, he was gradually able to respond to the jest in these overtures, aware now that he was being accepted rather than invaded. This kind of appreciation by the entire group later enabled Donald to initiate the ending of yet another unsatisfactory relationship.

Donald had also had to arrange separate quarters for his senile mother, because his father resented her and refused to care for her. Donald had in turn resented his "self-centered" father and his sister as well, who had participated little in making arrangements for the mother. In addition, Donald resented and rejected the father's own demands on Donald's time, noting with righteous anger that the father had ignored his last birthday, and that of Donald's son as well.

Donald was also angry at his employer, the head of a trucking firm, for playing patriarch to his employees. Feeling unappreciated, Donald had through the years harbored a smoldering resentment toward him. About two years before, he had confronted the employer and told him that he had felt discriminated against when raises had been given. When the employer offered him a bit more, Donald spurned it in such a way as to nearly lose his job. Since then, he had been wanting to leave, more than before, but found himself procrastinating, even though he felt the job was essentially a dead end.

Another group member, Paul, was one of its three remaining original members. His father, like Donald's, had rejected the mother, who was severely hypochondriacal, and had left her in Paul's care. Paul had come into group with a problem of impotence, and of impotent rages. He was a sensitive, intuitive, rather wispy and intellectualized teacher at a well-known art school. Thirty-eight years old, he came from a Maryland Presbyterian family of some wealth, and was the second of five children, the only son. His father had built up a successful manufacturing business from nothing. But Paul saw his father as a curmudgeon whose only contact with his son took the form of lecturing; worse yet, Paul felt that his father had always preferred his sisters to himself. This feeling that they were preferred had continued into adulthood, and had spread from the sisters to their husbands as well, even though Paul sat on the board of his father's company and drew an income from it to supplement his meager salary and income from private art lessons. In group, change began when he started to overcome his jealousy and dislike of one brother-in-law, whose determination when he replaced Paul's father as head of the failing family firm made him rather admirable in Paul's eyes, less like the hated idealized figure of his father, and more real and struggling. When Paul married one of his art students, Donald was impressed. Paul had been unhappy and frequently impotent with his previous and mothering girlfriend, a social worker. Now he seemed very happy and potent. Also, after I had accepted a very tentative invitation from Paul to visit one of his art shows about three years previous, Paul had grudgingly acknowledged that his father had also begun showing interest in his art and his shows, and had offered financial aid for several art projects, overtures which Paul somehow had never taken up. Gradually Paul became able to view his father as interested in his welfare, while before he had been totally convinced that his father would either ignore him entirely or take over any project dear to him.

Paul had a problem at work similar to Donald's: a longstanding frustration and rage at the founding head of his art school, a brilliant but quite paranoid man whose dripping sarcasm kept Paul and other faculty tyrannized and humiliated. About three months earlier, he had again voiced his desire to leave his position, if only he could find another situation of equal prestige. Like Donald, however, he had been unable to bring himself to write a resume, with its implication of change. In a group session following several in which they had shared this problem, each came back with good news. Paul had negotiated a series of interviews for a new apartment in a low-cost housing development, and had been accepted; he and his wife were tremendously excited at the prospect of moving from their tiny hole-in-the-wall to this spacious place with a view. But he was envious when Donald told of progress with his resume, conveying a buoyant feeling that "this was it!" Donald had also confided to the vice president of his firm that he was planning to leave; he was surprised at the vice president's efforts to keep him on and, if not, to help him find a suitable position. He was surprised also to learn that the president of the firm thought well of him. Shortly thereafter, the vice president confided his own marital problems to Donald. Donald seemed awed both by the trust placed in him and by the fact that an authority figure could be so like himself. This was very like Paul's discovery that his father was reachable. At the same time, Donald expressed some rather jaundiced feelings about therapy, especially his conjoint individual therapy, but without going into specifics.

In a later group session Donald sought to mobilize the other three men in the group to join with him; he felt that the six women were more vocal and interactive with each other than were the men. He also reproached me for attending more to a couple of the women in the group than to him. I pointed out to the men that they were not nearly as confrontive of me as were the women, and wondered why. There was only limited response at the time.

However, at the end of a subsequent session, Francine noted that the four men had talked—uncharacteristically but animatedly—with each other for most of the session. I asked her what this had signified; she broke up the group by responding, "They apparently have forgotten their place!" Paradoxically, she associated her playful response to a preference for watching her father's card games, rather than her mother's.

About two months later, Donald waxed enthusiastic about a fiftieth birthday party. He had been avoiding dating since his last breakup and had some concern about impotence, again as Paul had. Donald saw this birthday party as a restitutive event. The following session, Donald told of the success of the party. Later in the session, he casually asked Jim how he liked the party. Jim merely said he enjoyed it, and the group went on to other matters. It was not until the next time that it became evident to the group that Donald had asked Jim to *his* party, and that Jim had accepted. This information aroused some outrage among the group members, some berating Donald and accusing him—and, to a lesser extent, Jim—of secretiveness and "acting out." Donald thought all this over at length, but did not see its relevance to me at the time. But he was resentful of Jim for leaving him "in the lurch to deal with all these angry women"; several had expressed their disappointment and displeasure when he said he would not have invited them, since he was at the time seeking a rapprochement with men. He was taken aback at the strength of feeling they expressed, and began to wonder about his secretiveness and his surprise at their strong feelings about that. It seemed to come home to him, as if for the first time, how guarded he was with women, how much he feared their power, and how much he needed to join with other men to feel at all secure with women.

A word about Jim: Jim had been supportive of Donald's feeling about his boss and his job, telling how he had taken successful legal action against a large nonprofit institution that owned the building in which he had one of his two stationery stores. Jim, a good-looking, quiet midwesterner, a Protestant man of 40, was very reticent about himself. A recovered addict in conjoint treatment, he, like Donald, had a younger sister from whom he had been distant, as well as a father from whom he had been estranged. Without overtly trying, Jim had, from the start two years before, stimulated sexual fantasies in Pamela and Janice, the other two founding members of the group. Donald had been jealous over this. Jim's behavior in group came partly from a paranoid feeling toward me. This feeling had kept him an observer until a session the year before. During that session, he mentioned having only one aunt, whom he had not contacted for years, who lived in Madison, Wisconsin. He was about to stop talking, as was usual for him, when I told him I was going to Madison the next week (this was true), and asked if I could carry a message for him. Pamela, who shared his paranoid feeling about me, gasped at this, saying, "Are you for real?" But Jim had got my message. For the first time in group, his eyes teared; he went on to tell of his fondness for this aunt in a mystified, baffled tone, reflecting how out of touch he was with his motives for keeping his distance from her. Similarly, Jim offhandedly mentioned his tendency to stay out of touch with me, lest he misconstrue and be hurt by things he thought I had said, even when not to him directly; he had had to get his individual therapist to help him view me in a kinder light, so that he might stay in the group. Some time after this incident Jim became able to identify with me and to play. He sat by me for perhaps the first time in three years; during that session he noted wryly, in his quiet subdued voice, that I was wearing socks of two different colors. His observation caused much merriment in the group, along with offers from some of the women to take better care of me than I seemed to be getting. Intensified transference feelings were also in evidence.

It was in this same session that Donald was apologetic to Cordelia, a 45-year-old nurse from New Jersey, because he had not remembered the anniversary date of her husband's death, which had occurred shortly after she had joined the group and which Arlene, the other widow in the group, had called to the group's attention. I asked Donald why he *should* have remembered, and if it had anything to do with his birthday. Pamela, one of the women who felt most strongly her exclusion from Donald's party, asked him if he remembered the death of anyone important to him. After a few moments' thought, he recalled to his amazement an uncle who had been a warm and meaningful figure in his life when he was about ten. He had not thought of him in years. He mused silently, a bit teary and sad, recalling that time. Janice, a quite needy, depressed, and somewhat paranoid woman, pointed out that Donald's uncle was named Larry, and Cordelia's dead husband was Lawrence. Donald was not sure if this had been a factor in his forgetting. In the following session he reported with a sort of surprised air that he had not only sent a birthday card to his previously alienated sister, but had initiated a warm meeting with her which lasted several hours.

A crucial session occurred just before the Jewish holidays. I had not raised the question of our meeting during the holiday period until almost the end of the session. This late notice brought recriminations from Pamela, who voiced her hungry desire to have the session anyway, despite the fact that most members would be absent. I solved the problem by accepting Janice's suggestion of a later make-up session. I had handled it maladroitly; Pamela was miffed that I had seemed to defer to Janice and not to her. There was tension in the group, and the session ended there.

When we met two weeks later for an extended period that included the promised make-up session, there was, as might be expected, considerable anger in the group. Francine, an attractive 35-year-old lawyer, unmarried, who had been in the group about three months, was angry at Pamela. She felt that Pamela had slighted her after the previous session, while having seemed to want to talk on the steps outside the office. Group members had earlier commented on similarities between the two: their penetrating awarenesses of others, their intuitiveness, their prettiness, their hairstyles. This pairing by the group had seemed to please both women and had tempered Pamela's characteristic antagonism to a new female group member. In the present session, Cordelia too was angry at Pamela. Cordelia had not wanted the make-up session, which she attributed to Pamela's greediness. This seemed a hidden transference on Cordelia's part, from her young adult daughter to Pamela. She feared being drained by both of them, and the group helped her realize this. Paul too was angry at Pamela, feeling she had not given him a chance to voice his feelings about the missed session. Pamela fielded these responses adroitly, but turned her anger on me, saying that I had handled the situation badly and was "falling apart." Jim got up and shook her hand, agreeing that I had flubbed it. Janice kept trying to get some of the anger at Pamela directed at herself, but to no avail, even though it had been her suggestion that the group and I had finally agreed to. Later that same session, after someone had spoken of "closeness," Jim said to me, "What is closeness?" In a playful flash I answered, "Your smile right now!" As he had asked his question, I had glimpsed a new use of his mouth, fleeting and somewhat tremulous, but different from his usual wry expression, which had always seemed to say that he disbelieved the whole world. He nodded but said nothing further, and I made no further comment.

Arlene, a 40-year-old widow with three grown daughters, told a dream she had had the night before, in which her dead husband was talking to her but she was unable to hear. Nobody picked up on this dream, which was unusual for this group. Arlene was very bright and quick, given to homilies and quick, cogent appraisals of other people's problems. These she uttered in a brittle staccato voice, the words tripping along like Eliza, carefully skirting the thin ice of her own problems. When earlier in the session Norbert had remarked with regret that his three daughters were now on their own, Arlene had chimed in with a variety of stories about her own three daughters; I had remarked mildly that she seemed to have daughters for every occasion. She had made no immediate use of this remark, except to rush on pell-mell with some rational disclaimer, but the remark stuck with other group members, who offered this notion to her playfully whenever they felt she was fleeing from them. Later in the present session I brought the group back to Arlene's dream of her dead husband. Francine said, in an irritated way, "Oh we'll get to it later." She was still deeply preoccupied with strong negative transference feelings to Pamela, and with teary, warm, and tacitly positive feelings toward Norbert, the father *par excellence*. He was a 55-year-old research physicist, in the group about a year, who rarely spoke of himself, except occasionally to indicate his lack of pleasure in his wife, in sharp contrast to his pride in his three daughters. I had asked Arlene earlier in the session why she had not sought an individual appointment with me when her youngest daughter had become quite suicidal; she had answered that she had wanted to be "on her own." With my question, I had hoped to get her to talk more about her feelings toward men, rather than about an individual session. But Jim responded jealously to my question, asking why I had offered her an individual session when he had been waiting such a long time for one

I had promised him. (I try to have individual sessions with patients in conjoint treatment about once in two months.)

During the following session, the accumulated results of what had occurred in the make-up session began to emerge. Janice expressed her anger at me for allowing her to suggest cutting down on her individual sessions, a suggestion she took back less than an hour later. What she was not yet ready to reveal to the group was her jealousy that Pamela might pick up her individual hour. What she did say, however, was that she was thinking of ending treatment altogether before long, and had had a dream of both her mother and me dying. Jim helped her make the connection to termination. Donald claimed that it had not mattered much to him if we met or not, as did Norbert. Arlene began to speak of her overbearing mother, who used to come to her house and rearrange her furniture. It was clear that Arlene had also responded to her husband, and now to me, as a similarly preempting person, whom she must ignore. Jim said he had had to come to terms during the intervening week with the fact that he had not got, and might never get, an individual session with me. Then he talked with feeling he had never before displayed, either in the group or in individual sessions, of a sort of foster uncle he had had, a man he had cherished, but who repeatedly had not followed through on promised excursions. At the age of 11, Jim had suddenly become aware that this Uncle Joe was the oldest man he knew, older than his father, and that he would sooner or later die; he had therefore better not invest his feelings in him. By extension, since everyone would die, he had better not invest in anyone. "And so from that day forth," he said, "I haven't, even until now." The other group members were riveted in silent empathy with Jim, and with his unusually affect-laden revelation, even though it was apparently contradicted by the fact that Jim seemed truly fond of the ten-year-old daughter he shared custody of. In the same session, Jim told Cordelia of his fantasy of having been in an open grave, looking up and trying to push his way out. He associated the dream with his suicidal addiction and later recovery, and with the death of Cordelia's husband. Jim added that he had now begun to reach out by telephone to his estranged father and sister.

Cordelia's loss had also profoundly affected Paul, who had been confronted with the possibility of death when a serious tumor of the hip had been falsely diagnosed as malignant. Toward the end of the present session, Paul said he had two things to say. One was that he had gone to his new but still empty apartment by himself and had sat there for an hour, savoring its largeness and the view across the East River at dusk. In this he was identifying with Donald and his apartment. Then Paul presented his other remark, recounting with great relish and pride how he had become incensed at some arbitrary action by the director of his school, had confronted him in the faculty lounge in front of several other teachers, and had held his own throughout. He added, rather wonderingly, that the director had put an arm around Paul's shoulder the next day. But he was proud he had finally done what he knew he had to. Here he was identifying with Donald in relation to his boss, with Jim's self-revelation, and with Jim's having finally contacted his father and sister.

Pamela, also identifying with Jim, told of marked changes in her feelings toward her 15-year-old stepson, who had been stealing and taking drugs; she could now view him with empathy and concern, rather than as an adversary who interfered with her life. She also felt she might like to leave treatment soon. To this Janice responded, saying how much she would miss her, as if taking Pamela's very tentative statement as an accomplished fact. I suggested to Pamela that the anger directed at her had helped her to identify with her stepson, and possibly with a psychotic younger sister as well.

Pamela had come into individual treatment some twelve years before, complaining that she had been unable to find a career for herself in anything but teaching, which she hated, but which had been her mother's occupation. She was an attractive young woman, extremely bright and very quick in formulating her thoughts, with an undercurrent of bridled anger in her presentation of herself. One could sometimes not tell, from her rapid changes of expression, if she were laughing or crying, or both. She had come into treatment after having been told she was untreatable. She fled from individual treatment with me after about a year, to England, and was still frightened of her transference to me when she returned, sufficiently so that she could allow herself only group treatment for about a year and a half; only then was she able to resume individual treatment. At that time she was casting about somewhat hopelessly for a new career; following up on a lead from a man in the group, she got secretarial work in a pottery studio. Soon she began to try pottery making herself, and I was impressed by the results. When I rashly encouraged her to pursue it professionally, she was incensed to the point of halting her efforts completely for nearly a year; after that, she resumed her training and has since had several successful shows.

After two abortive relationships with men who were emotionally ill, Pamela took up with a rather passive and cold Jewish lawyer some sixteen years her senior. He had four children who were then living with his estranged wife. Eventually, he and Pamela married, Pamela got pregnant, his ex-wife left the United States and her children, and Pamela became the instant mother of four additional children. She survived this rather well, as she did the birth of her own child.

Pamela's initial complaints in treatment had included the fact that she had never had an orgasm, a lack that seemed related to her father's "inadvertent" exposures of himself during her childhood. She complained also of her compulsive groin-scratching, in imitation of her father. The oldest of five children, she had one sister, three years her junior who had had several psychotic episodes. Pamela herself sometimes lost her boundary and felt her face turn into her sister's.

I had introduced another patient, Jacqueline, part owner of an art gallery, into the group some three years after Pamela had come in as a founding member. Jacqueline came from Delaware, from a Protestant family, and had two older brothers and two older sisters. Her father, like Pamela's, had been away frequently during her early childhood, and both women had been left with quite depressed mothers. Both suffered from severe jealousies. Jacqueline, however, had had an older brother who had taken the father's place for her, but had also left in her the imprint of his sadistic sex play with her. Jacqueline had been able to marry, while still in college, but had been traumatized not too long after she had married by the suicide of a male classmate with whom she had had a brother-and-sister kind of flirtation-attachment. This trauma had led her to an abortion when she became pregnant by her husband, but later she had two children, both girls. When her second child was about two, her husband became psychotic. In time she was able to leave him, but only with the help of Pamela, other group members, and myself.

Although Pamela resented new members coming into group, she and Jacqueline sensed their special affinity for each other, one bond being their almost intractable anger, another being some homosexual attraction, along with intense jealousy of each other. This jealousy came to a head several times, and I had to step between them physically, in order to prevent mayhem. Nevertheless, each contributed a piece to the other's ego. Pamela's more rapierlike and socially adept uses of her anger taught Jacqueline to modulate her more physical, broadsword rages at me, at group members, and at the group, rages triggered by our supposed neglect of her. Jacqueline, in her blunt but intuitive fashion, could point out discrepancies in Pamela's accounts of her outside life, especially with her husband and with her sexual difficulties, and could get her to face these distortions more directly. Jacqueline, who prided herself on her fecundity, her sexuality, and her children, was enormously helpful to Pamela as the latter struggled over several years toward orgasm, marriage, and childbearing. Essentially, she helped Pamela to accept her incest-tinged sexuality. It is difficult to detail the many ways in which Jacqueline encouraged Pamela to find orgasm and to overcome fears of pregnancy and delivery. But jealousy overwhelmed Jacqueline after Pamela became pregnant, as her own most intense desire in life was to become pregnant again herself. She became agitated and asked to leave the group, which she did, taking with her the feeling that she had lost out in the competition to have a child. She also felt great anger toward me, though she continued in individual treatment. She seemed to feel that in the group Pamela had the exclusive on estimable marriage and childbearing. About two years later, while still in individual treatment, Jacqueline married a successful stockbroker and went on to graduate education in art history. For her, the group—especially Pamela—had been a valuable transitional object (Kosseff, 1975).

I had been fully prepared for a postpartum psychosis in Pamela, given her behavior and her dreams while pregnant. But this did not occur, and I suspect that it did not because of two factors. One was connected to life events, the splitting off of hated parts of herself into her husband's ex-wife and into the hateful demandingness of her seven-year-old stepdaughter, whom she contrasted to her own "angelic" baby daughter. The other factor was the presence of Janice in the group. One of four children and the next-to-youngest, Janice, like Pamela, was one of the group's founding members. Slightly paranoid, Janice was often openly expressive of seductive feelings as well as dissatisfaction and anger toward me, both of which were associated with a brother four years her junior. Janice still suffered from chronic mild depression after eight years of analytic work with a female analyst, and was now in conjoint treatment with me. Following Pamela's lead, she was able to marry. She decided, however, after long-drawn-out ambivalence, not to have a child. Between

Jacqueline's promotion of motherhood as a "second chance" for a self, and Janice's narcissistic need to have her husband all to herself, Pamela found an intermediate place. She gave birth without a psychotic break, became an excellent mother, but avoided sex with her husband for over a year thereafter, focusing her affections on her infant daughter. In the two years since, with help from the group, she regained a capacity for orgasm and, not without ambivalence, a much better relationship with her husband.

It took two thin egos, it seems, to make one fat one! This kind of pairing, when possible, of severely traumatized patients who have suffered similar traumatic experiences, but who differ as regards the effect on their lives and on their ego capacities, serves to bind each of the patients to each other and into the group, and enables each to negotiate the initial trauma of fitting into the group, a trauma that might otherwise prove overwhelming. Each supplies the other those bits of missing ego needed to make up a deficit.

In a later session of the group, Jim reported a dream in which he argued with me (a form of reaching out), and told also of persisting in several recent calls to his father, which was uncharacteristic behavior for him. Arlene told of her fantasies about two men who had shown mild interest in her, and of her ladylike efforts to encourage them. One was working seven days a week, she said, preoccupied "with holding on to his business," a phrase I repeated a bit later. Nonetheless she was hoping to be invited to his cabin in the Adirondacks that summer. Francine picked up on this and spoke of her own puzzlement about men. She wondered whether one could have a sexual relationship without commitment. She also proposed that the group adopt the phrase "Do you want to end up in the Adirondacks?" as a playful group slogan for a self-defeating search for a lasting relationship, a pattern she felt both she and Arlene had fallen into.

Just then Cordelia confessed that she had used the excuse of a professional meeting to stay away from the previous session. Her statement came while she was sitting by me, and I had sensed her mounting tension and inner pain as the others talked. I simply put my hand out between our two chairs, and drew her attention to it by quietly saying her name. She grasped my hand, welled up, and sobbed a few moments. Jim was flabbergasted at the quiet power of this offer, because of the intensity of Cordelia's affective response, usually so controlled. Cordelia was able to realize that missing the session had been a way of avoiding both her residual anger at Pamela and her hesitant desire to hug Jim in response to his fantasy about the grave and its connection with the anniversary of her husband's death. This was her first overt expression of desire toward a man since her husband's death. At this point she got up and hugged Jim. Cordelia's reaction seemed to jog Arlene's memory, and she recalled a dream about me which she presented as proud and perhaps mocking evidence that she was, at least in a dream, trying to fulfill my suggestion of an individual session. The dream was that she was standing on the street while I was in a doorway, and we held a session in that fashion. Janice suggested sexual meaning to the dream, but Arlene could not yet accept this. Group members also questioned Pamela about her decision to leave the group. She responded that her feeling was like "being pregnant," a full, good feeling, as if she "had got the group inside her." Paul told of his excitement about the prospect of a prestigious summer teaching job in an art colony, for which the director of his art school, among others, had recommended him.

I have described several microexamples of play: the women offering to rent Donald's spare bedroom; my telling Jim I would carry a message to his Wisconsin aunt; Jim and others joking about my mismatched socks; Arlene's "daughters for every occasion" remark; and Francine's "Do you want to end up in the Adirondacks?" I could add her saying to Donald, who was being a bit obsessional, that he was "shoulding" all over himself! Such bits of play tend to overcome resistance and enhance transference.

What makes the notion of play important is this: to the extent that patients view any treatment situation as a serious demand for change, for dealing with the "bad," the "failed," the "perverted" parts of themselves, they may experience the treatment situation (and resist it) as a distortion of their idiosyncratic need for time, space, and a unique manner of growth—that is, as the repetition of a parental demand to be something other than they are. But the need is there for "disengagement" from such fixed, frozen, and imperious behavior that renders the self unviewable, unreachable, unchangeable.

What does the foregoing imply for the work in group psychotherapy, for an object relations view of narcissistic and borderline patients, and for the group's value as an instrument for changes in the self through congruences and play? Just this:

Psychotherapy takes place in the overlap of two areas of play, that of the patient and that of the therapist. Psychotherapy has to do with two people playing together. The corollary of this is that where playing is not possible, then the work done by the therapist is directed towards bringing the patient from a state of not being able to play into a state of being able to play. . . . It is play that is universal, that belongs to health; playing facilitates growth and therefore health; healthy playing leads into group relationships [Winnicott, 1971, p. 38].

I should like to reverse that last statement, although both versions are true: group relationships lead into play, and healthy play leads to change and growth of the self.

GROUPING AND PLAY

Developmentally considered, play and grouping are both identity-making behaviors that begin almost at birth, so that there is an intrinsic connection between the two. Both require the presence of the mother. In play, she is at first the "subjective object" of the child's play, then a participant in play, and later a presence simply standing by while the child learns to play alone. Grouping begins when a parallel use of the mother occurs during the earliest proliferation of parts of the ego. The nursing infant is at one and the same time a lips-mouth-and-breast infant—an infant playing with the mother's breast and hair (Spitz, 1955; Padel, 1985)—and a scanning infant (Erikson, 1976; Padel, 1985) observing the mother, who in turn gazes upon the infant. "It is with the eyes that (maternal) concern and love are communicated, and distance and anger as well; . . . the eye blesses and curses" (Erikson, 1976, p. 316). Padel (1985) sees these simultaneous behaviors in nursing as the primitive origins of, respectively, the oral ego and the superego; he also postulates, along with Freud (1914), that this simultaneous sucking and scanning becomes, through a process of splitting, the basis for grouping:

At one extreme the individual may identify with mother and so enter on relationships in which he is more give than take (e.g. the baby holding out a piece of food to the mother); at the other extreme he may identify with infant-self and be receiver or taker rather than giver. . . . But the very fact of

being able to choose to identify with the one *or* the other
means that he also adopted a third position, from which he
could observe self and mother as a couple and be for a while
identified with neither . . . [p. 275].

If this is so, in terms of functional differentiations rather than
cognitive ones, it suggests that in earliest life—even before the father
is a major factor—there emerges a tripartite ego consisting of an
objective ego, a selfobject, and an observing ego. This proliferation of
the ego constitutes an internal group, later to be projected into the
outside world. "Pathology," says Padel (1985), "would start from an
inability, or from a lessened ability to take up any one of the three
positions; the normal ego is able to move between them" (p. 275).
Fairbairn (1952) amplifies this view of pathology as arising from
internalized affective ego-object relationships when failures to maintain essential closeness through all the developmental stages have led
to the defensive splitting off of disturbing affective parts of ego-object
connections, because of the intolerability of these attachments to
either the overexciting or the overcontrolling object, leading to
libidinal "stickiness or alienated forbiddenness."

Because of this etiological connection between grouping and
play, the group becomes a natural vehicle for reparative work on the
self when pathology is present. Though the group members and the
therapist are real objects, they represent internal objects and affectively colored relationships as well. Because, as Freud suggested
(1921), group members have all put the group leader in the place of
their ego ideal and identified with one another in their ego, group
situations greatly amplify the affective impact of these interrelations
and lead to identifications. "Play populates the world with people who
are identical with the split-off parts of the Ego" (Kardos and Peto,
1956, p. 107). The group provides that "intermediate area" in which
simultaneously and paradoxically the worlds of illusion and outer
reality can be acceptably intermingled (Winnicott, 1951; Deri, 1984).
When play is introduced into the group, there is an opportunity for
trial identifications, annulling traumas of the past, and for a narcissistic focus on play, canceling out for the time being narcissistic
withdrawals of a pathological sort. Objects can be possessed and
discarded at the same time; boundaries between self and nonself are
blurred; and there is a rapid, creative oscillation between what is true
and not true, real and illusory, object and symbol in the "magic

oneness" of the group feeling. There is oscillation, but there is commitment also. Because the group members are both real and not real, but safe "to play with," everyday anxiety is thrown "out of gear," freeing libidinal and aggressive impulses to emerge and be diffused in playful ways with the other group members. Internally, the individual can indulge omnipotent feelings playfully and yet permit the ego temporary loosening up and disintegration; during controlled fragmentations the individual dares to confront the previously terrifying possibilities of helplessness, accepting these split-off parts of the ego on a trial basis. "This joint sense of being both subject and object becomes the root of a sense of identity" (Erikson, 1972, p. 319).

In group play as in hypnosis, individuals can "lose themselves"— that is, they can lose the fixed, limiting aspects of the self and rise to challenges they might otherwise feel incapable of meeting. They find out as they do so that they have more power over their environment than they believed possible, while yet having to accept gradually that some things which they had dearly hoped for can never be. This process, paradoxically, often leads to greater ego integration. "The individual gains leeway for himself as he creates it for others; here is the soul of adult play" (Erikson, 1975, p. 132).

Dynamically, "play" has many aspects. It can be seen as the opportunity to make trial relationships, where there is relatively little fear of consequences or of being held forever to what one says or does. Play is therefore fun, where the most serious matters may be negotiated in a relatively light-hearted atmosphere, thereby reducing the "weightiness" that might otherwise cramp creative thought and action. Play implicates that which is human and warm, hopeful and free in us. Play it is that frees up that which is frozen and immobilized, and starts the spring thaw of "flowing" again, that peculiar dynamic and holistic state in which people feel they can act with near total involvement (Csikszentmihalyi, 1975). Play allows the patient to project parts of the self into the immediate world, to place them in others, and yet to recover them at will; play is a creative use of the whole personality in the search for the missing parts of the self. Play involves the sequence of movement from trust to trial to self, from nonintegration to integration. Play is an activity of search, in which the image and the "tone" involved may disrupt fixed perceptual images, and allow for shifts in orientation to objects and self (Schilder, 1944; Winnicott, 1971). Play involves the capacity to change the use of an object from a bundle of projections to a part of shared reality, and to put the object outside of the self, outside of what was once omnipotent control. Playing involves the body; objects are manipulated and an intense interest is generated that is connected with bodily excitement. The implication here is that the experience of excitement through play can be contained by the group. Additionally, few external objects are experienced as so central to the self as those representing the outcome of our own creative efforts, as in play, and in a sense the group is created by the play of its members (Rosenberg, 1979). Indeed, in Teutonic myths in which the world comes to a near end, it is the children, the only survivors, who reconstruct it through play (Lifton, 1976).

But how does the group both enhance and use play? Winnicott (1971) puts it thus: "The group life is experienced in the area of transitional phenomena, in the exciting interweave of subjectivity and objectivity and objective observation, and in an area that is intermediate between the inner reality of the individual and the shared reality of the world that is external to individuals" (p. 64). He is saying how the group life enhances play in relation to the self, and the growth of the self, in an area of interweave between people.

I will conclude by pulling together the evidence of the two preconditions for change in the self that I started with: congruences between group members and the notion of play.

For example, both Pamela and Jacqueline had depressed mothers and frequently absent fathers; both had early seductive experiences with a father or brother; both were pathologically jealous people; both had pervasive doubts about themselves and their worth and gave the appearance of waifs; both had chosen psychotic lovers; both had given birth to girl children; both had experienced the suicide of lovers. This is but a partial list of the congruences of their two lives. But the significance of what I have discovered about change in the self through group therapy, especially with more damaged patients, is this rather startling notion: transference is not enough. These two patients got better, I feel, as a result both of transferences (e.g., Jacqueline represented Pamela's psychotic younger sister, and Pamela the envied mother/ older-sister/ brother for Jacqueline) and of the actual congruences in their two lives and egos. One conclusion is that the group affords a unique vehicle for psychotherapeutic change. This it does by affording first-order change (more of the same) in the form of these "tight fits" of two or more selves, a tangle of emotionally congealed self-and-object, as with Pamela and Jacqueline, where the combined aspects, actual and fantasied, of the two selves get joined. This is more than mirroring, twinship, or transference alone, even though it includes all three; it is also the provision of large areas of a congruent and visible other self that helps make the group a unique agent for change, through the directness and immediacy of the introjections and identifications it affords. This can in part replace the frequent sessions and transference buildups particular to individual analysis, a form of treatment which nowadays we seldom have the time or money for (Schafer, 1968). It is, of course, not always possible to arrange for such congruences deliberately. But it does raise questions about a certain kind of homogeneity in this group, perhaps brought about by a preconscious and intuitive selection of its members, that may have contributed to its apparent efficacy.

Second-order change can also be seen to be occurring via the various pairings and transferences I have described, but I have tried to confine myself to a focus on the two preconditions—the congruences of group members and the groupwide provision of play—as potent forces for both anchoring and change in the self in the group. I will conclude by saying that second-order change can take place because of the paradoxical counternarcissistic force afforded by the group at play (Schafer, 1968), the force of the joined egos that confronts, neutralizes, and "disjuncts" the ongoing narcissisms, those mergings of self- and object representations that I have described in my group (Rochlin, 1973). How large-scale and how lasting the changes afforded each self are will of course vary from one individual to another in the same group.

What follows these two preconditions is—to borrow a phrase from Dr. Janet Kennedy—"a contagion of empathy" whereby change can occur. Thus, when there is present another self with both real and fancied congruences to oneself, and when this other self is presented in this more flowing sea of group feeling—this "contagion of empathy" in which the two selves meet—then there exists the possibility that the lost parts of the self will be found and that the self will be anchored.

REFERENCES

Csikszentmihalyi, M. (1975), *Beyond Boredom and Anxiety: The Experience of Play in Work and Games.* San Francisco: Jossey-Bass.

Deri, S. (1984), *Symbolization and Creativity.* New York: International Universities Press.

Erikson E. H. (1972), Play and actuality. In: *A Way of Looking at Things*, ed. S. Schlein. New York: Norton, pp. 311–338.

———(1975), *Life History and the Historical Moment.* New York: Norton.

———(1976), Psychoanalysis and ethics—avowed or ununavowed. *Internat. Rev. Psycho-Anal.*, 3:409–415.

Fairbairn, W. R. D. (1952), *Psychoanalytic Studies of the Personality.* London: Routledge & Kegan Paul.

Freud, S. (1914), On narcissism: An introduction. *Standard Edition*, 14:73–102. London: Hogarth Press, 1957.

———(1921), Group psychology and the analysis of the ego. *Standard Edition*, 18:69–143. London: Hogarth Press, 1955.

Jackson, D. D. (1968), *Therapy, Communication and Change.* Palo Alto, CA: Science & Behavior Books.

Kardos, E., & Peto, A. (1956), Contributions to the theory of play. *Brit. J. Med. Psychol.*, 29:100–112.

Kosseff, J. W. (1975), A beginning contribution in the application of object-relations theory to analytic group therapy: The group as a transitional object. In: *The Leader in the Group*, ed. Z. Liff. New York: Aronson, pp. 212–242.

Lifton, R. J. (1976), *The Life of the Self.* New York: Simon & Schuster.

Padel, J. (1985), Ego in current thinking. *Internat. Rev. Psycho-Anal.* 12:273–283.

Pines, M. (1981), Psychoanalysis and group analysis. Paper presented at the A.G.P.A. conference, Houston, TX.

Rochlin, G. (1973), *Man's Aggression: The Defense of the Self.* Boston: Gambit.

Rosenberg, M. (1979), *Conceiving the Self.* New York: Basic Books.

Schafer, R. (1968), *Aspects of Internalization.* New York: International Universities Press.

Schilder, P. H. (1944), Innate motor action as a basis of learning. In: *Play: Its Role in Development and Evolution*, ed. J. S. Bruner, A. Jolly, & K. Sylva. New York: Basic Books, 1976, pp. 1–25.

Schlesinger, H. (1981), The process of empathic response. *Psychoanal. Inq.* 1:393–416.

Spitz, R. (1955), The primal cavity. *The Psychoanalytic Study of the Child*, 10:215–240.

Watzlawick, P., Weakland, J., & Fisch, R. (1974), *Change: Principles of Problem Formation.* New York: Norton.

Winnicott, D. W. (1951), Transitional objects and transitional phenomena. In: *Through Paediatrics to Psycho-Analysis.* New York: Basic Books, 1975, pp. 229–242.

———(1971), *Playing and Reality.* New York: Basic Books.

Part II
Clinical Contributions

Introduction

The chapters in this section present a number of difficult problems commonly encountered in the conduct of group psychotherapy with borderline and narcissistic patients. In chapter 6, Gaburri convincingly illustrates the power of the group situation to provoke significant regression in vulnerable patients. He describes the development of a severe psychosomatic disorder that appears to reach delusional proportions in a member subjected to a not uncommon group "stress." According to Gaburri, such decompensations are manifestations of severe identity disorders which can present also as distortions of thinking. Such thought disorders are manifest both temporally (discontinuity of the self across time) and spatially (fluid boundaries as regards self and others). Using the object relations formulations of Bion, Gaburri notes that in basic assumption groups these thinking disturbances form the basis for a "protoidentity." Through introjective and projective mechanisms and the therapist's interpretive activity, the thinking disturbance is gradually resolved (as are the psychosomatic symptoms in his illustration) and the patient moves from this "protoidentity" to a more solid identity formation.

In chapter 7 Roth explores the vexing problem of an entire group of patients who do not meaningfully interact. Members talk to one another, but there is an absence of emotional engagement, and they do not generate new ideas about themselves. Roth, drawing on extensive clinical experience, presents a "fictive example" of a group interaction highlighting this lack of contact among members. The illustration will seem painfully familiar to clinicians working with such patients. Their lack of engagement and inability to form new ideas,

Roth argues, are best conceptualized as a latency period defense that has coalesced with earlier development deficits. This defense serves mainly to protect the members from the wishes and terrors of earlier periods in which anxiety was not mastered, basic trust (in both self and others) was not achieved, and moods were not reliably regulated. Roth suggests that traditional interpretations may only exacerbate the difficulties encountered in these individuals.

Bacal's contribution (chapter 8), reprinted from the *International Journal of Group Psychotherapy*, is an unusually lucid formulation of clinical material from significantly different theoretical perspectives. Reexamining two vignettes initially formulated from a traditional object relations–drive derivative vantage point, Bacal explores the group conflicts within the self psychology paradigm. The need of some patients for a twinship selfobject is emphasized here, but it is noted as well that other group members may require earlier selfobjects of the idealizing or mirroring sort. When these various selfobjects are unavailable, the environment may be experienced as conflicted and unempathic. The alternative explanations of clinical material presented here provide an excellent opportunity to explore contrasting theoretical positions.

Chapter 9 explores the importance of members' secrets in the group. Approaching the problem from a self psychological point of view, Morrison suggests that the inner experience of shame is an important determinant in keeping secrets, which may represent history, memories, wishes, impulses, or particular selfobject needs. Shame may be conscious or may emerge into awareness only during the treatment process, when selfobjects fail to respond empathically. Patients may expose their shameful feelings in group once a climate of trust and acceptance has been established. The therapist's task is to understand the process and accept the feelings rather than to interpret the content using a more traditional impulse-conflict paradigm.

The final chapter in this section (chapter 10) is Stone's exploration of affects in group psychotherapy. Beginning with a review of the contributions of Krystal and others to the understanding of affect evolution, differentiation, tolerance, and dedifferentiation, as well as the use of affect as a defense, Stone examines the contributions of object relations theory and self psychology to the understanding of affects in borderline and narcissistic individuals. The characteristics of the therapy group enable patients to reexperience their characteristic responses to affects and, through the interaction, to gain increased flexibility in experiencing and handling a variety of feelings. Within the group, affect contagion, norms, and interpersonal stimulation, particularly with regard to separations, competitiveness, and exhibitionism, contribute to the manner in which affects are experienced and displayed. Members' needs for selfobjects is a further stimulus to affective response. Clinical examples are presented to illustrate both defenses against the development of selfobject transference and responses to empathic failures on the part of selfobjects. These examples provide an opportunity to examine the therapist's tactics in helping members experience and manage affects.

6

Thought Disorders and Identity Disturbances Between the Individual and the Group

EUGENIO GABURRI, M.D., Ph.D.

It is not easy to define the borderline between narcissistic and identity disturbances. Normally what we label as narcissistic disturbances are rooted in an identity defect, and both identity defects and narcissistic disturbances are expressed as an alteration of thought function, especially in more serious cases.

A permanent identity defect often appears in the form of pathological thought organization, such as delusional thought processes. Less serious forms are expressed as slipping contact with reality, and transitory identity defects are often translated into an altered self-perception, as in depersonalization.

For the present discussion it is relevant that the so-called depersonalization phenomenon occurs in a physiological manner when an individual is in contact with a group. This phenomenon is characterized by two principal references. The first is a temporal reference; the individual has difficulty perceiving the self's continuity in time. The self changes and fails to maintain consistency over time. This is the case described symbolically in Robert Louis Stevenson's *The Strange Case of Dr. Jekyll and Mr. Hyde*. The second reference is a spatial one: the indefinite limits of the self. Freud (1921) described this as a relationship arising specifically from the individual's encounter with the group. For various reason, it seems that in this second case the ego is overwhelmed by mechanisms, or maybe by thoughts, emanating from a different, superindividual entity which alters and sometimes overwhelms the self (giving rise to depersonalization).

Note that in both cases this phenomenon is accompanied by a

common element—an uncanny feeling which the individual is able to distinguish from what is usually perceived as anxiety. At the root of this disorder lies not conflict, but a situation similar to what Freud (1919) described as the "uncanny." He considered it to be connected to the birth of the ego. If like Bion (1963) we define the mind as an "apparatus for thinking thoughts," in this case the apparatus seems to be delegated to a superindividual element presiding over the group functioning. Sometimes the relational space between the individual and the group is reduced almost to the point of leveling out completely. In these circumstances, also called "basic group assumptions" by Bion (1959), an individual, an idea, or a fantasy dominates the group. The group may appear as an offshoot of the individual or vice versa. Obviously, mechanisms of identification, introjection (Freud, 1921), and projection (Bion, 1959) come into play in these movements. Many authors agree that, due to these identificational exchanges, the group is particularly enabled to approach and potentially transform a narcissistic disturbance at its very roots in the identity. When the events of a small therapeutic group are inserted into a patient's identity disturbance, the reciprocal analysis of the two phenomena may favor a symmetrical reconstruction of the "apparatus for thinking thoughts" both in the group and in the individual. As I have earlier noted (Gaburri, 1981), certain structural disturbances of the ego can be recognized if we agree that thoughts produced by the group can be traced to the common identity matrix and narcissistic structure of the individual and the group.

Freud (1911) gave a basically temporal definition to thought. Thought is produced the moment that frustration from delay in drive satisfaction becomes tolerable. By contrast, Bion (1959) gives thought a prevalently spatial definition: a thought can be born where a "no-thing" experience can take place. The principal difference between these two conceptions lies in the fact that in Bion's the temporal evolution has to do with the formation of the container: that is, the place lending itself to be a "frame" of the "no-thing."

"No-thing" (absence of the object), therefore, does not mean "no reality" (absence of reality), but rather a very particular reality where past and present join to give rise to this momentarily empty four-dimensional frame. It is a "place" rather than a space, where the new thought can be contained. As the group as a whole evolves as a work group, this "place" can be formed. Here new thoughts join objects, persons, and different ways of solving problems.

Instead of providing a space for thought, a group formed according to the three automatic models described by Bion (1959) as basic assumptions would provide archaic forms of identity or, instead, a group protoidentity aimed at saturating defects in the group's identity structure. In these situations there seems to be no articulated connection between single member identity and group identity. Group identity, then, tends to assure rigidly "narcissistic" traits and to absorb the identities of the individual members. Members who condense within themselves the projective identifications specific to a particular basic assumption (that of the group's leader) personify the identity of the group itself. If the group lacks a work task outside itself (unlike such specialized work groups as an army or a church), this situation can result in delusional ideas and hallucinosis. In a basic assumption group, projective identifications of an evacuative type seem to act in an almost exclusive manner. They are kept in check by the group's narcissistic structure (by means of an obsessive-like thought) but are not contained by it (by means of a true thought).

The basic assumption group paired with its leader can be viewed as analogous to a case of twin transference (Bion, 1950). In both instances the formation of a mirrorlike double—an other self distinct from the ego but similar to it in all respects—leads to an archaic autoerotic fantasy that, through projective identification, encompasses the other as a homologous self.

Parallel to this, a situation develops in the group that is similar to a phenomenon described by Melanie Klein (1929) in her paper "Personification in Children's Play." According to Klein, a specific cathexis of play objects occurs in children's play (this is similar to the autoerotic narcissistic situation). This cathexis serves as a precursor of symbol formation. Bion (1950), speculating on "the personification of splits," asks, "Is it possible that the capacity to personify splittings of the personality is in some way analogous to a capacity for symbol formation . . . ?" (p. 20). I ask in turn, is it not possible that the basic assumption group becomes "personified" as such by its leader as in the situation of play objects? And might not the splits and the projective identifications be kept in check through this operation even in the absence of an ego structure (of work) capable of developing a "container"? If this is true and is adequately handled in the analyst's work, this fact might provide for the "presentification" of the proto-object elements Bion calls preconceptions.

It has been noted that in order to create a "no-thing" space, a child has to have had at least a minimal experience of realization. According to the Freudian model, the frustration resulting from delay in instinct satisfaction is intolerable without a memory trace of past satisfaction.

My hypothesis is that the basic assumption group and its leader, by mirroring each other reciprocally, constitute a first form of identity—a protoidentity meant to establish an initial embrionic experience of realization. With Bion we can say that this constitutes an initial form of "conception." To maintain this hypothesis, we must consider the possibility that the three basic assumptions coincide with the three instinctual instances described by Bion. They are: prolactic for the basic assumption of dependence, suprarenalic for that of fight-flight, and gonadic for that of pairing. The basic assumption might also link these instinctual instances to the three primal fantasies: seduction for dependence, castration for fight-flight, and primal scene for pairing.

The temporal succession of the basic assumption forms seems to function in the constitution of the work group. In this sense, the production of a basic assumption may be seen as a "primal nucleus of sense" (acting as a precursor to the identity of the work group's ego). This might be explained by the clinical fact that initial formation of the basic assumption, parallel to individual identity and thinking disturbances, produces relaxation and quiet, as if the violence of the conflict could be contained and dissolved in the sense included in that formation as a condition of the group's protoidentity.

The constitution of protoidentity through the basic assumption appears to some group members as a "realization" (Bion, 1970) favored by the interchange of projective identifications among members. This realization helps establish a "conception" played out in an intermediate space (perhaps Winnicott's transitional space) between dream and reality. The group seems to serve as an object (perhaps transitional) that personifies split parts, in line with the ideas of Bion and of Klein (1930). Precisely because of its ability to control conflict and to present primal fantasies, the basic assumption group realizes the "twin" of some members' split parts. For other members it is the object used to realize preconceptions through cognitive projective identifications.

For example: a panic situation of fragmentation and loss of identity together with the presence of a particularly violent conflict can create an evacuative emergency. This is presented through a fight-flight basic assumption, which serves as an object in the realization of other members' unsaturated preconceptions. This favors alteration of the fight-flight situation (suprarenalic drive based on aggressivity and castration fantasies) into one of dependence (prolactic drive based on seduction fantasies and the primary relation with the breast).

The dependence basic assumption in turn gives rise to that of pairing, and through these movements the work of the group eventuates in the creation of a potential container.

CLINICAL ILLUSTRATION

A group resuming its activity after summer vacation finds itself caught between two moments: the disappearance of a member without notice, and a new member's entrance into the group. In the first few sessions a violent conflict arises, the result of anger over the separation and of claustrophobic feelings experienced by some members. These conflicts occur mostly among members who have participated in the group for a long time and who experience their reentry as proof of their incapacity to achieve independence. The missing member participated in the life of the group only in recent months and then, without saying anything, no longer attended. Another member is getting ready to leave the group, having acquired a solid identity and a good level of independence. With the absence of the former member, a fight-flight basic assumption soon appears to control envious attacks on the "mature" member. These attacks tend to center around the idea that there is no difference between the more mature member preparing to leave the group and the less mature member who simply disappeared. This is meant to demonstrate that maturity results from chance external causes and "coups de main" rather than from the work of the group. These ideas are organized into a fight-flight basic assumption that gives a primary sense of cohesion to the group: "We should all take advantage of the mature member's termination and finish the group together." In this way, the mature member is equated with the member who vanished.

The organization of these thoughts can be compared to a form of delusional thought that on one hand helps control persecution anxiety and on the other blocks the organization of the work group. The leader of this basic assumption group rapidly becomes the weakest member present—Angelo. He suddenly personifies, by means of a somatic symptom, the evacuative mechanisms now prevalent in the group. This patient has been in the group for several years and lives in terror of ending up the one and only member, as one by one the others go away. He therefore tries to block any situation implying the separation of another member.

Angelo has a relapse of psychosomatic colitis, accompanied in this instance by serious symptoms of hallucinosis. He is obliged to spend many hours of the day on the toilet and at one point is convinced that he "sees" worms in his diarrheic feces: he has finally found the cause of his illness. Through this individual somatic realization of the fight-flight basic assumption, he hopes to find "escape" in a medical cure, even if it activates a thought disturbance.

In this situation the apparatus for thinking thoughts seems to be affected symmetrically in the individual and in the group. Through the somatic realization of the fight-flight basic assumption, Angelo counts on changing the therapist without changing the group. The desired medical therapy offers a primal nucleus of sense and momentarily alleviates the persecutory anxiety spreading both in his self and in the group.

The therapist introduces the analytic function by interpreting the worms as the hallucinatory realization of the members of the group. They are reduced to worms because of guilt feelings connected to their inability to help the member who disappeared. In reality, it is this member who must be escaped from, who has become "the other," the carrier of the fight-flight basic assumption.

In Angelo's mind the lost member stands for his own self, an unborn child never chosen from among the many unborn worm-babies in his mother's body. The leadership of the absent member (fantasied as dead) is made to pass onto the present member with the weakest identity. The weakest member manages this with an increase of anal evacuative solutions which seem to affect the entire group. The protoidentity resulting from the fight-flight basic assumption helps to keep the violent, envious conflict in check. It supplies a primitive image of sense as an alternative to the fantasies of fragmentation and claustrophobia that arose at the group's resumption.

A much more evolved patient, Emanuela, echoes this solution. In this period she experiences an intense desire for pregnancy and presents notable gynecological disturbances—violent menstrual periods occurring exactly in the most fertile moment of her cycle. These disturbances checkmate maternal desire. The emergence of this material (echoed in turn by other female members) permits the group to establish a symbolic equivalence between anal evacuation and menstruation. This occurs both as zone confusion in the group's mental area (Meltzer, 1973) and as the penis-feces-child equation.

The analytic function activated by this material mobilizes and transforms the projective identifications linked to the fight-flight basic assumption. A second patient, Rossella, who has identity problems connected to secondary narcissism, elaborates on a significant dream production. In her dream, the analysis is represented by a very powerful ship that arrives in port and starts machine-gunning a group of people united there, waiting for it. The machine gun fire paradoxically consolidates group cohesion and protoidentity. Otherwise, the group is composed of two antithetical subgroups—one pacifist, the other antipacifist. The ship confusedly machine-guns both groups, who instead of being wounded find a reason for cohesion. At the end of the dream, the captain of the ship sends a very attractive woman ashore with the precise intention of seducing the group, in light of the negative outcome of the machine-gunning.

This material relates the persecution felt by the group after the disappearance of one of its members to the persecution produced by the analyst's interpretation of Angelo's hallucinations. At the same time, this material allows the identity of the weakest member—now leader of the fight-flight basic assumption group—to move toward the analyst's identity as head of the work group. This passage takes place by changing the fight-flight basic assumption (represented by the machine-gunning ship) into that of dependence (the attractive and seductive woman).

This change is attested in the following session by another dream given by the same patient, Rossella. In it the patient has to get to the group and is being driven by Angelo. At a certain point Angelo accelerates abruptly, sending the car into a chicken coop and causing considerable confusion but very limited damage. This dream illustrates two complementary elements. On the one hand, fragmentation anxiety is checked by a less dramatic representation (the automobile accident is substituted for the fragmentation fantasy). On the other hand, there is a mobilization, a change from fight-flight to dependence (the need to arrive at the group).

In the meantime, several events have taken place in the group. Angelo, carrier of the hallucinosis disturbance, arrived one day complaining that the clinical and laboratory tests of his feces found no presence of parasites. This fact provoked lively discussion in the group. Another patient, Rina, pointed out the danger of proceeding in this way. She, too, had tried in the past to escape into a somatic disorder. She had even had a minor gynecological procedure performed, only to discover that it did not diminish her anxiety. This privileged a contribution from the more mature member, on the point of leaving the group. He noted how the group could have helped Angelo only so far as his "delusions" were concerned. Faced with a medical cure for Angelo's parasites, the group would have remained impotent, just as it had when faced with the disappearance of Marco (the missing member).

Thus, the group ran the risk of remaining a group of impotent parasites. Maybe the group could have helped if it had been used to cure its members' delusions; it could not cure the real worms, but maybe it could have cured the group idea to become "like worms" to combat and trample.

The improvement of Angelo's symptoms accompanied the arrival of a new member in the group, a girl who provoked a certain confusion in the group's established order. During the first session she had sat in the place Angelo usually occupied and had remained there. Angelo moved to a seat next to the analyst, occasioning a great deal of discussion and comment.

After the dependence basic assumption was established, following work on the chicken coop dream, elements of the pairing basic assumption began to appear. These were for the most part expressed through a dream reported by Emanuela. In it Emanuela showed a definite step forward regarding her homosexual and twinship problems. In her dream she is wandering around the city with an intimate friend, a figure who usually represents a twin, when through the window of a building she notices a mother breast-feeding her child. She convinces her reluctant friend to enter the house and there, before their eyes, is a sort of Holy Family scene. The child is at the center, surrounded by two parents and looking like a true, live Messiah.

The further passage to the pairing basic assumption, together with the messianic hope represented in Emanuela's dream, indicates the clear emergence of a work group. This is expressed through another dream production from Emanuela:

I was walking through my apartment with my husband, discussing the fact that the house was too small for a child.

Right in the middle of the conversation we notice another room next to the bedroom. We enter it and realize that it's full of old kitchen furniture that my parents had given me many years ago when, as a protest and to demonstrate my independence, I left home and went to live on my own. I no longer remembered that, in spite of the quarrel, my parents had given me the kitchen furniture. So we were surprised to discover that we already had space for the child. We had only to get rid of the old cupboards and leave a place for a crib.

On the individual model, the dream refers to the transformation of an oral reference (the kitchen) to a genital reference (the crib). But it seems to me that the dream's most important aspect is the discovery of a potential place where the future child-thought can be nestled and can find acceptance. A radical transformation, whereby the child inherits the "old furniture," can be seen as a selected fact when compared to the formless mass of worms that needed to be evacuated. Thus, a place for new thoughts represents the prospect of a work group.

The actual containing place is presented through the spatial reference noted earlier. This reference appears as a result of a transformation of the temporal reference (the memory not only of instinctual fulfillment but also of the good relations with the parental image). The patient has conserved this kitchen-memory during the fight-flight phase and now uses it to reconstruct a new space in the mind.

DISCUSSION

This material illustrates an evolution starting from a disturbance in group identity (the reaction to the summer break and the disappearance of a group member). The group identity disturbance is translated into a disturbance of the narcissistic condition allowing the production of several thought alterations. The succession of these alterations in the various archaic organizational forms of the group—the basic assumptions—enables a particular evolution. All of this translates into the representation of an empty space as "the place" for welcoming child-thoughts. What in our jargon is called the "work group" becomes emotionally "represented."

To summarize, the traumatic event which sets off the most violent thought disturbance is the absence of a group member when the group reunites after the summer break. Comparison with the missing individual creates fragmentation fantasies: just as one person disappears, so can the entire group from one moment to the next. Envious attacks on the more mature member then tend to equate him with the missing member. The destructivity of single members in relation to group thought rests on this.

At this point the most disturbed member elaborates a psychosomatic disturbance that "materializes" the psychotic defense prevailing in the group—the evacuative mechanism—and the group rediscovers an initial form of protoidentity in the fight-flight basic assumption. Angelo's evacuative mechanisms are assimilated into the general tendency of the group to displace all of its violent aggressiveness onto an external enemy—the worms that need to be killed with medical drugs. By providing an initial protoidentity, the fight-flight basic assumption alternatively favors the emergence of evacuative projective identifications and of knowledge-seeking, cognitive ones. This situation acts as a support to the split-off parts, permitting a primitive movement of "conception," the "personification-realization" of the parts. By supplying the group an archaic identity, the fight-flight basic assumption also controls the anxiety of fragmentation. If we agree that the dependence basic assumption contains the preconception of the breast, it is during the passage from fight-flight to dependence that the first potential transformation of the group occurs (the chicken coop dream).

It seems to me that this passage hinges on the same phenomenon described by Bion (1950) in "The Imaginary Twin." The group proposes itself as a mirrorlike twin for the patient, who through somatic disturbances in turn presents himself as a mirrorlike image of the group's mental health. We have here a symbolic equation between the mental state of the group and the somatic state of the leader of the basic assumption group. The leader of the fight-flight group personifies the primal fantasy of castration, which refers back to the primary separation experience of birth.

The analyst's interpretations of the group in the fight-flight phase inevitably contain persecutory potential for members settled in this protoidentity: this is what the dream of the machine-gunning ship represents. Analytic work on this material causes the leadership function attributed to the psychosomatic patient to pass to the ego function of the analyst. At this moment the more mature member finds his privileged space. He points out the group's impotence in curing the real worms and its (work) capacity to cure the worm delusions. In this way the psychosomatic member's destructive function can be brought back and reconstructed in a dependence situation. Similarly, thought function is taken from a very serious disturbance centered on evacuative mechanisms to a pregenital oedipal fantasy that oscillates between dependence and castration-impotence.

Rossella, who dreamed of the gunboat and the chicken coop, seems to personify the group's capacity to pass from an evacuative thought disturbance to the archaic preconception of the breast that is present in the basic assumption of dependence. Evaluating the material from a genetic prospective, we can conclude that from the oedipal ship emerges an approach to the problem of group "guidance."

Emanuela, who dreamed of the Holy Family and of the space for a newborn baby, personifies the group's capacity to use the further transformation to the pairing phase. The group evolves toward being a work group and seems to anticipate a realistic symbolic capacity. A thought disturbance centered on fragmentation, and therefore on reality judgment, is thereby transformed into a judgment disturbance centered on choices and opportunities. The problem is shifted from judging whether something exists to judging whether something is one's own. From an initial, mirrorlike function of the twin type, the group moves toward fraternal differentiation.

In my experience, it is impossible to determine to what degree this movement is due to the intrinsic qualities of the three basic assumptions. That is, their sequence as presented here cannot be said to be typical. In other clinical situations, the sequence could be quite different. It can be said, however, that movement toward a work group is more likely to happen in the presence of reciprocal movement among the basic assumptions. The risk here is that the group might crystalize along the lines of one of them.

As seen, changes among the various basic assumptions favor transition of the various identity forms. The identity of the analyst is included and can pass through the identity of the basic assumptions group leader. This transitional operation permits mobilization of the various forms of projective and introjective identification. In this way, the various types of preconception may find a group space for realization. The experience of realization (or conception) allows the creation of a memory trace in the group. On the temporal plane, this will then be useful in tolerating frustration and, on the spatial plane, will favor the construction of a container.

REFERENCES

Bion, W. R. (1950), The imaginary twin. In: *Second Thoughts: Selected Papers on Psycho-Analysis*. London: Heinemann, 1967, pp. 3–22.
———(1959), *Experiences in Groups*. London: Tavistock.
———(1963), *Elements of Psycho-Analysis*. London: Heinemann.
———(1970), *Attention and Interpretation*. London: Tavistock.
Freud, S. (1911), Formulations on the two principles of mental functioning. *Standard Edition*, 12:218–226. London: Hogarth Press, 1958.
———(1919), The uncannny. *Standard Edition*, 17:219–256. London: Hogarth Press, 1955.
———(1921), Group psychology and the analysis of the ego. *Standard Edition*, 18:69–143. London: Hogarth Press, 1955.
Gaburri, E. (1981), Il gruppo e il pensiero. *Gruppo e Funzione Analitica*, 3:57–74.
Grinberg, L. (1985), Bion's contribution to the understanding of the individual and the group. In: *Bion and Group Psychotherapy*, ed. M. Pines. London: Routledge & Kegan Paul, pp. 176–192.
———Grinberg, R. (1975), *Identitad y Cambio*. Barcelona: Paidos Iberica. 1980.
Klein, M. (1929), Personification in the play of children. In: *Internat. J. Psycho-Anal.*, 10:193–204.
———(1930), The importance of symbol-formation in the development of the ego. *Internat. J. Psycho-Anal.*, 11:24–38.
Meltzer, D. (1973), *Sexual States of Mind*. Perthshire: Clunie.

7

The Group That Would Not Relate to Itself

BENNETT E. ROTH, Ph.D.

Clinical observations over the last two decades suggest that narcissistically disordered patients have a particular claim on the students and practitioners of psychoanalytic group psychotherapy. These patients represent the largest number of nonpsychotic individuals who seek out group psychotherapy and the greatest percentage of those who then prematurely leave groups. In general they are individuals who have great problems in understanding and affecting interpersonal intimacy and trust. These problems, while having developmentally early origins, coalesce with latency and cognitive defenses, and result in the incapacity to generate reflective ideas. Ironically, the same defensive conditions that draw these patients to the group modality render them unable to use the therapeutic group process. In prematurely leaving treatment they unwittingly contribute to our ignorance about how we have failed them and reduce our therapeutic ability to effectively treat similar patients.

Some unusual circumstances in a psychotherapy group have led me to reconsider a number of issues concerning certain types of narcissistic problems that obstruct therapeutic group functions. Among these issues are premature leaving, the requirements of psychoanalytic group psychotherapy, and the varieties of narcissistic defenses that result in "unrelatedness." As with most advances in clinical theory, initial understanding begins with the recognition of a problem. Readers looking for technical solutions will likely be frustrated for at this time I am content simply to describe some of the unique group-related problems.

LEAVING THE GROUP

Leaving the group, whatever the motivation, is probably the most radical form of not relating. Less drastic solutions to patients' problems always seem available, yet they seem fixed on this radical solution. A patient's leaving or entering a psychotherapy group has an immediate impact on the group dynamics. This is felt by group members as changes in lateral patterns of transferences and alliances. Premature leaving as a separate dynamic is a radical refusal to relate. It unsettles the group and often leads to a decrease in the felt trust toward both the group and the group therapist. While not all patients are compatible with every group, the number of patients who prematurely leave group psychotherapy, particularly analytic group psychotherapy, is quite significant. Equally significant is the fact that this phenomenon, as it occurs in private practice, has largely been ignored in the literature and remains unstudied. There are a variety of clinical reports, or studies of other populations, that contain important clinical evidence about the reasons some patients leave. This kind of leaving should not be confused with a planned process of termination, which has its own dynamic, or with dropping out of the group in its early stages. A recent review by Klein and Carroll (1986) may be consulted.

Accumulated clinical data that precede the act of prematurely leaving reveal overdetermined erotic, aggressive, or narcissistically tinged events that, while thought provoking, are not sufficient to explain the need for departure. In addition, explanations by the group therapist are postmortem, offered in the absence of all witnesses, and lacking objective phenomenological evidence. Further, most accounts of a patient's departure are resolved without considering the kind and quality of the patient's expectations, transference attachment, and working alliance vis-à-vis either the group or the therapist. Important distinctions between the patient's real and transference conflicts are blurred and if reported are generally couched in a defensive explanation. Group therapists, in print or in supervision, usually defend themselves narcissistically against separation and humiliation. The most frequently employed defensive maneuvers here are self criticism and open accusations against the departed group member. Such defenses may serve to maintain temporary group cohesion or self esteem in the remaining group members. This defensiveness obscures crucial dimensions of the group's narcissistic functioning, the emergence of a working negative transference in the group, and analysis of the countertansference reactions of the therapist. As they appear in print, accusations directed against the patient who has left appear in many indirect forms, and usually include a pejorative diagnosis or a statement of patient deficit as if the diagnosis or deficit were not previously known. Explanations are rarely made in clinically useful terms of the patient's failed struggle to achieve either real or transference attachments and intimacy, either to the group or to its members.

All theories are bound by the conceptualizations of their time, and clinical theories are no exception. Our current theories of analytic group process and dynamics stand very much in need of completion. Few clinicians are satisfied with their predictive or explanatory power when confronted with the multidetermined complexity of a group interaction. Strikingly absent from the literature on group therapy, with a few exceptions, is a perspective drawn from theories of development, either psychoanalytic or psychological. This is even more striking since natural, educational, social, and religious group membership forms part of the developmental history of all members of society, and part of the early transference to the group leader. The core theoretical issues of group interaction, of the dynamics of an individual's regression in the group and the gathering of multiple or hierarchical transferences and resistances, are still inchoate and enigmatic when applied to the treatment of certain patients with narcissistic transferences and resistances. My initial attempts to grapple with specific kinds of behavior in groups of certain narcissistic types (Roth, 1982) is one of the few bridges to this current volume.

Group therapists of various theoretical orientation have been treating the more difficult narcissistic patient for longer than the current psychoanalytic interest in these patients. Some groups because of their composition, and some group therapists because of their optimistic character style, have been effective as therapeutic agents or engineers. Some patients with the same diagnosis are "better group risks" than are others. The fundamental issues of psychoanalytic group treatment and group techniques for such patients remain as a mystery or are as yet unarticulated and unstudied.

The treatment of many patients in a group setting continues to be based on vague ideas and unsound (group) techniques, often drawn too closely from theories of dyadic treatment. While some understanding of the meaning of the individual behavior and dyadic events from psychoanalysis is useful, it is not clear that the unique structure of group therapy and group regression readily permits a direct application of dyadic dynamics. Such applications may be a form of group resistance. Another problem exists in the tendency of group therapists not to discriminate among different types of borderline or narcissistic patients, or to rely on DSM descriptions as if these possessed specific relevance for therapeutic treatment or tactical intervention.

There are many profound issues in treating the contemporary patient, and one place to start is with the sensitive insight that most patients with narcissistic problems report about their negative stance to group membership: that there is something paradoxical and seemingly impossible about the task of belonging to a psychotherapy group. Yet we encourage these patients to engage in a sustained effort to resolve this paradox by using the group for and against themselves, by being for and against the group, embracing it in order to live and enjoy while loosening from it in a nonpathological way to go on with their separate and individual lives.

PSYCHIC REQUIREMENTS FOR MEMBERSHIP

We can deepen our understanding of the paradoxes of group membership by investigating the multiple requirements for group membership. To be a member of any group requires some form of psychic change in the individual. The dynamics of regression and the narcissistic exaltation of the leader that were originally made explicit by Freud (1917, 1921) remain verifiable with neurotic patients. However, Freud's theory of groups was framed before his formulation of the structural model and the general emergence of a theory of the development of the ego and object relationships. The essential narcissistic group dynamic—that group cohesion occurs by taking the leader in place of the ego ideal—lacks explanatory value and takes different courses when more characterologically disturbed patients are considered. Idealization as a dynamic, with its various defenses and its multiple origins, remains crucial in understanding some groups' behavior. However, the phenomenon of idealization does not exhaust the narcissistic dynamics of analytic psychotherapy groups.

To become a member of a psychoanalytically oriented psycho-therapy group requires both specific psychic capabilities and psychic potential. Among these capabilities is a tolerance for the sustained ambiguity and anxiety occasioned by the unrevealing group therapist. At the same time the group participant attempts to remain "open" to new emotional understanding in a supportive or exploratory multi-person environment. With narcissistic patients, who have a tendency to idealize the leader or, conversely, to defend against idealization, there is likely to be no tolerance for therapist ambiguity. With this intolerance is their defensive readiness to project and identify with an unarticulated part of the entire group interaction.

Successful outcomes of analytic group therapy depend on the patients' healthy mastery of conflict and anxiety within the confines of the positive transferences within the group. Successful outcomes also require the ability to take these changes outside the boundaries of the group. Rarely is an analytic psychotherapy constructed to offer regressive satisfaction of original primary needs, dependency wishes, or idealizing fantasies, since those wishes remain irrevocably in the patient's past. For an analytic group to be functional there must be a tension between gratification and frustration. Therapy groups in which attempts are made to satisfy primary needs or idealizing fantasies are likely to become psychologically addictive or narcissistically perverse. The same may be said of group therapists who employ the group to gratify their own needs with group members who are in a transference regression. Briefly, a perverse relationship exists when a part-object relationship becomes both narcissistically and erotically charged and these psychic regressive charges are turned into directly satisfying action (Arlow, 1986).

In general, analytic group psychotherapy evolves through seemingly intricate psychological processes, both within and among the individuals. These interactive processes, which are called "group dynamics," partially depend on regressive recall within the group of multiple transferences. In addition to the regressive transference recall a (regressive) shift in ego functions is also precipitated. Self-reflective awareness and the ability to verbalize that awareness must be episodically available and enable the sharing of distortions and both failed and successful attempts to achieve pleasure and mastery. This basic ego capacity of verbal therapeutic work, occurring in the absence of psychomotor discharge, leads to many adaptive changes. These changes occur in the group functioning of the patients, in the patients' ego capacities, and in their functioning outside of the group setting. This desired change in ego functioning is achieved only to the extent that the participants are able to effect a minimally trusting relationship in the group, be reflectively aware and eventually to communicate that awareness while in the regressive psychic state common to all group membership. In analytic psychotherapy groups, activity other than verbalization is prohibited, which puts greater pressure on the dynamics of speech and the process of verbalization. Silent learning, learning that occurs in the absence of verbalization, has a stronger tendency to be narcissistically distorted, as it is held apart from the reality testing functions of the group. Motoric actions in a group are more directly charged with other impulses usually of an erotic or aggressive nature. Although some forms of silent learning occur voyeuristically in every group the specific problems of silent learning in group psychotherapy deserve separate study.

An additional problem of technique in analytically oriented group psychotherapy with narcissistic or borderline patients is posed by the nature of their ego problems and capacities. By diagnostic definition, their capacity to trust, their self-awareness and their object-seeking behaviors are often severely limited. Frequently these are replaced by extremely powerful defensive and externalizing operations. These defenses impel the patient to concrete action or emotional discharge rather than reflection. The presence of this mode of narcissistically defensive ego structures places these patients at the brink of a type of regression that must be very strongly defended against. This means, in my experience with these patients, there are severe limits placed on any reflective verbal therapeutic work and an immediate readiness to attempt to use the group for repetitive emotional discharge, or acting in, which has little lasting therapeutic value. Therapeutic tension, the tension between gratification and frustration, is difficult to maintain unless the group therapist has a great tolerance for acting out.

Any group dependent on self-reflective awareness and the capacity to verbalize that awareness places an impossible demand on these narcissistically traumatized people. Often their unsuccessful attempts to comply with this requirement while actually defending against it creates additional intricate defensive processes in the individual and in the group. These defenses bring to the surface of the group severe anxiety, intensely felt projections, or outbursts of narcissistic rage and regressive transference anger. These outbursts are often accompanied by accusations of being deprived, treated badly, or having their reality problems ignored.

Those with more severe narcissistic problems face additional psychic problems. Their wish for and fear of a symbiotic relationship with the group leader or with group members precipitate a terror of confronting their fearful wish to lose their identity in the group. On most occasions, patients who experience a terror of dissolution have little ability to trust the group therapist and to remain in the group to sort out the meanings of their wishes and fears. Further, there is often little time to psychically hold that experience in the group and compare their terror with the reality of other group members' similar experiences. Too often such patients are impelled to leave the group very rapidly in order to dispel their fears of dissolution and relieve psychic tension.

Other conflicts are generated that make it difficult for these patients to remain in the group. They have a marked tendency to feel overwhelmed and usually a long history of, acting to reduce overwhelming anxiety and depression. This is a recurrent tendency. Often they seek literal satisfactions rather than sharing a more mature ability to convert conflict into a verbalizable wish or fantasy. Consequently, they deny responsibility for the impulsive actions they take in the group and project the blame outside the self. These complex defenses stand as a barrier to reflective awareness and as a protective shield against severe ego vulnerability and superego shame and guilt.

Caught between a frustrating reality and failed coping and adaptive behaviors, the new group member is in a vise of externally and internally generated anxiety; literal-minded attempts at adaptive solutions have yielded only more problems in reality and greater narcissistic vulnerability. The painful personal experiences that ensue become the motive for the reconstructive work of therapy. At the same time, their psychic inability to "contain" their own experience becomes the occasion for an increase in both defensive behavior and impulsive actions. Sometimes these actions are a search for an idealized object, but all too often doing or acting is better than having the experience and its emotional consequences. In general terms, the increase in defensive behaviors is played out in the group setting and can have a painful effect on other group members and the transference network in the group.

It is a very important requirement for effective membership in a group that patients have some capacity to observe their own behavior and feelings and to be receptive to various forms of interpretation without feeling too humiliated, shamed, or criticized. Some participants are willing and able to engage in self-observation despite the regressive pulls in the group. Others too often are more willing to observe other's behavior in the group and to make observations that satisfy complex character needs; this bars them from effective membership and participation in the group. Bion (1952) has made important distinctions within this phenomenon in describing the "work group" and "the basic assumption group." However, in terms of the exhibitionistic-voyeuristic balance, within both individuals and groups, if it were true that every individual in a group was but an observer that group would be waiting for a subject who might never arrive. The well-known drama *Waiting for Godot* uses this insightful premise. In this voyeuristic group situation, members distance themselves and become objects waiting for a subject. Conversely, if everyone seeks at once to be the subject of attention, investigation, and help, this competitive exhibitionism would create an equally impossible group situation, sort of a Tower of Babel effect.

THE NARCISSISTICALLY STRUCTURED GROUP

When an individual presents narcissistic problems in the group therapy situation, very rapidly a number of defensive operations are evoked in other members based on their narcissistic transferences to that individual (Roth, 1980). When the therapy group is composed of a number of these patients, the evoked narcissistic defenses and transference dynamics take on a geometrically increasing group intensity. Problems with basic trust and the safety of participation are at the core of these dynamics. In homogeneous groups composed of people with similar conflicts, or at moments in which there is a confluence of narcissistic defenses, increasing fears of "being in the group" invariably occur. Usually there is an intense and threatening narcissistic conflict over how to retain one's individuality while remaining in the group.

From another perspective, although we are accustomed to speaking of psychic boundaries as if they were fixed, clinical observations reveal that these patients are prone to rapid and intense boundary fluctuations. In a group situation, these patients experience a partial or very deep regression depending on the particular mix of neurotic and narcissistic conflicts and the manifest and latent conflicts in the group at a given time. One frequent outcome of this oscillation in regressive experience is the development of a group culture. The function of a group culture is either to avoid or to precipitate the narcissistic breakdown of the group. One sign of the existance of a group culture is a style of character relatedness that emerges, which not only protects the idealization of the leader, but serves as a stubborn group characterological defense.

Within any group culture there is no absolute freedom. Extreme psychological forces operate that assign to certain individuals particular and well-defined stereotypical roles that have characterological and narcissistic significance. As a result of boundary problems and the narcissistic wish to be defined only by external events, some narcissistic patients welcome the group role assigned them. It supports a group identity and serves to dampen intolerable affect and anxiety. Sometimes the group role assigned an individual is compatible with that person's character style and experiential history, but at other times the individual feels forced into a role that is not a good fit. An individual group role is used at different conflictual points in the group history. More often the role assigned is an aspect or part of the person's identity. Because such patients need to relate to part-object representations, these roles are often acted out in extreme ways.

The individual subjected to group pressure to assume a role has often come to the group with an expectation of what would happen and tends to make that expectation a self-fulfilling prophecy. A form of part-object group defensive relatedness is seen here that has not been previously described. When group needs are congruent with the individual's character defenses or character problems, this poses a difficult technical situation that often requires the intervention of the group leader if group-syntonic behavior is to be made dystonic. In doing this there is always the risk of disruption and upheaval both in the overall group-role dynamic and in the individual, because part-object identity definition serves to reaffirm boundaries for that individual and, in some form, for the entire group.

Any time group-syntonic behavior is made dystonic, not only do object constancy and expectancy become uncertain, but group compatibility is disturbed. This in turn results in disequilibrium in the group's object relations. I have previously described one such process involving scapegoating (Roth, 1980). With patients who have preconstancy problems, group-syntonic role identity occurs more frequently than is imagined and is extremely sensitive to disruption, as they are developmentally sensitized to object expectancy. Some examples of group identity phenomena may be recognized by the character images they evoke; "the professional helper," "the group clown," "the silent screen star," "the secret keeper," "the group prisoner," "the stalking horse," "the pretender to the throne," "the fine tuner" (the person who changes the emotional meaning of any exchange in the dialogue), "the love seeker," "the litigator," and "the nay-sayer" are but a few of the part-object transference role behaviors seen in groups. Sometimes a missing part-object group role is identified with and played out by the group therapist as a result of unanalyzed character defenses and narcissistic pressures in the group. A healthy ego function lacking in the group may also be consciously assumed by the group psychotherapist without it turning into a role, but this should be done only temporarily until the group is ready to assume this function.

Taken as a group event, the playing out of roles actively prevents the members from emotionally examining the defensive manifestations of their character or sense of self and thereby prevents the emergence of new meanings and understandings within the group. In other words, insight and change are avoided and the defended and vulnerable aspects of the self or the self-image are protected by role behavior. From the perspective of the group members, a part of another member's self is taken for the whole of that person, so that contradictory or ambivalent elements also present as part of that person's identity are unrecognized and prevented from emerging in the group.

Clinical Illustration

In one of my therapy groups a patient would actively interview group members who were new or who told complicated stories. He would single-mindedly, gently, and persuasively gather all the facts he could. The group tolerated and silently approved of his behavior, as it satisfied complex defensive needs for them. When I called this behavior to their attention, one group member said he was reminded of Edward R. Murrow; thereafter the patient was "doing a Murrow" whenever he manifested this behavior. Over the course of many years' membership in the group, this direct questioning revealed itself to serve many complex defensive functions. It allowed him to keep the group on an "all I want is the facts" level of interaction and to prevent him from exploring the intense nature of his curiosity and its possible meanings; to avoid stranger anxiety; to reverse his fear of being questioned about things he did not want to tell the group; to prevent him from talking of things about which he was doubtful; to allow him to keep hidden his own guilt feelings; to substitute action for reflection and remembering. It should be noted that the group vicariously identified with the active and defensive nature of his individual behavior, and that a long period of working through was required for both the individual and the entire group.

THE GROUP THAT WOULDN'T RELATE: A DESCRIPTION

I have taken this descriptive path to set the stage for examining a particular set of circumstances that emerged in a group therapy situation. Stated simply, the group did not relate to itself; that is, the people in the group did not relate to one another as people. They spoke to one another and at times of crisis attempted to help one another, but they simply did not relate to one another in any meaningful psychological way. There was no mad choreography of feelings and projections to sort out, no clarifications to make, and no emotional threats to blunt. The group work was slow, tedious, and characterized by tepid complaints or quasi-helpful remarks and dialogues that seemed psychologically irrelevant. A form of defensive passivity dominated the interactions so that spontaneity was almost completely absent, as were emotional or self-revealing responses, unless specifically asked for. The therapist's prospective physical absence, which in other groups evoked acting out or memories of abandonment, was met here with either relief or indifference. Countertransference images, such as being under glass or in a plastic bubble, offered little aid in terms of avenues of interpretation. The group members themselves, while moderately successful in the world, were uniformly unsuccessful by any therapeutic standard in their personal or intimate lives.

Object relationships outside the group therapy situation were dominated by repetitive acting out; that is, the actions of these people lacked reflective awareness. Serial relationships predominated among the single patients. While mostly unarticulated, the more permanent social relationships were empty, emotionally blunted, or fundamentally unequal. With little exception, the members of the group seemed to have a limited capacity to evaluate realistically their "significant others." This indicated a compromised capacity for attachment and reality testing. Each of these people seemed to have limitless capacities to adapt passively, without an outward appearance of anxiety, anger, or other defenses, to situations that occurred in the group. Coexisting with this passive adaptation were extreme tendencies to be self-critical and self-blaming, and to accept the accusations of others with a lack of healthy perspective. Ego weakness of a particular kind predominated, and was clinically manifested in a tendency to feel overwhelmed and at the mercy of some external force or object.

Interpersonal relationships of a meaningful, equal, or reciprocal nature seemed limited or absent. Certain issues of control predominated: of distance between objects; control of the presence or absence of the object; and control of oneself and one's feelings. Patients alternately felt that they could not expect to be loved for who they were or demanded to be cared for in ways that could never be met. They faced these prospects either with painful silence, feeling no depression or sense of loss, or used simple rationalization and justification as a defense. Sometimes they responded by reporting earlier events that proved to them that their lives were not really in their control: that they were severely traumatized as children; or that they were good patients. Mourning seemed either impossible to start or, having started in childhood, impossible to resolve. Conflictual events that they brought into the group and that became the subject of discussion were treated at a "safe" emotional distance rather than experienced, and there was a limited range of elicited feelings. Individuals reporting conflictual events were often told by other group members what they should do to simply resolve the conflict. The more clever members were then able to manipulate the group, after they presented a conflict, either to arrive at conclusions they had already reached in private or to support actions they had already taken of which the group was unaware.

In sum, this group never moved beyond the initial stages of becoming a group. Maintaining a static distance from one another, they constantly attempted to deal with experiences that were outside the group or outside themselves. They did not appear fragile or stubborn in their resistance but seemed to be caught in a short repetitive cycle, starting out from and returning to the same psychological defensive point. Any opportunity was ignored to move below the surface of events to emotional meanings or self-revelation.

Underneath this surface behavior each member seemed to be clinging to defenses that were fixed much as a photograph is fixed. I assumed that this defensive stance of the group was the result not only of a defensive regressive splitting but also of what appeared to be their "felt" permanent incapacity for further development. Their capacity to understand one another empathically was severely limited. Empathy between group members remained at the level of vague projection, offered indirectly and silently absorbed by the person to whom it was directed.

Intervention by the group therapist in the form of empathic remarks, confrontations, or explications of meanings was absorbed in much in the same manner—never to be heard or seen again by the individual for whom they were intended or by the other group members. In repetitive situations, responsibility for an event was defensively located outside the self so that there was also an inability to learn from experience: whatever happened was simply someone else's fault. A major task of group interaction was neglected: the group would neither study itself nor allow itself to be studied.

My own reaction to this encompassing style of interaction was complex. Had I unconsciously formed a homogeneous group with an unknown dynamic? Curiosity about the group predominated over any other feelings. I could not really explain why this group would not become involved in some form of analytic work, would not move from its initial stance of self-protection and resistance, would not move to an anaclitic object-seeking position or become curious about itself. It was clinically obvious that the very phenomena enumerated in this description of their functioning was integral to the adaptive functions of the group as a whole and of its individual members. It was, I suspected, a clinical analogue to prior and current object relations in which emotional neglect or emotional absence, coupled with a sense of overstimulation, played a significant role. To thera-peutically disturb these fixed adaptive patterns of object relating would generate great pain and anxiety in the group members, and it was inappropriate to do so aggressively. At the same time, the members of the group seemed to have very little capacity to read their own anxiety or to tolerate painful feelings in themselves or others. Yet the phenomenon of unrelatedness had to become the subject of a group therapeutic alliance, that is, their unrelatedness had to be observed by the group members themselves and worked with as an essential element of their dynamics. I was certain, based on prior events, that continued interpretation and clarification would serve very little therapeutic purpose other than being received as a superego accusation. Educating the individuals to be group members seemed to be essential; it was the way to make manifest their hidden dynamics.

A DEVELOPMENTAL EXPLANATION

Current psychoanalytic thinking has drawn attention to the process, purpose, and structuralization of psychic individuation as dependent upon both real and psychic variables that occur very early in the child's development. Preoedipal experiences are the essential psychological building blocks for later psychic structures. Among the important variables that affect this interactive process are the empathic relationship between mother and child; the quality of maternal caretaking and identificatory processes that depend on mutual cuing; the balance between developmentally early frustration and gratification; the capacity to move toward significant others such as the father; and the ability to adapt to timely affective experiences with reality.

Out of these early interactive experiences the core structures of the body ego emerge (Weil, 1970), as do two very important psychological characteristics: (1) the individual's basic mood which emotionally colors and titrates all experiences that are crucial to ongoing psychological development and (2) a basic sense of trust in oneself and in others.

In addition to these interactive variables, the emerging function of anxiety and affect in its complex signal function interacts with preoedipal variables and plays a significant role in the ongoing development of defenses and adaptations. These variables contribute to the ability to learn from experience, to have a sense of trusting curiosity first about reality and later about the self, and to the ability to achieve separation from primary objects and thereby experience a variety of intimate relationships—mutually trusting and gratifying— with new people.

The individual's ability to learn from experience is particularly important in determining how patients function in a psychotherapy group; it reveals the individual's cognitive style and the cognitive processes used in processing external and internal information, as well as the intensity of the patient's urge to repeat traumatic experiences in the transference, and the manner in which external interpretations are received and internal insights arrived at. In the treatment of narcissistic patients in group therapy, the ability to learn from experience is particularly important, as the interactive mix of patients and setting make acting out—that is, acting without thinking—a regular occurrence (Glatzer, 1962).

Learning, in particular about oneself, involves the taking in of experience, an internalizing process that represents and encodes experience, making information personal, useful, and available. Any part of this cognitive process can be interfered with by psychic conflicts and trauma. Experience is not simply incorporated in pure form; rather, it is filtered through the unique and complex transference dynamics of the moment, as well as the more permanent personality structure and cognitive style of the individual. For example, the distortion of actual therapeutic remarks is a frequent occurrence with narcissistic patients, who are defensively unable to "take in" what is stated without changing the original words and converting them into a criticism.

THE LATENCY PERIOD

The latency period has been overlooked as contributing to the development of group cohesion and a working group alliance. While most adaptive learning occurs in the developmental framework of the preoedipal period, the crucial developmental test of the individual's psychological style of learning occurs in the few years immediately following the oedipal period. Thus latency also coincides with the first few years of the child's school experience. It is at this time that the child begins to amass the cognitive tools that are needed to learn. Learning as a psychological event never becomes completely autonomous or conflict free, since it is affected by mood and anxiety as well as by the ability to delay gratification and maintain attention. From a psychological perspective, this period of time extends into preadolescence.

During latency the child's sense of reality becomes more complex. Psychic boundaries are expanded to include extrafamilial demands, and the ability to adapt to these demands reveals, by displacement, any prior separation anxiety. Preexisting internal psychic structures from the oedipal and preoedipal periods are built up, and the rudiments of cognitive style begin to emerge. It is not by accident that the early forms of group therapy in this country were conducted with latency age children; it is precisely at this time that cohesive groups are formed and the ego becomes educable (Scheidlinger, 1982).

For the group members under discussion it was to become

evident that a normal latency period did not occur. All of their parents had problematic relationships with both spouses and children. There was little sense that during latency these patients had a functioning family unit, either as a working and emotionally cohesive group or as having the potential to become one. Rather, what emerged was a picture of individuals in lonely and isolated struggles against a severely traumatic reality, with little sense of any pleasure in being together as a family. The prevailing lack of basic trust was manifested in reports of perceptual vigilance and wariness with regard to parents or siblings. Reality, it seemed to them, provided good enough reasons for this lack of trust. Such family conditions are frequently the natural occasion for the development of disorganizing paranoid defenses, yet true paranoid feelings never developed. Rather, in their place was an undifferentiated readiness to withdraw from humiliating reality into fantasy accompanied by a feeling of hopelessness (deidealization) about the parent and concern about what to do. One aspect of this adaptive defense, often apparent in the group, was the outward display of an inappropriate wary calmness on the part of the group members and a tendency to impulsively act without thinking. While fantasy and withdrawal into silence or calmness are commonplace defensive reactions, too often there was no surface evidence that the patient was under stress or that a strong nonverbalized emotion was present. As well, it was very difficult at these times for them to engage in a dialogue, and language usage became highly defensive.

Affective wary calmness and the absence of felt anxiety is not uncommon at the initiation of a group or immediately after a separation. The duration and persistence of this group stance, in conjunction with yet another defense, made the group take on a rather telling quality. I have mentioned that the members of the group had a pronounced tendency toward projection of "bad" feelings and other externalizing defenses. In addition, they were often successful in reality, or on the verge of being so, which clearly indicated areas of conflict-free functioning. Yet for each member there was an absence of ideas, a concreteness or literalness of thought, accompanied by a reacting responsiveness that created another level of flatness to this group's interaction.

In summary, the defensive behaviors in the group presented a complex and puzzling problem. While the natural form of regression in a group takes on the properties of wishing for an omnipotent leader, in this group certain characterological forces operated against the natural development of this form of therapeutic regression. First, almost all of the patients had a parental figure whom they consciously did not trust, and there was a basis in reality for their emotional wariness. Second, defenses were such that both the here-and-now affects and attachments to new objects were resisted, almost totally precluding any feelings about what was occurring in the group. In sum, these patients resisted being vulnerable to a regressively recalled omnipotent figure and to their own experience. While this regressively recalled figure appeared to be paternal, their failure to establish emotionally resonating relationships within the group and to the other members indicated an earlier, perhaps cumulative, problem in trusting their mothers.

A HYPOTHETICAL CLINICAL EXAMPLE

At this point I have given a developmental perspective on certain forms of learning problems that stem from basic trust issues. These issues are exacerbated by the continued presence of latency defenses and are best revealed by a clinical example. For this purpose, I have created a dialogue that draws on a number of similar events that actually occurred in the group I have been discussing. As with any written report of clinical interactions, nuances of tone, affect, and response are lost, as well as the freshness of impact upon the therapist. The words alone in this example will have to stand for the events, and the reader may supply the emotional texture.

Miss A. The last time this happened, I didn't tell you anything about it so this time I will. . . . I'm going to miss the next two weeks. . . . I mentioned it last week at the end of the group but I did not tell you why. I'm making plans to visit my father next week.

Mr. B. The last time you brought along your boyfriend. Is he going with you this time?

Mrs. C. Are you still going out with him? I thought you had stopped seeing him.

Miss A. No, I am going alone.

Mr. B. I didn't understand, after everything you told us about how you hate your father, why would you want to see him?

Miss A. We are a bicoastal family and . . . well . . . we became one after they divorced and . . . there is a conference in San Diego where my father lives. I am going to spend a week at the conference and a week with him while I visit friends.

Dr. R. Do you think this vacation has anything to do with my vacation next week?

Miss A. The conference is the week after you're away. . . .

Mr. D. You made it sound as if the conference was next week.

Mr. E. My father slept in the same room as me after my mother died and I couldn't sleep all night.

Mrs. C. Did you sleep in the same bed?

Mr. E. No, I had twin beds . . . and I told him that my sleep was important to me—I couldn't go to work so exhausted—and he would have to get his own apartment.

Miss A. My father has a big house and we will have separate rooms and separate bathrooms. . . . Even if we are in the same house I don't think we'll see much of each other, but it's cheaper than spending money on a hotel.

Mr. D. Who is going to take care of your children for two weeks?

Miss A. I thought I told you that my sister is going to stay with them. I don't know what the fuss is about; I'm just going to see my father.

Dr. R. That's the first time I've heard any feeling in your voice!

Miss F. Even if you have a father that beats you or is angry at you . . . it's better to have a father. When mine died I felt so guilty that we had no relationship.

Miss A. Did your father beat you? I'm asking . . . because . . . you know my father was always angry at me.

Miss F. No, but when my parents were getting divorced I saw a lot of violence. They were always screaming at each other. I couldn't let him touch me even after they divorced.

Miss A. Do I have to pay for the two weeks that I'm away? You know I don't have very much money because I'm divorced and a lot of the money I have pays for getting my degree.

Mr. G. I'm going to see my mother and I won't be here for two weeks after Dr. R. gets back.

AN ANALYSIS OF GROUP DIALOGUE

Much can be made of this dialogue, if it can be called a dialogue at all. For present purposes this fictive exchange will be regarded as if it really occurred. From a therapeutic perspective nothing is pursued and very little is clarified. This is so although the group has been together for a long time, over four years, and each knows the other's history and problems quite well. There is nothing overtly bizarre about the interchanges, and yet there is the constant tone of complaint and feelings of simultaneous participation, banality, and evasiveness. Everybody has something to say and almost everything is ignored that might lead beyond the surface of events. What is said is mundane, empathically blunted, factual, and repetitive. I am using this "multilogue" not only to convey the tone of the group, but also to demonstrate their paucity of ideas and adherence to surface facts. Typically, they make no attempt to explore a reaction or to give additional meaning to what is being revealed. It can be assumed that a great deal of material of an affective or fantasy nature has been precipitated by Miss A.'s announced plans, and is going on below the surface in some form. However, none of it emerges in the group in a form, discursive or nondiscursive, that makes it available for analytic group work. Certainly, many ideas and hypotheses are aroused in the therapist's mind, and perhaps in the reader's, but none of these appear in the group.

The fantasies, fears, and feelings of group members remained beneath the surface of their mundane dialogue, and continued to, because of a lack of coherence from one group meeting to the next. There was a felt reluctance to move toward empathic closeness or sharing, and individual defenses of privacy were never violated by any attempt at intimacy or emotional commonality. My upcoming vacation was not the occasion of regressive recall, and the "reporting" of events as a shared group resistance continued unabated.

THE ABSENCE OF IDEAS

This group's lack of capacity to form ideas, abstract ideas in particular, is an important defense whereby the symbolic form and meaning of thought is disavowed, making progress through interpretation nearly impossible. The object relationship from which symbolic meanings arise is also defended against. This process results in what has been called "a shallow transference," a transference with shallow attachments and no unconscious commonality that effectively binds the group together.

A reflective idea is a complex psychological event for which certain psychic structures and a confluence of psychic operations are required. Among the first of these is the experience and recognition of some primary affective relationship between external objects and the self. This kind of mental event requires that both the object and the event be mentally represented, then distinguished as separate entities, and then reflected upon in a manner that permits a subjective evaluation of what each is in reality, as well as what each is in different conceptual frameworks. New ideas are essentially new meaningful mental connections between the self and its mental representations, or between the self and events in reality.

The absence of ideas that is common to certain forms of narcissistic disturbance is caused by a developmental disruption in the internal representational process. The traumatic disruption affects either the initial ability to subjectively represent the event or the ability to reflect upon differences between the actual mental events or among the objects in different represented events. The constant, repetitive questioning characteristic of some narcissistic patients arises from their inability to hold on to ideas, an ability caused by these disturbances in representational processes. Frequently these also involve an inability to "link" internal events with external ones; to know who they are in relation to other objects. They cannot be their own reflective subject and perceive a link that mediates between them and objects in reality. The seeming evasiveness of certain patients when confronted with what they have said is another form of this disturbance. They cannot mentally hold (that is, represent) what they have said or done. In other words, they are not a constant subject for themselves over time. Literalness of thought, aside from its defensive functions, may also represent a failure in accepting their own narcissistic experience. For example, Miss A. was not simply "making plans"; she was actually going to California. She had never mentioned "her sister" to the group and had in a prior meeting spoke openly of her wish not to visit her father. She could not, at the time of her speaking, discern the differences between her current and past statements, or between concrete plans and hypothetical ones. Interestingly, the group would not bring these discrepancies to Miss A.'s attention.

HAVING IDEAS IN THE GROUP

To have an original idea is to make a new affective connection between psychic events and objects in psychic space or over time. To have an original idea in the group requires a partial resistance to the powerful regressive pull into a merged group consciousness and unity with the group leader. For the patient with a neurotic psychic structure, regression and ideas are at opposite poles of a continuum. Original ideas—that is, spontaneous thoughts or novel connections among familiar ideas—serve as a partial resistance to regression into group unity that creates, at that moment, a mental separateness from the group.

The narcissistically traumatized patient's psychic structure is more prone, because of structural weakness, both to wish for and fear the regressive pull of the group toward unity. This fearful wish may be experienced jointly with other members of the group. One result of the defense against being vulnerable and needy (losing one's self) is to defend the boundaries of the self, which entails a resistance to accepting anything from the group. To be accepting is to allow the experience of an individual need and the paradoxical wish for both merger and separateness vis-à-vis the group leader. This is a particular problem for narcissistic patients because, by dint of their history, they seem to intuit that giving by the analytically oriented therapist has as its intent, not unity or completely sating a need, but the achievement of individual separateness. That is, regression toward group unity is resisted by some form of primary self-defensiveness or group separateness that prevents the group experience from becoming personal and meaningful (Freud, 1921; Bion, 1952). One proactive way to be separate is to have or to think one's own ideas and thoughts about oneself and the other objects in reality. To require little, to offer little, to not be seen, and to learn nothing is a defensive way of being separate.

Group therapeutic processes depend on the basic human need to reach out to people and for social relationships. This basic core transference is first expressed in nondiscursive behaviors. Within a group there are usually discursive and nondiscursive forms of reaching out toward members in reality to create a familiar social, transference, or regressive relationship. One therapeutic expectation of this process is that it will generate new ideas and new meanings about "old" relationships and the "old" self in relation to objects. In the general course of group events, ideas about the other members of the group, or the group therapist, generally appear first, just as recognition of the outside initially appears in mental development (Katan, 1961).

Ideas about the self—insight or self-reflection—usually occur in the individual's development, and in the group's as well. Insight is defined, in this context, as the ability to take oneself as both subject and object of thought. Ideas about the self occur when group members have sufficient psychic structure to be less concerned with their own boundaries, or with their wishes and fears about the leader, or with merging into group unity. When the boundaries between self and other fluctuate under the narcissistic tension of either intensely felt need or the fear of being merged into a group, it is often not possible for these patients to distinguish between the ego or self as subject and outside objects. Ideas are not possible when the distinction between self and object is absent; only illusion is possible.

At times of openness and vulnerability to the group, powerful externalizing defenses, the product of structural deficits, are mobilized that exaggerate the importance of the outside. A part-object relationship thereby exists between aspects of the self and externalized aspects of the self. At such times, insight is impossible because the self is emptied of its objective-subjective balance by the powerful externalizing defenses. In this group, ideas were prevented by defenses protecting against traumatic reexperience of unmet needs, by deep and fearful wishes for unity and separateness, and by the loss of subject-object differentiation.

MISS A. RECONSIDERED

Let us return to Miss A. and her representation of conflicts with her father as a concrete example of these defenses in operation. She had been in constant conflict with the group rules and hence the group leader. Her most recent problem was her failure to tell the group about a conflicting appointment she had set up at exactly the time the group met. She expected to be chastised for her transgression by the leader, thereby reviving adolescent struggles over being criticized by her parents, but instead was simply asked why she had not "talked about" her plans. She could not tell whether the group cared about her presence or her conflicts. She could not distinguish a "new" external object from her internal representations. Her representational confusions were real. Her real father had died when she was nine and her mother had remarried, yet she always referred to her stepfather as "her father." In a parallel manner her boyfriend was a source of ambivalence for her children, and she was unable to acknowledge that they had the right to their own feelings as she herself had defended against consciously held ambivalent feelings toward her own stepfather.

Miss A. often directly asserted that I did not understand her needs and wishes but rarely spoke with feeling when she made the accusation. She sat opposite me in the group, always particularly attentive to me. She often told me I was wrong for treating everyone differently. She completely dismissed the idea that these events in the group had any bearing on events in her "real life" and blatantly refused, when invited, to explore her reactions to my behavior or to explore the meaning of her remarks. "Real life" was a term she used frequently, and neither I nor the other members could determine its meaning for her. In her remarks I was a vague object of some disdain and was openly useful to her only in that I was somehow responsible for the group's meeting. Miss A. had left prior treatments because "they weren't helpful," and yet she wanted me to be "a helping therapist." In the group for more than two years, she rarely spoke of her sister or her boyfriend and always offered direct suggestions to anyone with a problem. As in the group example, she rarely responded emotionally to anything said to her but would respond only to factual remarks. Later in treatment, when I became the object who constantly deprived or frustrated her, I experienced having some transference value for her. In many ways Miss A.'s behaviors were not extremely different from that of other members of the group.

DISCUSSION

I have described the style in which this particular group functioned, and related this functioning to the capacity for experiencing a safe regression in group psychotherapy. A safe regression is a significant element in the formation of ideas about the self in relation to others and therefore to the nature of all group functioning. The clinical nature of narcissistic regression in groups can be immediate or seemingly fixed. Immediate regressions in the group rest on an inability to recognize new objects in the group situation as being different from the transference to old objects. Patients' immediate transference illusions and self-illusions are accepted by them as real. However, often with narcissistic patients there is an immediate revival of a fixed wary unrelatedness, indifference, or narcissistic withdrawal indicating an early disturbance in reaching out to new objects and fears of loss of the self. One product of these early narcissistic defenses is an incapacity to form new internal and external relationships and hence an absence of new ideas.

The members of this particular group functioned without a meaningful dialogue for a considerable period of time and could not empathically share their conjoined experience. They remained unable to make the group experience theirs, to possess it, use it, and find useful ideas in it. They related by factualizing their relationships with the other members of the group and the group itself. Looking for facts that explained behavior, they were unable to establish an emotional framework of meaning for these facts and behaviors. This mode of relating served as a protective psychic reaction to avoid reexperiencing the pain of multiple childhood traumas. An element reinforcing their behavior was their need to protect their ability to withdraw into fantasy or illusion and their concomitant inability to reality test these fantasies prior to acting on them. This dual defense severely compromised their ability to establish intimate relationships, with themselves or with others, particularly of a reflective and verbal kind. Still another related outcome of their developmental fixedness was their need to keep the external world of objects, and their transferences, constant.

The simultaneous appearance of all of these complicated defenses led to a thin veneer of partial relatedness and extreme self consciousness rather than self-awareness. The temporary group summation of these defenses resulted in extreme vulnerability to humiliation and shame, and further defenses against being seen (exhibitionism) or having their fantasy lives revealed. Many times the patients had the appearance of latency age children or early adolescents engaged in a form of parallel verbal activity. They talked at each other rather than to each other, and seemed to engage with a part fantasy about another person rather than effectively relating to the whole person in reality.

Many authors (Glatzer, 1962; Scheidlinger, 1964) have suggested that the individual's dynamic relationship with the group as a separate psychic entity echoes the earliest wishes toward the preverbal mother as a psychic entity. These wishes include the desire for a blissful unity with the mother and other varieties of preoedipal configurations related to maternal caretaking. In the dynamics of this particular group, not only were mothers as real objects in the patients' lives not spoken of as psychic entities, but the kind of regression that would possibly yield such wishes was actively defended against. The wish for oneness with another could be understood only by inference and through identificatory processes and object choices. While clinical inference is not reliable by itself, one can only suppose that the absence of direct referential material to the mother and the patients' incapacity for closeness had direct bearing on a number of early psychic defenses.

One additional element of the group's behavior reveals something of importance in this regard. The group members had exceptionally limited capacities for pleasure and play with objects in reality. It seemed likely that no significant transference person enjoyed them, played with them, or took pleasure with them. If we consider the members' vigilance to fathers as leaders, suppliers, guardians, and rule makers, as sources of power and information but not of warmth and pleasure, it is possible to infer, from the absence of passion toward the father, a mother who was cold and distant, depressed, inadequate, or otherwise unavailable when these patients were infants. People cannot be warm if they have not been warmed, cannot give if they have not received, cannot be intimate if they have never felt close to another, cannot please if they have never been pleasured. Clinical material that emerged in sessions years later confirmed complex identity problems with sexual pleasure and intimacy as well as sexual functioning.

PROBLEMS OF TECHNIQUE

We generally assume that the continuing presence of a patient and accepting therapeutic attitude will permit the unfolding of group processes that will eventually allow the patient's resumption of psychological growth. But certain patients with severe character disturbance, who load the group process with threats of aggression or violation of individual psychic boundaries, prove this generality to be untrue. The normative unfolding process, in fact, was not the case with this group, as defenses against emotional relatedness seemed to harden over time, bringing the expected group processes to a halt at the surface of material. In order to move this group toward self awareness and self-acceptance, additional therapeutic activities were used in an attempt to bring this defensive behavior into the confines of a group alliance.

It was evident that the members' reality testing had been partially compromised; reality had not been explained to them as children and group interaction therefore remained puzzling and inchoate to them. As a therapeutic strategy, reactions to events in the group were explained to them in terms of the participants' history, or affective components of the interaction were verbally identified. For example, in the fictional illustration above, Miss A. might have been told, "There are fears and anxieties and perhaps fantasies that have been generated in the group by the idea of your spending time with your father. After all, many people in this group have had problems with their fathers and stepfathers." Alternatively, I might have said, "Aren't you starting a fight about money the way that you and your mother fought with your father about money?" Or perhaps, "It's better to fight with me about money in the group than start a fight with your stepfather about money again."

The technical problems of interpretation with such individuals are complex, in part as a result of the rapidity with which they shift identificatory patterns and the literalness with which implied meanings are often accepted. Both the shifting identifications, and the cognitive literalness are, I believe, the direct result of the child-mother estrangement and other drive-related inhibitions. Horowitz (1987) has reached similar conclusions regarding insight-resistant patients in dyadic treatment. He cites the tenacity of latency defenses as the cause of this resistance. Cumulative trauma and traumatic family conditions, I would add, culminate in a faulty or incomplete latency that occasions severe superego problems. Horowitz cautions against the search for "earlier and earlier" causes for pathogenic responses. In this regard I believe that the overt influence of the Kleinian mode of interpretation has obscured more accessible group phenomena at the surface and has often led to reductionistic analytic thinking that too often is welcomed by such patients, as it is similar in both form and content to latency defenses. Narcissistically traumatized group members who are at all bright can employ analytic stereotypes as a defense against reflecting on their individual emotional experience.

In this group, interpretations and direct confrontations were experienced as an attempt to subjugate individual members to the demands of the group leader and to the establishment of a sadomasochistic relationship. For example, the intent of the last hypothetical interpretation—"It's better to fight with me . . ."—might be construed as an invitation to quarrel. Such remarks often lead to further withdrawal of affect and fears about aggression emerging in the group. Additionally, it is a great test of a therapist's flexibility to determine rapidly, in the midst of a shifting group situation, which style of intervention is empathically appropriate at a given time and with a given patient. With this group, I confess, empathically incorrect interpretations occurred with great frequency. In retrospect, it may be said that therapeutic leverage was obtained only after an extended period of time during which I was able to help group members with reality problems and to point out their behavioral patterns without directly addressing genetic material that might make them feel overwhelmed and vulnerable.

Finally this group was able to move from its initial position and become more related. Many kinds of technical intervention are possible with people who have problems with intimacy. However, it is clear to me that by approaching the problem from an intrapsychic perspective it was possible to help the members of this group begin to recognize both the nature of their complex problems and their emotional impact on others in the group. The latter recognition is a first step in subject-object differentiation within the group. Simultaneously, as certain members made progress, powerful defensive forces were unleashed that caused other members to oppose the movement toward intimacy and clarity.

Those with less capacity to change became more secretive in the group. All therapeutic efforts to keep these members involved in the group process elicited only short-term effects. It later was discovered that these members became even more vulnerable; outside the group they increased their masochistic acting out while keeping this behavior from the group. Three members of the original group left over a period of six months. Each of them left in a different way, but each seemed propelled from the group as an act of self-defense, an attempt to hold on to their psychic structure.

CONCLUSION

In an attempt to understand the phenomena of group-related problems with intimacy, I initially hypothesized that premature leaving is correlated with the same narcissistic problems that prevent intimate interactions in the group situation. I assumed that evidence of these problems would be discernible at the level of group dynamics. However, I neglected an important therapeutic consideration— namely, that the improved functioning of some group members might occasion the need to leave in others. I also failed to anticipate that there might not be surface evidence of a growing sense of personal incompatibility as regards the group's functioning and motives, both conscious and unconscious.

To move on with one's life, to grow and disentangle one self from archaic conflicts, transferences, and objects, can represent a profound psychic threat to people who must remain affectively distant and must keep a constant psychic reality. For these patients any hopeful invitation or situation contains too many psychic threats. While we would like to believe otherwise, not all people have the same capacity to change. Severe pathology may result not only in a restructuring of the personality but also in a loss of the capacity to think and to change. Pathological structures and distortions have to be understood, in the final analysis, as reversible or irreversible. Most important, pathological forms of grandiosity and idealization must be understood and distinguished from idealizations that have the potential to grow and undergo change and integration into the personality through analytic group psychotherapy.

In conclusion, it may be said that from a clinical perspective patients who struggle with attempts to find or secure their own identity in analytic group psychotherapy will experience paradoxical fears inherent in the group situation. They must be both for and against the group, and must be able both to join with it to find themselves and to separate from it to protect themselves. How they do this in our presence, and what our response is to their struggles, is the core therapeutic question.

Important theoretical work on idealization remains to be done. Freud's formulations on idealization in groups and Kohut's later work from the perspective of the dyadic situation are particularly relevant to the emergence in group psychotherapy of the dynamics of idealization. The problems of overidealization (Greenacre, 1966), failures in idealization, and fear of idealization contribute to the core transference dynamics of a therapeutic group.

REFERENCES

Arlow, J. A. (1986), Panel on identification in the perversions. *Internat. J. Psycho-Anal.*, 67:245–259.

Bion, W. R. (1952), Group dynamics: A review. *Internat. J. Psycho-Anal.*, 33:235–247.

Freud, S. (1917), Mourning and melancholia. *Standard Edition*, 14:243–258. London: Hogarth Press, 1957.

———(1921), Group psychology and the analysis of the ego. *Standard Edition*, 18:69–143. London: Hogarth Press, 1955.

Glatzer, H. (1962), Narcissistic problems in group psychotherapy. *Internat. J. Group Psychother.*, 12:448–455.

Greenacre, P. (1966), Problems of over idealization of the analyst and the analysis: Their manifestations in the transference and countertransference relationship. In: *Emotional Growth*, Vol. 2. New York: International Universities Press, 1971, pp. 743–761.

Horowitz, M. (1987), Insight and its failures. *Psychoanal. Quart.*, 1:177–196.

Katan, A. (1961), Some thoughts about the role of verbalization in early childhood. *The Psychoanalytic Study of the Child*, 16:184–188. New York: International Universities Press.

Klein, R., & Carroll, R. (1986), Patient characteristics and attendance patterns in outpatient group psychotherapy. *Internat. J. Group Psychother.*, 36:115–132.

Roth, B. (1980), Understanding the development of a homogeneous identity impaired group through countertransference phenomena. *Internat. J. Group Psychother.*, 30:405–426.

———(1982), Six types of borderline and narcissistic patients: An initial typology. *Internat. J. Group Psychother.*, 32:9–27.

Scheidlinger, S. (1964), Identification of the sense of belonging and of identity in small groups. *Internat. J. Group Psychother.*, 14:291–306.

———(1982), *Focus on Group Psychotherapy*. New York: International Universities Press.

Weil, A. (1970), The basic core. *The Psychoanalytic Study of the Child*, 25:442–460. New York: International Universities Press.

8

Object Relations in the Group from the Perspective of Self Psychology

HOWARD A. BACAL, M.D., F.R.C.P.(C)

The terms "object relations theory" and "self psychology" are to some extent misnomers. That is to say, both terms are not entirely adequate designations of the paradigms or set of ideas to which they refer, although I had not realized the extent to which this was so until I began to think about them in the context of their relevance to the group. It then also struck me that I really regarded psychoanalytic self psychology very much as an object relations theory and that in the years prior to my discovery of Heinz Kohut's work I had in some ways functioned in my own therapeutic work as if object relations theory was a psychology of the self. I am sure that I am not the only one who has made these observations.

There is in fact no coherent object relations theory.[1] The origin of the term has been variously attributed to Ferenczi, Klein, Balint, and Fairbairn, and has been used by them and by others to denote an

---

This chapter was first published in the *International Journal of Group Psychotherapy* (1985), 35(4):483–501, and is reprinted with permission.

[1]While the term itself may appear to be an unfortunate choice in that it conjures up dehumanized images of relatedness, we must remember that it did not originally connote its current colloquial meaning of "interpersonal relationships." Rather, it appeared to have been originally coined in an attempt to shift the focus of study onto the relationship between the instinct and its object, rather than on its source or on its aim. It is likely that Melanie Klein had some significant influence on the choice of the term. Object relations theory, for her, is not only a relatedness between people—for which the term "interpersonal relationships" would be better—but also includes "relationships with parts of people," that is, part-objects, and relationships between internalized wholes and parts of people; "internal object relations." Instinctual forces remain central in Kleinian object relations theory.

emphasis in psychoanalytic theory on aspects of human relatedness rather than on instinctual discharge.

Notions of object relations were in fact around from the very early days of psychoanalysis. One need name only a few concepts central to psychoanalytic theory, such as transference, resistance, countertransference, and the Oedipus complex, to demonstrate convincingly that psychoanalysis has always been a psychology of relatedness, that is, an object relations theory. However, Freud's theoretical emphasis continued to rest on a drive-and-defense paradigm despite the fact that his clinical findings and associated clinical concepts clearly pointed to problems of relatedness as central to psychopathology. The result of this discrepancy led over time to a widening gap between classical psychoanalytic *theory* and some of the *practice* of psychoanalysis and psychoanalytically determined psychotherapy. Object relations theory evolved to fill in this gap, but the interesting and perhaps inevitable form these theories took was that, although their authors came to emphasize relational aspects of psychopathology, almost all of them agreed that it was the pathology of drive derivatives which gave people trouble in their object relationships.[2] However, this was only half the problem that prevented the development of a "true" object relations theory. The other half was the persistence, in the psychoanalytic world, in regarding narcissism as a defense against object relations as well as against object-love. To put it bluntly, the analyst's attitude toward his patient's "narcissism" as basically selfish prevented him from hearing, and thus from evolving a systematic theory based on the legitimate developmental needs of the self in relation to objects throughout life.[3]

---

[2]The significance of the relationship of the instinct or drive to its object became most fully elaborated in the theories of Melanie Klein and her students, particularly with respect to the vicissitudes of the relation between the destructive instincts and their part and whole objects. More recently, Otto Kernberg, Vamik Volkan, and others have made significant contributions to this dimension of object relations theory as it articulates with ego psychology.

[3]Freud's observation that "the finding of [an] object is in fact a re-finding of it" (Freud, 1905, p. 222) was a statement used by Michael Balint in support of his refutation of Freud's notion of primary narcissism (i.e., objectlessness) as a basic state of affairs (Balint, 1968, pp. 35–76) and to substantiate the validity of his notion of a primordial object relatedness between the infant and the mother from the very beginning ("primary love"). But he too seemed unable to free himself from the notion of narcissism as a state of moral weakness (translated into more sophisticated terms—a defense against loving object relatedness); and so he never could develop his interesting theory of primary object-love (Balint, 1939) into a psychology of the selfobject relationship.

Freud (1921) in his group psychology paper states that "in the development of mankind as a whole, just as in individuals, love alone acts as the civilizing factor in the sense that it brings a change from egoism [i.e., narcissism] to altruism" (p. 103). It is evident that from this perspective the notion of a maturing "narcissism"—what we would today call a maturing self in its relation to selfobjects—simply could not be entertained. This remained true even for people such as Balint, Winnicott, Fairbairn, Guntrip, and Jacobson, whose theoretical concepts came to lay stress on the importance of relatedness for the optimal development of the ego, or the "self."

As I have mentioned, well before I learned of Kohut's work I considered some object relations theory to be "psychologies of the self" and to some extent worked from that frame of reference. I well remember Jock Sutherland's weekly staff seminars at the Tavistock Clinic in the 1960s where he repeatedly and vividly drew attention to the enormous gap that remained between our theories and our clinical practice, and that when it came to object relationships (which was what clinical practice was in fact all about) the notion of the "self" and its problems just *had* to occupy a central position as we addressed ourselves to actual work with our patients. I was, with Sutherland, typical of quite a number of analysts whose clinical practice was a few uneasy steps ahead of the theories on which it was based. Since then, Sutherland has cogently summarized the object relations theories of Balint, Winnicott, and Fairbairn (Sutherland, 1980), in which the importance of relatedness between the child and its (mothering) environment is stressed as basic to the healthy development of the individual and where the concept of the self begins to occupy an increasingly important position in object relations theorizing. However, many of us continued to remain a few uneasy steps ahead of these people as well. My personal familiarity with the work of Balint and Winnicott has led me to conclude that neither of them evolved a comprehensive developmental psychology of the self in relation to its objects, both because they had to find a place for Freud's drive-centered theory in their own schemata and because they could not become "self-centered" enough to consider the notion of the "narcissistic" object or selfobject as of legitimately central importance to the self *throughout the life cycle of the individual.* They thus remained hung up on the one hand, on the overriding importance to the development of psychopathology of the maladaptation of the *infant's* maternal environment—as did Bowlby, which was acceptable—and on the

other hand, on the criterion of maturity being the establishment of
the primacy of object-love (which for them was not primarily a
libidinal attitude but rather concern for the object) into which the
"narcissistic" need must be transformed. It is my impression that
Fairbairn came closest to a true relatedness theory—one without
reference to the drive as central—but his theories never gained a wide
audience, partly because of their conceptual awkwardness, partly
because Fairbairn worked in isolation in Scotland with no selfobjects
except Harry Guntrip to support or market him, and also because, at
the time they were published, his considerable theoretical departures
from classical theory constituted too much of a threat to the idealization of Freud to be taken seriously by the majority of the psychoanalytic community. Fairbairn also, however, did not grapple with the
significant issue of narcissism, which is so central to a theory of object
relations.

The work of Heinz Kohut, which could be regarded as an object
relations theory—of the centrality of the relationship of the self to its
selfobjects[4]—could not have come about without a significant change
in our conceptualizing of narcissism. Without doubt, Kohut's new
view of narcissism as essentially comprising a developmentally legitimate object relation ranks with his emphasis on the empathic stance in
data-gathering and interpretive intervention as his most seminal
contributions to the theory and practice of psychoanalysis and psychotherapy. For Kohut, narcissistic needs are not regarded as selfish
but comprise basic needs of the self in relation to *selfobjects*—objects
which are experienced as belonging to the child as more or less
extensions of himself, and who are responsively available to fulfill
functions which meet developmental requirements for self-esteem
regulation. The phase-appropriate empathic responsiveness to the
child's selfobject needs is essential for the cohesion and development
of its self—more particularly, of the "bipolar" aspects of the self's
unique capacities and ambitions on the one hand and the identifica-

---

[4]Ego psychology added important perspectives to our clinical work in that it
placed emphasis on the ego's problem of adaptation to the demands of external reality
and introduced into theory and practice the notion of the autonomous functioning of
the ego and its conflict-free activities, such as may occur in thinking, locomotion, etc.,
activities which were conceived of as associated with the experience of a "self." But the
self was still regarded as an experiential content of a mental apparatus. That is, in
Hartmann's work the self is regarded as a component of the constituents of the
tripartite model of the mind with its drive and defense problems, rather than as a
central or supraordinate construct in the personality.

tion with and pursuit of leading ideals on the other. Kohut described two kinds of selfobjects (Kohut and Wolf, 1978): "those who respond to and confirm the child's innate sense of vigor and perfection; and those to whom the child can look up and with whom he can merge as an image of calmness, infallibility and omnipotence. The first type is referred to as the mirroring selfobject, and the second as the idealized parent imago" (p. 557). Selfobject (or narcissistic) needs have a "driving" force of their own (Kohut, 1978); and healthy "drives"—oral or genital—are regarded not as primary motivators but as appetites (Basch, 1981), and these and their associated affects are expressions of an intact self.[5] It is important to distinguish between the affects and appetites which are the vigorous experience and expression of an intact self, and the *driven* need for gratification of a sexual need or the satisfaction of revenge prompted by a narcissistic rage which comprise attempts to reconstitute an injured self. The sexualization or aggressivization of the selfobject needs of a fragmented self often constitute a desperate attempt to reach and compel the selfobject to respond in a way that will restore the integrity of the self.[6] Thus, what we see as persistent sadism, hatred, destructiveness, envy, perversions, addictive states, and oedipal pathology can be understood as the symptomatic expressions (i.e., breakdown products) of a self that has become significantly conflicted, enfeebled, distorted, or fragmented by varying degrees and kinds of failure of selfobject responsivity over the whole range of childhood developmental relatedness.

For Kohut, "the primary psychological configuration (of which the drive is only a constituent) is the experience of the *relation* between the self and the empathic selfobjects" (1977, p. 122; italics mine), and "our interpretations about the idealizing transference and the mirror transference are statements about an intense object relationship, despite the fact that the object is invested [narcissistically]" (1971, p. 228).

The essence of a psychoanalytically understood therapeutic process, then, from the point of view of self psychology, basically becomes not the resolution of conflict but the filling in of structural defects. The well-studied neurotic manifestations of oedipal pathology are

---

[5]See Fairbairn's notion that "instinct" is not the stimulus to psychic activity, but itself consists in characteristic activity on the part of a psychical structure (Fairbairn, 1946).

[6]Normal aggression, from the perspective of self psychology, is the legitimately experienced assertiveness, or reactive anger, of the intact self, not a primary destructiveness directed toward others (or to the self), as in the classical Freudian model.

regarded from the perspective of self psychology as selfobject relations that have become conflicted as a result of unempathic, inappropriate responses on the part of the selfobject milieu during that phase
of development (i.e., oedipal self pathology).

The main impetus for the discovery, as well as for the study of self
pathology arose out of Kohut's experimenting with accepting his patients'
"narcissistic" attitudes toward him as legitimate transference needs or
longings—*selfobject transferences*—in patients whose treatment seemed to
founder when they were interpreted as pathological defenses or resistances against object-love or object-hate. Conceptualization of the selfobject transferences entailed a significant shift in the ambiance or
atmosphere of treatment in that it demanded a new kind of relational
perspective and responsiveness from the therapist.[7] In other words, the
defects in the self produced by faulty responses of selfobjects lead the
individual to establish what Kohut called transferencelike states, where he
looks for selfobjects in his later life to provide him the responses which he
missed, in order to repair the self. These are designated as "selfobject
transferences" in relation to people called therapists, and "selfobject
relations" with respect to others. Thus, while the psychopathology of the
patient was noted, it called upon the therapist to utilize his empathically
gathered data to consider demands which formerly were regarded as
"narcissistic," as failed developmental needs reactivated in relation to
others as selfobjects.

As students of group configuration and group process, we might
agree that the notion of the centrality of the self and its relation to
selfobjects for personal growth and development should have been
invented by an analytically trained group psychotherapist. As group
psychotherapists, we attend, par excellence, to interpersonal phenomena, and our analytic methodology of data-gathering—empathic
immersion in our patients' complex mental states—should have
alerted us to the deepest psychological significance of the interpersonal interaction, namely, the need for the (belated) responsivity of
selfobjects. Perhaps, in our understandable endeavor to make maxi-
mum use of our medium, the group, we lost sight of the depths of the
individual's perspective. Perhaps, in our emphasis on the importance

---

[7]This has been expressed aphoristically by Evelyne Schwaber in her description of
the essence of Kohut's notion of the introspective-empathic perspective in treatment as
one "which is tuned more sharply to how it feels to be the subject, rather than the target
of the patient's needs and demands" (Schwaber, 1979; see also Wolf, 1976).

of maturation of our patients' actual object relationships, we became "too much" behavioral scientists and "too little" empathic investigators.[8] While Kohut did not have experience in groups, his rigorous use of the empathic-introspective method, in the face of failures with certain kinds of difficult patients, allowed him to listen to his *patients'* theories more clearly. And what he came up with, essentially, was a confirmation of the importance of the vicissitudes of interpersonal interaction on the development of the self: "The self [as] the core of our personality, has various constituents which we acquire in the *interplay* with those persons in our earliest childhood environment whom we experience as selfobjects. A firm self [results] from optimal *interactions* between the child and its selfobjects" (Kohut and Wolf, 1978, p. 414; italics mine). When a self is established in treatment as a result of transformation and internalization (transmuting internalization) of the selfobject functions of the therapist, the patient will feel able to function independently. Kohut (1979) emphasizes, however, that "some need for selfobjects remains in all people throughout life and that it is characteristic for a healthy self that it can . . . turn toward the support of selfobjects." Although these views recommend themselves to the attention of group psychotherapists, we are only in the beginning stages of applying the concepts of self psychology to groups (Stone and Whitman, 1977; Harwood, 1980; Paparo, 1981).

Goldberg (1982) has emphasized that the psychological self is a construct which, developmentally regarded, arises out of relationships; and that it needs to be conceptualized "as a functionally or operationally separate focus of various relations, which relations are always part of a psychological matrix," a notion with which I think Foulkes would have agreed. The state of the self, its cohesiveness and sense of well-being, depends on the quality of the self-selfobject relationship at any moment and over time. Comparably, in the group, the state of the self in this sense depends also upon the quality of the relationship between the self and the selfobject matrix of the group.

Freud (1921) believed that group formation and group cohesiveness are associated with "a limitation of narcissism" (p. 102); "if an individual gives up his distinctiveness in a group and lets its other

---

[8]From the perspective of object relations theory, the focus is on the quality of the relationship, while from the perspective of self psychology, the focus is on the experience, within the self, of the object and its relationship with the self.

members influence him . . . , it gives one the impression that he does it because he feels the need to be in harmony with them rather than in opposition to them—so that perhaps after all he does it '*ihnen zu Liebe*'" (p. 92). (A footnote tells us that this is an idiom meaning "for their sake"—literally, "for love of them.") That is, for Freud, in the group the individual moves to give up his narcissistic need for the love of others. However, harmony comprises two different voices singing the same tune; rather than being a hallmark of altruism or object-love, the renunciation of distinctiveness in the group, as far as it goes, is better understood as a primitive or archaic form of object related-ness, probably best conceptualized by Balint's notion of "primary love," in which there is a felt identity of need, belief, and so on between infant and mother, and by Kohut's notion of an archaic merger of the self with its idealized and merging-mirroring self-objects.[9]

In effect, for Kohut (1976) "group processes are largely activated by narcissistic motives" (p. 840) which, as he has indicated, are in fact very much object-related in that they entail the need for responsive-ness from selfobjects on all levels of relatedness. The individual's selfobject needs in joining the group relate to his need to be very much just one of the members of that group (that is, to belong) and also to be special within that group.

From the point of view of self psychology, three selfobject transference needs can be identified as operating within the group. That is, the individual will look for three kinds of relationships with others to restore and maintain a sense of self and to enhance its development. In the group situation, however, selfobject transference needs will to some extent be in conflict. In addition to the wish for harmonious merger with idealized selfobjects (experienced as other individuals or the group itself), the emergence of mirroring needs—the wish to be recognized for one's distinctive capacities and talents—may give rise to a tension state within the individual with regard to the bipolar needs of the self; this will affect his relationship with other members and with the group as a whole.[10] The struggle between these is in turn modulated or exacerbated, as the case may be, by a third

---

[9]In a previous paper (Bacal, 1981), I attempted to elaborate the similarities and differences between the primitive object relations theories of Balint and Kohut.

[10]This, I believe, should be regarded not as an artifact of the group situation but rather as the demonstration of a significant, universal psychological issue which is to some extent obscured in the individual psychotherapy situation.

form of selfobject transference, which, like the other selfobject transferences, becomes, in respect of other group members, also a selfobject relationship. This type of selfobject transference, or selfobject relationship, which was initially called a "twinship" or "alter ego" transference by Kohut, was considered the midpoint on a maturation continuum of the mirror transference (the continuum comprising merger, twinship, and mirror transference proper, in that sequence). However, some of us have come to think of this type of transference as a distinct form of selfobject relatedness for which the designation "partnering" (Tolpin, 1981) is probably more appropriate. It reflects a need to form a link with a "partner," or buddy, where the mutual recognition between felt equals provides a sustenance to the self not quite offered by the meeting of needs for idealization and mirroring. It is likely that this form of selfobject need arises from deficiencies of phase-appropriate responsivity mainly during the adolescent period. Tension can arise between the need for this kind of selfobject relation in the group and the individual's need for experiencing others as idealized selfobjects, since, if the need for merger with the idealized selfobject is intense, the disparity between the self and the idealized selfobject makes a feeling of partnering relatedness with the selfobject understandably difficult. Tension can also be expected to occur between needs for a partnering selfobject relationship and needs for the mirroring response of the selfobject, since the satisfaction of the latter can preclude the experience of equality which is so essential to partnering selfobject relatedness.[11]

However, patients in group therapy will have less difficulty in establishing the selfobject relationships they require, since in the group the opportunity for selfobject relationships with various group members can modulate this effect of "conflicting" selfobject needs. When there has been deep failure of the idealizing selfobject needs, as well as of the partnering function of the selfobject, the dyadic therapy situation can present almost insuperable difficulties in transmuting internalization of the functions of the selfobject. In this situation the individual cannot allow the shoulder-to-shoulder experience of the therapist as a partner to evolve, for fear the therapist will crumble as

[11]For example, when the question of using first or last names between patients and therapists in the group becomes an issue rather than simply a matter of local convention or preference, it could be understood in the light of the implied conflict between needs for partnering selfobject relationships and for idealized selfobject relationships—on the part of both patients and therapists. That is, it is both a transference and a countertransference issue.

the needed idealized selfobject, nor can he allow the complete evolution of an idealizing transference, lest partnering needs be frustrated.

A comparison with Bion's notion (1961) of the group subcultures of pairing, fight-flight, and dependency could be entertained. While Bion regards these configurations essentially as reactions against the work group, selfobject theory would look upon pairing as the selfobject need for partnering, and dependency as a need for idealizing selfobject relationships and/or primitive merger with archaic selfobjects. Shifts between the subcultures of pairing and dependency could be regarded as determined partly by the ascendancy within the group of the predominating selfobject need and partly by the sort of conflict I have just mentioned. A fight-flight subculture could then be understood as the development of a defensive organization within the group that is mobilized against the pitfalls of the others.

It is evident that as a result of the conceptualization of the selfobject transference, the concepts of defense and resistance are understood somewhat differently in selfobject theory than in traditional psychoanalysis. Defenses and resistances (the manifestation of defenses in relation to the therapist), rather than constituting attempts to ward off the awareness of drives or wishes for object relationships that are frightening because unacceptable, are regarded as attempts to protect the self against the experience and expression of selfobject needs that would expose the individual to retraumatization; that is, they repeat, in the here and now, traumas sustained in childhood through significant selfobject failure.

In keeping with my impression that a number of us have sometimes functioned intuitively in our therapeutic work on the basis of the centrality of the self in considering object relations (in contrast to drives as the central working construct), without a theory to guide or legitimize our work, I decided to review the clinical examples Sheldon Heath and I used to illustrate the Tavistock method of group therapy fifteen years ago (Heath and Bacal, 1968).[12]

There were two examples in that paper. The first was an example of the first session of a new group of two men and four women:

After preliminary remarks about the procedure for calling the group from the waiting room and the holiday period and

[12]The case examples are in fact from my groups.

times, the therapist fell silent. The group was silent for about two minutes with most of the members looking at the therapist. One woman began to interrogate the other members as to their occupations. The anxiety in the room then seemed to go down. Several members volunteered that they would prefer another job to the one they had, and they joked with apparent anxiety. This, in turn, decreased when they switched onto how they spent their spare time relieving their boredom, for example, dancing, television. One married woman talked of what she and her husband did, for example, going to his club. A man who had separated from his wife talked of how he couldn't get people to be interested in him. The young woman who was "running" the group said she couldn't get people interested in her either. The therapist interpreted that they were talking about how to relieve feelings at home and at work and that they were letting someone be a substitute leader (the required relationship) in order to avoid talking about their feelings in the treatment room, i.e., *those needs to be cared for by himself* (the avoided relationship) *and that they did all this because they wished to avoid the anxiety should these needs not be fulfilled by the therapist*[13] (the calamitous relationship). The therapist then went around and pointed out how the woman had to handle her dependency needs by herself assuming leadership, how the married woman dealt with hers by describing how her husband cared for her, and the lonely man expressed his by complaining that no one was interested in him. He interpreted that all of these, as well as their talk about preferring other jobs and their attempts to relieve boredom by entertainment, were defenses against the anxieties associated with the expression of their dependency needs toward the therapist [pp. 25–26].

Were we to have engaged in theoretical discussion of that example at that time, we would probably have formulated that the patients' problems reflected either a regressive shift from competitive strivings to preoedipal dependency issues, which could be understood in terms of oral-drive concepts, or that we were in fact dealing with a

[13]The italics are not in the original version, but have been added to highlight aspects of the interpretation that can be seen in the light of selfobject theory.

primitively organized group whose members were, at bottom, defending against anxieties associated with primitive instinctual drives. Whichever we would have come to regard as primary (oedipal or preoedipal) at any moment in the group, we probably would not have stressed theoretically what I believe we understood clinically: namely, the patients' fear that if they did not take care to defend themselves against the possible traumatic repetition of failure to meet their need for the caring interest from selfobjects—other group members and the therapist—they would experience varying degrees of the anxiety of the unsupported self, an anxiety that Kohut termed "disintegration anxiety."

I find it particularly interesting that in the discussion section of that paper we questioned "the validity of one of the premises in this [theory of] therapy, i.e., that whatever we observe is always primarily defensive in character. Some of the observations may be samples of the kinds of relationships that people are consciously or unconsciously striving for" (p. 29). In this particular example, the patients in the group are, from the perspective of selfobject psychology, apparently struggling with yearnings and failures in respect of mirroring and partnering selfobjects. Interestingly, the response to the therapist's intervention indicated that issues over failures and yearnings in respect of trustable idealized figures were likely, at that moment, to be paramount in the group.[14]

The second example in the paper was taken from a group that had been meeting weekly for a year and a half:

> There were four patients present. Miss A. was telling the group about her date over the previous weekend and commented that if she thought of marrying this man, who is not Jewish, her mother would do everything to stop it. She went on to talk about the many ways in which her mother clung to her and showed disapproval of her behavior. The whole group took up the theme. Mr. V. said that his mother would have been horrified if he had married someone who

[14]The result of the interpretation was that the young woman who "ran" the group said angrily that anyone would do what she had done. Another woman member talked of her lack of trust in people. The man who was separated from his wife turned to the group leader and asked for permission to smoke. The young woman went on to talk in an angry manner about how one needed to sound out people first before one could trust them.

was not Catholic. Miss R. described how her mother actually spoke in a disparaging way about her fiancé because he was non-Catholic, implying that he was an outsider who would understand nothing. Mr. L. told the group that he had in fact married a non-Jewish girl, and his family had taken a long time before they came around to accepting her. The therapist made the following interpretation: Whereas the group was talking about the unfavorable reaction of parents, particularly mothers, to their forming a permanent sexual liaison with someone of another faith (the required relationship), what they did not see was that here in the group there were two Jews and two Catholics . . . and he wondered whether they were really discussing these outside situations to avoid feelings and thoughts about each other (the avoided relationship) because this "parent"—the therapist—might react unfavorably (the calamitous relationship). The therapist then went around and pointed out the three relationships for each member, e.g., whereas Miss A. talked about an inhibited relationship with a non-Jewish man (the required relationship) to which her mother would react in the particular way she described, she couldn't talk about her wish for this sort of relationship with the other male group members because the therapist-parent might smother her with restrictive disapproval [pp. 26–27].

In his interpretations, the therapist stressed his patients' inhibition of the expression of sexual wishes which they regarded as unacceptable to the therapist-mother; the response of the patients was dramatic:

Miss A. and Mr. V. began to confront each other (Mr. V. with considerable anxiety) about their sexual thoughts and wishes about each other. Mr. V. remarked that he had thought of going to bed with her and had talked jokingly about this outside the group after the last session. Miss A. wondered, nervously, whether he was circumcised [pp. 26–27].

The material, in this instance, was understood clinically as well as theoretically in terms of drive and defense issues, and the patients responded on that level. However, if the therapist had not regarded

the relief of sexual inhibition (the avoided relationship) as the target
of his therapy, but rather considered that his group was expressing
their complaints and anxieties about the empathic opacity of selfobjects—more specifically, parents and potential partners whom they
needed to be more like them (i.e., the expression of a wish for
twinship, or partnering selfobject responsivity)[15]—the direction and
content of the session might have become significantly different. One
can also see, in this example, the possible development of a conflict
between partnering selfobject needs on the one hand, and idealizing
and mirroring selfobject needs in the transference on the other,[16] as
described earlier in this chapter.

The essential difference, then, between a traditional object relations psychology and a selfobject relations psychology in the group
could be summarized as follows: within the framework of the former,
one works through the defenses against the anxieties of expressing
wishes for unacceptable forms of object relationships in the group,
which are related to unconsciously warded-off instinctual drives, as in
Ezriel's paradigm (Heath and Bacal, 1968; Ezriel, 1973); by contrast,
when using a self psychology framework, one works through the
defenses against the anxieties associated with expressing developmentally phase-legitimate selfobject needs; and then one attempts to
understand the meaning of the reactions of group members to the
leader, other members, and the group when they fail to respond
adequately to these needs for them to function as selfobjects.

An important implication of selfobject theory, then, for understanding both object relations in the group and their interpretation, is
that the individual's frustrated reactions to others (including so-called

[15]Alternatively, one could still have taken the sexual content as the significant
aspect, but from a self psychological point of view—that is, regarding the defended-
against expression of normal phase-legitimate sexual wishes of the self as due to the
fear of unempathic responsivity of the therapist (i.e., failure of the mirroring
selfobject). In terms of the therapeutic process, what the therapist chooses for his
interpretive focus is inevitably always the result of an admixture of his capacity for
empathically determined introspection and whatever constitutes his working theoretical framework. As the above discussion demonstrates, the material in this second
example could be interpreted in at least two different ways utilizing the framework of
self psychology. A third way of regarding the patients' struggles from this perspective
comprises their feeling caught in the web of the mother's (therapist's) need for them to
function as *her* selfobjects.

[16]There is evidence for the implied need for the mother to be right (idealizing
need) as well as for her approval of the child's assertion of distinctiveness—for
example, with regard to choosing a sexual partner who suits *him* or *her* (mirroring
need).

acting out) are pointed out not primarily as distorted or maladaptive but that they are understandable reactions to the patient's experience of selfobject failure and can be specifically related to thwarted developmental needs which are repeated in the here-and-now inter- actions within the group.

In summary, therapeutic intervention would therefore give sub- stance to (1) the significance of defenses as protecting the self against the effects[17] of frustration of the underlying need for selfobject relatedness within the group—a relatedness that forms the basis for the resumption of the growth of the individual; and (2) the recogni- tion of the inevitable disruption of the selfobject relations between group members and selfobject transference to the therapist and to the group as a whole, and their interpretive understanding. These elements would constitute the task of the therapist and, as happens in the group, would be carried out by other group members as well. It is important to emphasize that interactions in the group which constitute the inevitable frustration of selfobject needs must be optimal, so that transmuting internalization and structure-building can occur rather than trauma and further enfeeblement or fragmen- tation of the self. The leader's role is of course crucial in creating a group climate in which this can occur.

According to Kohut (1977), "No implication of immaturity of psychopathology must . . . be derived from the fact that another person is used as a self-object—self-object relations occur on all developmental levels and in psychological health, as well as in psychological illness" (p. 188). In a paper in which he traces the developmental line of selfobject relations, Wolf (1980) writes:

A healthy oedipal phase [is] . . . characterized by parents who are empathically in tune with the child's erotically tinged needs and who, through appropriate controlling and sooth- ing responses, aid the youngster in the task of integrating his uncomfortable tension. . . . During adolescence the need for selfobject relations usually is met to a large extent, if not totally, by the peer group . . . [from whom the adolescent may derive as a selfobject] the confirmation for his phase- appropriate grandiosity; equally important, he may develop

[17]Disintegration anxiety, associated with enfeeblement, depletion, deflation, fragmentation.

an idealizing selfobject relation with the peer group idol. When internalized,[18] the latter strengthens the pole of values and ideals of the bipolar self and may well set the direction for choice of vocation and of mate [pp. 127–128].

A question that is sometimes posed with regard to selfobject theory is this: how does the individual develop the capacity for concern that is so important for mature human relationships? The answer to this question has been, up until the development of selfobject psychology, through the transformation of narcissism into object-love. Wolf (1980) and Ornstein (1981) offer alternative answers: "When . . . the self attains the capacity for becoming a relatively independent center of initiative . . . it is then also capable of recognizing the relatively independent center of initiative in the other—the 'true object' of the classical framework" (Ornstein, 1981, p. 358). Ornstein emphasizes that the continuation of selfobject needs through life is entirely compatible with the notion of the development of the capacity to recognize and accept the independence of others: "Optimally, in the state of health, the self may flexibly fluctuate between these two forms of relations to its objects" (p. 358). Wolf has introduced the notion of *reciprocal* empathic resonance with one's selfobjects as maturation of selfobject relations occurs. While not offered in this context, the idea could well stand as an alternative to the theory of the transformation of narcissism into object-love as a way of explaining the development of mutuality in interpersonal relationships. Since the development of a vigorous and cohesive self is regarded as the outcome of a series of optimal relationships with its selfobjects, one of the therapist's most important functions will be to facilitate reciprocal empathic resonance as a coordinate of the spontaneous reactiveness that comprises the vitality of the therapeutic group.[19]

REFERENCES

Bacal, H. (1981), Notes on some therapeutic challenges in the analysis of severely regressed patients. *Psychoanal. Inq.*, 1:29–56.

[18]To this, of course, I would add the importance of internalizing partnering selfobject relationships in adolescence.
[19]I have dealt with this particular issue extensively in another paper (Bacal, 1981).

————(in press), Reactiveness and responsiveness in the group therapeutic process. In: *The Expanding World of Group Psychotherapy*, ed. S.Tuttman. Madison, Conn.: International Universities Press.

Balint, M. (1939), Early developmental states of the ego: Primary object-love. *Internat. J. Psycho-Anal.*, 30:265–273.

————(1968), *The Basic Fault.* London: Tavistock.

Basch, M. F. (1981), Selfobjects and selfobject transference: Theoretical implications. Delivered at the Progress in Self Psychology Conference, Berkeley, California, October 3, 1981.

Bion, W. R. (1961), *Experiences in Groups.* London: Tavistock.

Ezriel, H. (1973), Psychoanalytic group therapy. In: *Group Therapy 1973*, ed. L. Wolberg & E. Schwartz. New York: Intercontinental Medical Books, pp. 183–210.

Fairbairn, W. R. D. (1946), Object-relationships and dynamic structure. *Internat. J. Psycho-Anal.*, 27:30–37.

Freud, S. (1905), Three essays on the theory of sexuality. *Standard Edition*, 7:125–245. London: Hogarth Press, 1953.

————(1921), Group psychology and the analysis of the ego. *Standard Edition*, 18:67–143. London: Hogarth Press, 1955.

Goldberg, A. (1982), *The Self of Psychoanalysis in Psychosocial Theories of the Self*, ed. B. Lee. New York: Plenum.

Harwood, I. (1980), The application of self psychology concepts to group psychotherapy. Paper presented at the Twenty-first Annual Meeting of the Los Angeles Group Psychotherapy Society.

Heath, E. S., & Bacal, H. A. (1968), A method of group psychotherapy at the Tavistock Clinic. *Internat. J. Group Psychother.*, 18:21–30.

Kohut, H. (1971), *The Analysis of the Self.* New York: International Universities Press.

————(1976), Creativeness, charisma, group psychology. In: *The Search for the Self*, Vol. 2, ed. P. Ornstein. New York: International Universities Press, pp. 793–843.

————(1977), *The Restoration of the Self.* New York: International Universities Press.

————(1978), Narcissism as a resistance and a driving force in psychoanalysis. In: *The Search for the Self*, Vol. 2, ed. P. Ornstein. New York: International Universities Press, pp. 547–562.

————(1979), Notes on definitions for workshop on self psychology (unpublished).

————Wolf, E. S. (1978), The disorders of the self and their treatment: An outline. *Internat. J. Psycho-Anal.*, 59:413–425.

Ornstein, P. (1981), The bipolar self in the psychoanalytic treatment process: Clinical-theoretical considerations. *J. Amer. Psychoanal. Assn.*, 29:353–375.

Paparo, F. (1981), Self psychology and group analysis. *Group Analysis*, 14:117–121.

Schwaber, E. (1979), On the 'self' within the matrix of analytic theory: Some clinical reflections and reconsiderations. *Internat. J. Psycho-Anal.*, 60:467–479.

Stone, W., & Whitman, R. (1977), Contributions of the psychotherapy of self to group process and group therapy. *Internat. J. Group Psychother.*, 27:343–360.

Sutherland, J. D. (1980), The British object-relations theorists: Balint, Winnicott, Fairbairn, Guntrip. *J. Amer. Psychoanal. Assn.*, 28:829–860.

Tolpin, M. (1981), Threatened self cohesion: A contribution to the understanding of difficult patients. Paper presented to the Ontario Psychiatric Association, Section on Psychotherapy. November 21, 1981.

Wolf, E. S. (1976), Ambience and abstinence. *Annual of Psychoanalysis*, 4:101–115.

———(1980), On the developmental line of selfobject relations. In: *Advances in Self Psychology*, ed. A. Goldberg. New York: International Universities Press, pp. 117–130.

9

Secrets: A Self Psychological View of Shame in Group Therapy

ANDREW P. MORRISON, M.D.

Shame is considered by many to be an external, public, interpersonal phenomenon. For instance, Nathanson (1987) suggests that where there is shame there is always a shamer. Others (e.g., Spero, 1984) emphasize the role of "audience" in the shame experience. Certainly this public view of shame frequently occurs, especially as it is experienced in groups. However, I suggest that shame may also reflect an internal, intrapsychic process, a failure with regard to the ego ideal as manifest by "the eye turned inward" (Morrison, 1987). Internalized shame often reflects narcissistic vulnerability, and may occur in group as well as individual psychotherapy.

Several authors have applied a self psychological framework to the understanding of groups (Stone and Whitman, 1977; Harwood, 1983; see also Chapter 8). I believe that internalized shame, and the secrets and hiding which result from it, can well be understood within the framework of self psychology, and that this perspective can usefully be applied to shame manifestations in therapy groups. I will first review some essential factors in self psychology as they relate to groups and then consider shame in group therapy from that viewpoint. I will then present several illustrative case vignettes from a therapy group I have conducted, and finally will consider some clinical implications in the treatment of shame.

This chapter is an elaboration of a presentation made to the Panel on Shame in Group Analysis at the meeting of the American Group Psychotherapy Association, New Orleans, February 1987.

SOME ESSENTIAL FACTORS IN SELF PSYCHOLOGY

Kohut (1966, 1971, 1977) has suggested that psychoanalytic (and, implicitly, group) theory overemphasizes the importance of object relations and object love, while minimizing the attendant state of the self and its cohesion. He has referred to object relations as mere "social psychology" (Kohut, 1972), which he contrasts with a hypothesized narcissistic line of development. Implicit in this view is the conviction that object attachment and love need not be a given, primary goal of the self but rather may serve as only one of the self's several needs to establish cohesion, stability, and positive self-esteem. This perspective on object relations and attachment must be considered a central theme for Kohut, as he constructed his conceptualization of the self and moved toward his ultimate view of the self as supraordinate to the structural ego, superego, and id (Kohut, 1977).

Selfobjects

One of the major tenets of self psychology is the concept of the "selfobject," which is clearly differentiated from the libidinal (or what I have referred to as the "configurational") object. Kohut (1971) defined the selfobject as an extension of the self which provides the functions necessary for establishment of a cohesive, stable, and valued self. Thus, the selfobject is necessary to provide the need-fulfilling functions that establish self-structure or identity. Again, the selfobject and its functions must be distinguished from the configurational attributes of the object of object love and object relations.

The mirroring selfobject, most frequently the earliest selfobject function to develop (Morrison, 1986a), represents acceptance and affirmation of the infantile self. It is empathic, responsive reflection of infantile needs, including enthusiastic joy and affirmation of the infant's age-appropriate grandiosity and exhibitionism. This function, which has been referred to by Stern (1985) as "empathic attunement," is usually provided by the mother; it represents the configurational object in its least differentiated form.

The idealized selfobject (or idealized parental imago) represents the toddler's quest for merger with the omnipotence and perfection of the selfobject, thus providing for powerful protection and soothing. The idealized selfobject function tends to develop later than the mirroring function, is frequently provided by the father, and, according to Kohut, represents the second pole of the "bipolar self." It offers a second chance for the establishment of self-cohesion. The idealized selfobject presents an opportunity for early movement toward identification with the configurational object and is in part created through projective identification of the ideal self into the minimally differentiated selfobject (Morrison, 1987). Stone and Whitman (1977) have similarly noted that primitive grandiosity is projected onto another, who then becomes all-powerful and protecting.

The alter-ego (twinship) selfobject, initially classified by Kohut (1971) as a form of the mirroring selfobject, was elevated in his posthumous book (Kohut, 1984) to the status of a more mature form, a central part of the "selfobject matrix" that surrounds adults as they progress through maturity to old age and death. It reflects the sense of sameness from which individuals participate and interact with their human environment, the element of shared humanity and empathic resonance which, in maturity and health, sustains each of us as we strive toward full actualization of our self and our capacities. This function is particularly relevant in the experience of a cohesive, well-working group, and bears some similarity to Bion's concept of pairing.

The search for selfobject functions, and, thus, the priority of narcissistic vulnerability, is revealed during treatment through the development of selfobject transferences, in which the need for mirroring, idealization, or twinship emerges. Kohut (1971) has emphasized that the predominance of narcissistic needs becomes evident through the emergence of selfobject transferences. In addition, it is through selfobject or empathic failure that most therapeutic impasses occur. These failures are experienced by the patient as a discontinuity or break, a problem in the therapeutic relationship. They are not failures in therapeutic technique but rather the experienced repetitions of failures of the selfobjects of childhood to meet infantile, age-appropriate needs for affirmation or merger. Therapeutic work consists in careful assessment with the patient of what was felt to be a "glitch" in therapeutic communication, and resolution of the experience of therapeutic failure. It is my belief that the need exposed by the experience of selfobject failure most frequently generates vulnerability to shame within the transference. Bacal (see chapter 8) has similarly noted that defenses against shame are generated to protect the self from the expression of selfobject needs, which expose the individual to the fear of retraumatization.

Empathy and Empathic Failure

Empathic attunement represents a means of observation and understanding, related by Kohut to "vicarious introspection," through which therapists inform themselves of the patient's experience-near feelings and thoughts. According to Kohut, empathy is the means by which therapists become aware, through attention to their own feelings and associations, of what the patient is actually experiencing. Empathic attunement is particularly important in group therapy; through it the group therapist becomes aware of the impact on individual members of the current group process and the meaning of specific group interactions. The use of empathy for understanding is closely related to the second stage of projective identification (the container/processing stage), in which the therapist internally recognizes and contains the projected affect or introject eliminated by the patient (Grotstein, 1981; Morrison, 1986b). Empathic appreciation of shame as a painful affective experience, or as a projected, disavowed feeling internally recognized by the therapist, is a central manifestation of empathy, and is particularly relevant in group interaction.

Again, it is important to emphasize what empathy is not: it is not primarily sympathy, gratification, or action. It does not imply what one should do to or for the patient. What the therapist does with empathically derived knowledge or information will vary from situation to situation. For example, if one recognizes empathically that a given patient has had a predominant experience of parental acquiescence to outrageous demands, the therapist may decide to confront and "stand up to" the patient's continued verbalization and "grabbing center stage" within the group.

As noted above, empathic failure reflects the patient's experience of not feeling understood, accepted, or soothed, and always constitutes a break in the therapeutic bond. This need not imply any failure in technique on the therapist's part, but represents a challenge to understand and work through the rupture in therapeutic work. In fact, as described by Kohut, optimal sequences of empathic failure provide an opportunity for structure-building, for the internalization of selfobject functions by the patient to provide a stronger capacity for self-soothing, acceptance, and cohesion.

SHAME IN GROUP THERAPY FROM A SELF PSYCHOLOGICAL VANTAGE POINT

Shame may be considered either the reflection of wishes, thoughts, and actions resulting from overwhelming grandiosity and exhibitionism—described by Kohut (1971) with regard to the "vertical split"—or the self's failure to attain an internalized ideal. Such failure may be experienced as a defect of the self, especially with regard to the perceived shape of the actual self in comparison with the ideal self (in Freud's terms, the ego ideal). Shame, whether conscious or disavowed, is the central affective phenomenon of narcissistic conditions (Morrison, 1986a), much as guilt is pivotal to the neuroses. Shame will be experienced in regard to weakness, failure, inferiority, and defectiveness of the self, and represents, from an object relations perspective (Spero, 1984), manifestations of critical internalized objects, or what Kris (1983) has called punitive unconscious self-criticism. Shame is revealed through terms applied to the self—such as "stupid," "pathetic," "contemptible," or "insignificant,"—which frequently reflect narcissistic vulnerability.

Sensitivity to shame reflects developmental sequences of repeated empathic failures by primary selfobjects in mirroring, idealization, or twinship functions and is often a manifestation of the felt need for such unfulfilled responses from the later selfobject environment. This developmental perspective on shame clearly emphasizes environmental failure—that is, the failure of parental selfobjects to meet the developing self's age-appropriate needs. It should be noted, however, that the grandiosity and exhibitionism leading to shame as described by Kohut closely resembles Freud's delineation (1905) of voyeurism/exhibitionism as a primary manifestation of early libidinal drives.

One major impediment to the treatment of shame is the fact that shame characteristically leads to concealment of the real or imagined failures and inferiority feelings which generate it. Because of the discomfort that shame elicits in the therapist, and the frequent lack of resolution of shame feelings in the therapist's own treatment, an unconscious collusion between participants frequently leads to avoidance of shame elements in psychotherapy. This may be especially true in group psychotherapy, where the potential reminders of previous selfobject failures, and the generation of their related needs, may be multiple. Another way of considering the prevalence of shame in groups is that shame and humiliation are frequently precipitated by here-and-now empathic failures by the multiple significant players who populate the group. However, because of the tendency toward concealment, shame frequently is bypassed in group interaction.

Selfobject manifestations are generated by the group-as-a-whole, by the group leader, and by the other group members. Each group member, particularly those with pressing narcissistic issues, will search for figures within the group to supply unmet selfobject needs for mirroring, idealization, and twinning. Since the group itself cannot always function as an optimal selfobject, the selfobject figure identified by a given member (i.e., the group-as-a-whole, the leader, or another member) will often fail to assume satisfactorily the ascribed role, a failure that leads to outbursts of narcissistic rage. This rage frequently represents a response to the underlying shame generated by the very recognition of need as well as to the shame in response to actual selfobject failure. In addition, those patients determined to confirm their own shame as an outlet for rage will no doubt be able to find shame-eliciting responses within the group.

Here again I want to note the similarity of the twinship selfobject function to Bion's notion of pairing in a group, as well as the similarity of idealization to Bion's notion of the dependency group. Needs for the belated responsivity of designated selfobjects are generated in the group in an attempt to rework or relive earlier traumatic experiences with parental selfobjects that have led to a lack of, or weaknesses in, self structure. From our standpoint of shame, this quest can be described as an attempt to use the selfobjects offered in the group to alter the shape of the actual self in the direction of the wished-for ideal self. With regard to the more mature selfobject need for empathic attunement with others, individual change during the progress of group therapy can be considered in terms of movement from the need to be special to a desire to be one of (or merged into) the cohesive group-as-a-whole (see chapter 8).

Manifestations of shame in groups are multiple, as noted also by Alonso and Rutan (1988) in their recent paper. Before elaborating on these, however, I want to emphasize that feelings of shame, and their precipitants, are frequently concealed from the group until structured selfobject functions and relationships as well as a sense of trust, have developed within the group. This secretiveness often leads to the generation of personal secrets, both conscious and unconscious, which may represent the most important sources of individual shame and self-loathing. Not infrequently, shame will be hidden behind manifest defenses, including anger and rage, contempt and envy, depression and humiliation (Morrison, in press). In essence, secrets are often preserved, and shame concealed, until an atmosphere within the group is established which conveys conviction of individual acceptability (which in turn fosters self-acceptance), in spite of weaknesses, failure, inferiority feelings, and defects. Vicarious detoxification occurs through the observation of others revealing their "shameful" secrets (Alonso and Rutan, 1988, p. 9), thus fostering a sense of "sameness" within the group. This sense of acceptance is a crucial element in the successful treatment of shame; without it, continued concealment is to be expected. Acceptance and shame contrast with the quest for forgiveness that accompanies guilt, a factor leading frequently to confession, another reason that guilt has been so much more accessible in treatment than has shame.

What are some of the explicit precipitants of shame in group treatment? First of all, as noted above, the multiplicity of potential selfobjects in groups brings with it the possibility of multiple selfobject failures. These include projections and perceptions of rejection, ridicule, insignificance, and nonempathic interpretation, which lead to the shame equivalents of feeling pathetic or invisible. Related to experienced selfobject failures in the group is the evocation of the self's needs, particularly with respect to dependency. Dependency needs–frequently experienced in groups—often serve to expose the self as vulnerable, weak, and inferior, generating manifest shame.

One specific precipitant of shame in groups is the particular nature of group-as-a-whole interpretations. With a focus on themes emerging within the group, the group therapist often uses issues raised by one member to generalize to concerns shared by the group. While such interpretations provide useful foci for the group-as-entity, they not infrequently bypass the individual needs of the member who has expressed the theme. Thus, personal needs to feel special, to be empathically mirrored, or to idealize may of necessity be ignored in favor of the group theme. This leads inevitably to an individual experience of selfobject failure by the leader, with resultant shame. Finally, some narcissistically vulnerable group members may express to the group reactively grandiose feelings and demands for attention. According to Kohut, such feelings of themselves lead to internal shame, as the ego is overwhelmed by the disavowed grandiosity represented by what Kohut terms the "vertical split." In addition, however, such demands may generate responses of anger, rejection, and ridicule within the group, enhancing the intensity of shame.

I have mentioned some characteristic defenses against shame, and suggest that the group therapist become acquainted with them, search them out, and move toward acknowledgment of the underlying shame. As Kohut (1972) has emphasized, narcissistic rage represents the self's lack of control over the internal and external object environment, and the resultant urge to "wipe out" the offending selfobject, toward which no empathy is possible. I agree with this view, suggesting only that the selfobject offense that precipitates rage is a case of empathic failure leading to shame. Thus, in most cases of narcissistic rage, shame is the underlying precipitant and should be elaborated and interpreted as its subjective source.

Depression, as delineated by Bibring (1953), reflects feelings of helplessness, inferiority, and failure. These qualities inevitably lead to feelings of shame, and sometimes to the suicides that Kohut has associated with "guiltless despair" and depletion. Unfortunately, the underlying shame is often bypassed in therapeutic work on depression, leading to incomplete resolution. In the group, the opportunity is present to get to the shame that so frequently leads to depression, a fact that should be interpreted by the group therapist. Finally, shame may frequently be masked by expressions of envy and contempt toward the group, the therapist, or other group members. Envy reflects a sense of comparative individual inferiority and, hence, shame. Contempt frequently occurs through the projective identification of a disavowed, shameful feeling about the self (e.g., helplessness, passivity, inferiority, failure), or a painful, negative introject, into another group member-as-container, who is then subjected to contempt or loathing. This can be recognized by the tenacity of the expression of contempt toward the other, or the inability of the contemptuous group member to leave the loathed other alone. Therapeutic work may consist of helping the projector recognize that the contempt felt toward the other represents a disavowed, loathed aspect of the self, and of facilitating the reinternalization of that feeling.

CLINICAL ILLUSTRATIONS

Shame, then, often leads to concealment, frequently reflected in secrets maintained by group members until they come to trust the group and to feel acceptable to the leader and other members (through "vicarious detoxification" and recognition of other members' shared shame). Shameful feelings often relate to events considered unacceptable by the self, or to self-contempt and loathing, and may not be revealed until the middle, cohesive phase of group treatment. In this section, I will describe several examples of shame-induced secrets taken from a once-weekly psychotherapy group of vulnerable, professional, nonpsychotic adults who worked hard on issues of intimacy, self-regard, self-delineation, careers, and interpersonal relationships.

It is relevant here to attempt a distinction between neurotic and narcissistic shame. Neurotic or secondary shame, which tends to be temporary and episodic, usually reflects passivity following retreat from oedipal strivings, assertiveness, and competition, and is experienced as a feeling of public, external failure to achieve a goal or ideal. Narcissistic shame, by contrast, is primary and internal (Levin, 1971) and permeates the sense of self as unworthy, inferior, insignificant, and pathetic. In each group of patients, shame may be experienced consciously, or may be unconscious or disavowed. The clinical examples to follow primarily reflect the exquisite narcissistic vulnerability of these group members, as well as their response to perverse character traits.

Susan

A large, Hispanic, middle-aged, married woman, Susan entered the group to work on low self-esteem, an ungratifying marital relationship, and difficulties in work situations. She had been fired from an administrative position with a public service agency, and emphasized her difficulties working with men, especially those in positions superior to her own. She had been in individual psychotherapy several times, and wanted now to try group in order to alleviate these problems. In the first sequence of group meetings, she dolefully told of her work problems, blaming her male bosses for her difficulties. She blamed her husband, who had been hospitalized several times for suicidal gestures, for her unhappiness at home. After several weeks of elaborating painful details, the group confronted her with her tendency to "tell stories," accusing her of not looking at her own contribution to these difficulties. Initially this caused her to fall into a sullen and withdrawn silence that lasted for several meetings.

Gradually, however, she began to emerge from her self-imposed exile. She tried to examine her own role in her life situation and attempted to make helpful comments to other group members. As the group experience deepened for Susan, she developed an idealizing selfobject transference toward the group and the therapist, expressing gratitude and comfort at feeling helped and understood in ways not experienced in individual therapy, and contained and supported by the cohesiveness of the group. She became extremely sensitive to absences or lateness by other members, and was uneasy at the prospect of admitting new members to the group. Any disturbance or change in the structure of the group seemed intolerable to Susan.

During the intake interviews that preceded her joining the group, Susan had revealed several shame-producing secrets she had not yet mentioned to the group. Intermittently in the past, at times of stress, she had been sexually promiscuous, picking up men in various settings for "one night stands"; this had led to several dangerous encounters and one robbery. Her own mother, and a beloved older friend who had raised her, had each suffered severe depressions; her mother had abandoned her, and her friend had died on a trip when Susan was an adolescent. She recalled episodes as a latency child in which her mother had brought men home, and had been sexually intimate with them in her presence. She related these traumatic memories to her fear of men and sex, and to many difficulties she experienced with her husband. During those initial interviews, the therapist had understood (and verbalized) Susan's shame over these experiences, and over her related episodes of promiscuity. While her early deprivation, traumas, and subsequent behavior demonstrated severe disturbance, her capacity to engage and her commitment to work had encouraged the therapist to invite her to join the group.

However, Susan concealed all of this history during the long initial phase of group. The therapist appreciated Susan's sensitivity about her past and did not confront her regarding its concealment. However, as her trust in the group-as-selfobject evolved, and as she developed a twinship relationship with another group member, she finally was able to reveal these painful experiences during an emotional and shame-filled meeting. (In an earlier session, in response to another member's comments about his sexual activities during a marital separation, she had alluded to her promiscuous episodes.) On this particular evening, the group was pushing Susan to discuss her marital anger and pain. At first she blamed her husband for his impulsivity and psychological problems, but then her eyes teared as her gaze dropped toward the floor (the facial expression of shame), and her voice softened to a near whisper. Holding back tears, she recounted her painful experiences with her mother, and then sobbed as she described the circumstances under which she had learned of her beloved friend's death. She described her despair over that loss, and then her shame over her mother's exploits and feeling herself to be an "abandoned" girl in the neighborhood. The group appreciated Susan's delicateness and reality at that moment and empathized (and sympathized) with her feelings, as other members revealed childhood experiences of deprivation. Pauline, for example, told of continuous humiliation by her mother, who had taunted her being overweight and compared her disparagingly with her brother.

Thus, the group demonstrated acceptance of Susan and her painful, shame-filled feelings about her past, and she in turn expressed great relief at being able finally to unburden herself and reveal these experiences to the group. At this point the therapist's only comment was something like "How hard, how painful it must have been to reveal this aspect of your past, to have carried it around inside of you in here for so long without feeling that anyone could accept your humiliation. What a relief it must have been to have been able to share it with the group." Thus, the therapist attempted to mirror Susan's experience, rather than to interpret prematurely her sexual behavior and its sources.

This example illustrates, I believe, the role played by hiding of shameful secrets in group until trust in the group selfobject functions has developed. The therapist's response demonstrates the importance of respect for patients' need to maintain secrets until such trust has developed, and for tactful, empathic identification and acceptance of the shame that accompanies such secrets. Indeed, Susan elaborated her early life experiences during several subsequent group meetings. As she became more comfortable with her revelations, interpretation and confrontation became possible and useful. Her experience of maternal intrusiveness and inappropriateness was linked with her marital and work difficulties, her sexual experiences, and instances of angry projective identification toward other group members.

Derek

A mental health professional in his mid-thirties, Derek entered group to work on symptoms of depression, low self-esteem, and social isolation. During evaluation he said he had few friends and wanted to figure out why. Like Susan, Derek revealed the perverse manifestations of major character pathology. He was in a stable homosexual relationship about which he expressed deep shame. "I don't think of myself as homosexual," he said. He also described, with embarrassment, his retarded brother, and a previous long-term relationship with a girlfriend who had a visible chronic illness. His father had been an aloof "workaholic" who was frequently absent from the home. His mother, about whom he expressed considerable loathing, had been intrusive and controlling. Related to this history, he described himself as being very self-conscious with other people. He felt stiff and different in comparison to others, and emphasized his embarrassment about his brother and his former girlfriend.

When he entered the group, Derek had presented himself as a competent professional, a problem-solver for others. Rather quickly he formed a twinship transference with a group member whose creative talents he seemed to admire. During the opening phase of group, he often remained silent and somewhat imperious, saying very little about his own self-doubts. Tentatively, however, he began to speak of his self-concerns, particularly as they related to his feeling of social isolation. Feedback from the group indicated that members found it difficult to understand how someone as apparently competent and "together" as Derek could feel so badly about himself.

The first concerns he shared had to do with his homosexual relationship. What if his colleagues at work found out about it? What would they say? He elaborated his fears of revealing this relationship—his secret—especially since he wondered whether he was truly homosexual. The group first questioned this concern. So what if people guessed that his friend was also his lover? Derek was obviously moved and provoked by the thought that others, including members of the therapy group, might accept the nature of his attachment. However, this idea then led to a useful consideration of the differences between acceptance within the group and less tolerant public responses in matters of sexual identity. While certain secrets are best maintained outside, they could be explored, along with Derek's painful sense of difference, within the confidential envelope of the group.

This accepting attitude led to memories of shame and humiliation when Derek had brought friends home during high school. He had felt "ridiculous, pathetic" when his friends were exposed to his intrusive mother and defective brother. He then reminisced about his sick girlfriend, and his concerns that others would associate him with his girlfriend's "defect." The group's response to these painful feelings was one of accepting interest, concern, and probing inquiry. Gradually, Derek acknowledged that, at least within the group, he might not need to feel like such a "freak" about his various shameful associations.

After further work on shame about his family, his former girlfriend, and his current lover, Derek finally revealed his most closely hidden current secret—a wish to become a "big brother" to a neighborhood child. He elaborated his fear that his lover would reject and abhor this secret plan. He also revealed that he had quit his recent individual therapy because his therapist had questioned this wish; he reported that he had doubted whether Derek could provide adequate companionship without becoming sexually stimulated and involved. He discussed this matter with great hesitation and manifest embarrassment, and seemed relieved, both by the group's acceptance and encouragement to explore his desire to care for children, and for the opportunity to unburden himself of previously hidden feelings.

The therapist's response to this self-revelation was, "It sounds both discouraging and degrading to have heard this from your therapist. It's hard to understand where those concerns might have come from. Let's explore your own self-doubts about being a big brother, and your hesitancy to bring this up, both in here and with your lover. I wonder what the group is thinking?" An active discussion about Derek's dilemma then ensued, as he palpably relaxed. He clearly felt unburdened and affirmed by the interested response of both the group and leader. Subsequently he did discuss his wish with his lover, who was receptive and interested. He began investigating his various options, and kept the group informed of his progress on this project.

It seems to me that Derek felt mirrored, accepted, and understood by the therapist and by the group-as-selfobject as he shared his pain and humiliation about his past life and his current wishes to be helping a needy child. In this process, he developed an idealizing selfobject transference toward the therapist, which was accepted silently rather than being interpreted prematurely. Within this context, questioning and interpretation of the relation of his self-doubts and shame to his "contemptible" view of his family and lover, and resultant negative internalizations, could begin. He did not wish to explore further his homosexual gender choice; this wish was accepted by the group.

CONCLUDING REMARKS

In closing, I wish to note the particular role of projective identification in the expression of shame manifestations as played out in group interaction. I have previously discussed projective identification in couples' groups (Morrison, 1986b), suggesting that groups in general provide a particularly fertile field for this phenomenon. I believe that shame is frequently revealed and expressed through projective identification into one or another of the group members, the leader, or the group itself, as reflected in the shame defenses of rage, contempt, or pity. This perspective is particularly relevant in groups of more difficult patients, for whom shame may be less tolerable and more fundamental than for the neurotic. It will be important, therefore, for the group leader to recognize underlying shame, help other members contain and understand the projections, and help the subject to recognize and accept as his or her own the dysphoric, projected affect (in this case, shame).

What needs to be said, then, about the treatment of shame in group therapy? First of all, I think that shame must be expected, searched for, and accepted, both in the group members and in the therapist. The therapist must respect the need for protection of secrets kept from the group, which may have been revealed during intake interviews, until such time as the individual develops trust in the group's evolving therapeutic atmosphere. At such times, themes of shame and humiliation should be recognized and articulated, leading, as it frequently does, to a sense of great relief and unburdening. Shame feelings are frequently contagious, and may lead either to expression of shame by other members, to further concealment within the group, or to manifestations of the shame defenses outlined earlier. Finally, each group member, as well as the group therapist, must face and deal with their own shame—their failures, defects, and feelings of inferiority. Without this searching and sharing, no therapy group will have completed its task.

REFERENCES

Alonso,. A., & Rutan, J. S. (1988), The experience of shame and the restoration of self-respect in group psychotherapy. *Internat. J. Group Psychother.*, 38:1–14.

Bibring, E. (1953), The mechanism of depression. In: *Affective Disorders*, ed. P. Greenacre. New York: International Universities Press, pp. 13–48.

Freud, S. (1905), Three essays on the theory of sexuality. *Standard Edition*, 7:130–243. London: Hogarth Press, 1953.

Grotstein, J. (1981), *Splitting and Projective Identification*. New York: Aronson.

Harwood, I. (1983), The application of self psychology concepts to group psychotherapy. *Internat. J. Group Psychother.*, 33:469–487.

Kohut, H. (1966), Forms and transformations of narcissism. *J. Amer. Psychoanal. Assn.*, 14:243–272.

———(1971), *The Analysis of the Self*. New York: International Universities Press.

———(1972), Thoughts on narcissism and narcissistic rage. *The Psychoanalytic Study of the Child*, 27:360–400.

———(1977), *The Restoration of the Self*. New York: International Universities Press.

———(1984), *How Does Analysis Cure?* Chicago: University of Chicago Press.

Kris, A. (1983), Determinants of free association in narcissistic phenomena. *The Psychoanalytic Study of the Child*, 38:439–458.

Levin, S. (1971), The psychoanalysis of shame. *Internat. J. Psych-Anal.*, 52:355–362.

Morrison, A. P. (1986a), Shame, the ideal self, and narcissism. In: *Essential Papers on Narcissism*, ed. A. P. Morrison. New York: New York University Press, pp. 348–372.

———(1986b). On projective identification in couples' groups. *Internat. J. Group Psychother.*, 36:55–73.

———(1987), The eye turned inward: Shame and the self. In: *The Many Faces of Shame*, ed. D. Nathanson. New York: Guilford, pp. 271–291.

———(in press), *Shame, The Underside of Narcissism*. Hillsdale, NJ: Analytic Press.

Nathanson, D. (1987), Shaming systems in couples, families, and institutions. In: *The Many Faces of Shame*, ed. D. Nathanson. New York: Guilford, pp. 246–270.

Spero, M. H. (1984), Shame: An object relations formulation. *The Psychoanalytic Study of the Child*, 39:259–282.

Stern, D. N. (1985), *The Interpersonal World of the Infant*. New York: Basic Books.

Stone, W., & Whitman, R. (1977), Contributions of the psychology of the self to group process and group psychotherapy. *Internat. J. Group Psychother.*, 27:343–360.

10

On Affects in Group Psychotherapy

WALTER N. STONE, M.D.

There is little dispute that in successful psychotherapy therapists must pay considerable attention to methods of exposing, activating, or containing affects. Therapists explore these affects using a linear model, the two ends of the continuum being (1) the patient's suppression of unwanted feeling and (2) the patient's expression of volatile and often disorganizing feeling. It is generally understood that in optimal functioning affect is contained somewhere in the middle. This view is expressed by Lane and Schwartz (1987): "much of psychotherapy consists of helping patients to clarify what they are feeling, understand the origins of their feelings, and tolerate their intense emotional states better while minimizing the tendency to exclude these states from conscious awareness" (p. 133). To this it should be added that a patient's ability to identify, channel, and thereby master strong affects for constructive or creative purposes is a central developmental achievement.

However, at this time a coherent theory of affect does not exist. As Knapp (1987) has stated, "psychoanalytic contributions to the study of emotion have resulted in a profusion of clinical detail and a confusion of theory" (p. 227). While psychoanalytic models have attempted to develop a framework for understanding affect development, regression, tolerance, and defensive use, this framework—derived from a dyadic treatment modality—is still a partial and emerging structure. For group therapists it is particularly incomplete: it includes neither unique group phenomena, such as emotional contagion, nor the impact of group development and dynamics on individual group members.

In this chapter I will review some of the central concepts of affect development from psychoanalytic theory and infant behavioral observation, with a focus on effects in borderline and narcissistic patients. I then will examine the impact of group membership on affects for these individuals. The work of Krystal (1974, 1975, 1978) will be used as a framework for this theoretical review.

THEORY

Affect Evolution and Differentiation

According to Krystal (1974), affects evolve from an undifferentiated somatic matrix. Expectable development requires separation and differentiation of affect states, as well as their progressive desomatization and verbalization. Simultaneously, the growing child gains the capacity to experience a range of feelings without experiencing excessive inner disruption or disorganization. Individuals become familiar with distinct feeling states (e.g., anxiety, depression, shame, guilt, joy, pleasure) and a variety of other negative or positive affects which they are able to utilize in the service of the ego. The ability to tolerate affects of considerable intensity and to use them in attaining goals or managing conflict is an indicator of maturity.

The earliest phases of affect development are described in terms of the infant's irritability (Schur, 1969) and as experiences of pleasure or unpleasure (Novey 1959, 1961). Infants seem to achieve gratification and experience pleasure in reaching out with eyes, hands, and mouth. Failure appears to produce unpleasure. Pleasure and unpleasure states are communicated "in body terms to the mother, who with varying degrees of success and through her own affective, felt experience, responds to the infant's situation, thereby constituting and defining the biological unit, mother-infant. The biological unit thereby becomes psychobiological" (Engel, 1962, p. 90).

According to Krystal (1975), affect differentiation begins through interaction with the mother.

> The infant experiences his affects passively as if they were emanating from the mother. When he has good feelings, he experiences them against a background of his maternal-object representations, which (he feels) must signify that it is all right for him to have the good feelings. When he feels

distress, he must turn to his mother for an evaluation of the *meaning* of his discomfort. . . . Quite likely, identification with the parents, and imitation of their way of dealing with their emotions becomes the most important determinant of the patterns the child will develop for himself [p. 194].

As development continues, ideational aspects of experiencing become part of a complex affective-ideational constellation of inner objects. The progressive affect differentiation is related to self- and object representation, libidinal organization, and motor-neurological development (Schmale, 1964).

Further key organizing periods for affect differentiation are the phases of separation-individuation, latency (when the individual begins to verbalize affects), and adolescence (when the upsurge of sexuality and growth intensifies feelings and the adolescent begins to master the feelings of depression, anxiety, and shame). Adolescents also have the task of learning that it is permissible and helpful to take over parental functions, including self-soothing attitudes and containment of pleasurable affects.

Successful emotional development continues throughout the life cycle, including the second half of life, and brings feelings to a point "where there is adequate affect tolerance, and where affects are experienced mainly as signals to oneself and not as a means of controlling others or as attacks. Under these circumstances, affects function mostly 'silently' (i.e., unnoticed), and play their key roles in perception and motivation" (Krystal, 1974, pp. 123–124).

Affect Tolerance

Affect tolerance is gradually accomplished through the use of a number of temporary strategies or defenses which permit relief and later integration. Krystal (1975) includes among the adaptive defenses

transient consciousness modifications, shifting of attention cathexes (self-distraction), eliminatory or cleansing fantasies, or compensatory acting out. There are also a variety of self-administered or "object involving" methods of comforting or "mothering" oneself. Where such modes of behavior are experienced as prohibited and therefore inaccessible objects, drugs or placebos may have to be used to circumvent inner barriers (inhibitions) resulting from repression [p. 182].

The developmental achievement of tolerating affects involves an ability to recognize affects, use them as signals, and then make a "judgment" regarding how the feelings should be managed. On close inspection, individuals vary considerably in their capacity to tune into the meaning and the impact on others of direct emotional expression. Some may ignore the impact of expressing feelings and respond to an inner imperative "to get the feelings out." Others may fear responses to any display of affect and in consequence contain or inhibit their feelings. In both circumstances, affects may be identifiable, but they cannot be tolerated.

A patient's need to express affects, particularly angry responses, is misleading and derives from anal analogies (i.e., one rids oneself of the affects). Krystal (1975) disagrees with treatment strategies that encourage direct affect expression: "the only possible help patients can attain is to learn to tolerate [their affect]" (p. 188). Nevertheless, despite the limitations of merely expressing feelings, individuals feel better having temporarily expressed anger or rage. Dynamically, such expressions counter feelings of being wronged and helpless and may gratify revenge fantasies. Both dynamics assist the individual in reestablishing an internal balance.

Affect Dedifferentiation and Affect as a Defense

Vulnerable individuals may experience affect dedifferentiation, particularly resomatization and deverbalization, in response to stress. In a severe regression, individuals are unable to describe discrete feelings and instead express affects in a vague, blurred, or incomplete fashion. The dedifferentiation may be expressed also through a variety of hypochondriacal or somatic symptoms. As Krystal (1974) notes, "it has not been possible for me to find an example of impairment of affect verbalization without there being some evidence of resomatization of affect" (p. 103). Regressed individuals, like those who are developmentally stuck, may be unable to specify their feeling states or may experience only somatic responses. Under these circumstances they may need considerable direct assistance in verbalizing and differentiating their emotions.

Affects in themselves may evoke defenses. Krystal (1975) describes this process as part of an individual's developmental sequence: "First he develops the emotion in question, and then reacts to having it. He becomes either frightened of it and/or angry about it, thus building it up into a panic, rage, or other affect storm" (p. 207). If it becomes overwhelming, then the individual may wall off emotions, develop psychic numbing, a loss of vitality, a feeling of deadness, or dissociative reactions. One feeling response evokes another—e.g., the hurt feeling of being ignored evokes the angry response to the hurt. The unraveling of the various layers becomes very complicated.

Anna Freud (1936) addressed this transformation of affects: "The analysis and the bringing into consciousness of the specific form of this defense against affect—whether it be reversal, displacement or complete repression—teach us something of the particular technique adopted by the ego" (p. 39). The child according to her "may exhibit indifference when we should have looked for disappointment, exuberant high spirits instead of mortification, excessive tenderness instead of jealousy" (p. 39). One affect may replace another, and part of the therapist's task is to examine the relationship between the affect states (Novey, 1959). Anger is often used to cover over other feelings. As one patient noted, "Sometimes I become very angry when I'm scared." Another stated: "I can't stand people getting close to me. I get angry and shove them away." Feelings of humiliation or shame often are experienced as unbearable and are walled off with a variety of feeling responses. Similarly, disgust or scorn may cover and protect against other feelings. Excitement and mobilization for action may be an indicator of difficulty in containing affects which are only momentarily perceptible. In the therapeutic process, attention to the precipitant for intense affective states will often provide important leads in uncovering fleeting or previously hidden feelings.

AFFECT IN BORDERLINE AND NARCISSISTIC DISORDERS

Borderline States

Kernberg has a preeminent place in the hierarchy of authors discussing borderline individuals. His object relations theory, which significantly modifies drive theory, theoretically links affect to drive derivatives activated in the interaction between infant and object (primarily the mother). Of borderline conditions he writes that "the main etiological factors appear to be the excessive nature of primary aggression or aggression secondary to frustration, to which probably certain deficiencies in the development of primary ego apparatuses and lack of anxiety tolerance contribute" (Kernberg, 1975, pp. 34–35). In Kernberg's formulation (1976), the splitting of good and bad objects must be maintained in order to protect the positive introjections and identifications from destruction by the internal aggressive drives and the associated affective coloring. Novey (1961) adds that borderline individuals have difficulty with cognitive integration of affects:

> in the borderline state . . . it may be substantially more difficult to establish coincidence between their internal representation of objects and the objects of time-space [external objects]. . . . In this group of patients, particularly, one can see the essentially affectional nature of their relationship to self and others with only a modicum of intellectual conceptualization [p. 29].

Blanck and Blanck (1974) placed borderline developmental difficulty in the period of separation-individuation: "the broad concept that borderline phenomena have their origin in failures in development in the separation-individuation phase is central to precise diagnosis and treatment of these problems" (p. 60). Horner (1979), while partially disagreeing with the concept of innate aggression, proposes that "anger and hostile aggression result from the failure or the inability of the environment to respond to the infant with good enough empathic caretaking to protect the child from excessive frustration and from overwhelming traumatic states" (p. 279). This formulation suggests that the ego deficit has preceded the separation phase but does not become manifest until the stress of that period. Adler (1985) concurs: *"the primary sector of borderline psychopathology . . . involves a relative developmental failure in formation of introjects that provide to the self a function of the holding-soothing security"* (p. 4). Without stable introjects, separation triggers regression which, in Adler's view, the individual experiences as a critical sense that the self is alone and very near to disintegration. This formulation helps in understanding the "restitutive" or "stabilizing" intense clinging, demanding, or entitled positions that borderline patients assume when they fear disintegration. Under these circumstances, affect differentiation is lost and in its place global, less organized affects emerge.

Narcissistic Disorders

The interpersonal aspects of affect regulation have been of interest to theorists of the psychology of the self (Kohut, 1971, 1977, 1984; Socarides and Stolorow, 1984). The self acquires an ability to pursue ambitions, goals, and ideals through an interaction with the selfobject, who is experienced as functionally part of the self. Socarides and Stolorow (1984) have posited that "selfobject functions pertain fundamentally to the integration of *affect,* and that the need for selfobjects pertains most centrally to the need for phase-appropriate responsiveness to affect states in all stages of the life cycle" (p. 105).

Beginning in infancy, the infant actively attempts to interact with others. Infant and mother cannot act indifferently to one another. The joy in both is noticeable when mutual and successful reciprocity takes place. "The empathic observer sees two selves, mother and child, actively evoking responses in each other that are experienced by both as satisfying states of the self" (Wolf, 1980, p. 121). The need for the growing child to have selfobject responsivity to needs for mirroring and for merger with an idealized selfobject continues within a phase-appropriate responsiveness. In reaction to inevitable empathic failures, the child gradually develops the capacity for self-regulation and control over disruptive affects. More chronic empathic failures lead to affect dedifferentiation with feelings of emptiness, of dullness, and, in more intense situations, of fragmentation and dissolution of the self.

One of the central emphases in the psychology of the self is the delineation of poorly differentiated affects. These feelings, described as generalized dullness, or anhedonia, or loss of vitality and interest, are to be distinguished from depression. Stern (1985), in a review of behavioral studies of infants, described a group of affects which he labeled "vitality affects." These do not fit into the ordinary taxonomy. They "are better captured by dynamic, kinetic terms, such as 'surging,' 'fading away,' 'feeling explosive.' Different feelings of vitality can be expressed in a multitude of parental acts that do not qualify as 'regular' affective acts: how the mother picks up baby, folds the diapers, grooms her hair or the baby's hair, reaches for a bottle, unbuttons her blouse" (p. 51). These studies and those of a more theoretical nature from self psychology have placed an emphasis on vague affects which may persist into adulthood and signal a defective development of the self. However, Stern's formulations raise a question regarding the potential of some generalized feelings (vitality affects) having a separate developmental line which would not ordinarily be transformed into more specific feelings like love or hate. These preliminary observations will have to await further studies for confirmation.

GROUP DYNAMICS AND AFFECTS

The change from a dyadic to a group psychotherapy format adds significant dimensions to the exploration of affects. Each group member experiences the impact of the group-as-a-whole and the interpersonal transactions with peers and authorities as a stimulus to fantasies and affects. This discussion will focus on the group dynamic processes of emotional contagion and norm setting as they impact on borderline and narcissistic patients. These dynamics are especially relevant to the patients' responses to the separations, the exhibition-ism (grandiosity), and the competitiveness that are inherent in membership in a psychotherapy group. In this section group and individual dynamics and their interaction will be explored as they impact on the experiences of the disturbed patient.

Emotional Contagion

A significant aspect of an affective experience in groups is the phenomenon of emotional contagion. The rapid spread of emotion among group members is readily observable and indeed is a universal experience. According to Freud (1921), "There is no doubt that something exists in us which, when we become aware of signs of an emotion in someone else, tends to make us fall into the same emotion; but how often do we not successfully oppose it, resist the emotion, and react in quite an opposite way? Why, therefore, do we invariably give way to this contagion when we are in a group?" (p. 89). Freud answered his question by positing that suggestibility, the basis for contagion, is "an irreducible, primitive phenomenon, a fundamental fact in the mental life of man" (p. 89).

The recognition of the phenomenon of contagion has influenced group-as-a-whole theoreticians. According to Rioch (1970), in a review of Bion's writings, mobilization of affect is a fundamental pressure from which basic assumption behavior arises. The contagion processes are described by Whitaker and Lieberman (1964): "there are times when shared feeling emerges so rapidly that one is hardly aware of the associative links. In fact these appear to be short-circuited, often because one is seeing more or less simultaneous reaction to some event which operates like a trigger" (p. 287).

Verbal and nonverbal channels alike contribute to the rapid spread of affect in groups. Infants recognize and respond to affect states in others and will smile in response to a smile and broaden it in response to similar behavior on the part of the adult (Stern, 1985). Rycroft (1956) has suggested that emotionally perceptible internal responses have an "intrinsic tendency to evoke either an identical or complementary response in a perceiving object" (p.469). In groups, emotions may flow through the membership, and sudden shifts from one feeling state to another are not unusual. A warm glow of tenderness or affection spreading throughout the group may follow from a poignant story. Anger can be shifted to pity or sorrow with a few brief words. These are responses that occur not only to the words of a story, but to the entire presentation, including tone of voice, posture, and facial and bodily expressions.

For borderline and narcissistic patients the fear of affect contagion is a significant dynamic. In research exploring the reasons for premature termination from groups, Yalom (1985) cited fear of emotional contagion as an important contributing element. He stated that some dropouts "had been extremely affected by hearing the problems of other group members" (p.242). Yalom suggested that these patients' anxiety and fear of being alone led them to be vulnerable to being influenced. These observations are concordant with those of Adler (1985), who posits that the fear of aloneness is at the core of the borderline's defect. However, this fear is countered by the wish for contact, which is of such intensity that the patient fears disintegration of the self. These dynamics are prominent in the initial phases of group formation, when the fear of contagion is compounded by the fear of loss of self in the amorphous unknown mass of the group. The dangers for these patients may precipitate premature terminations, or contribute to a prolonged entry phase during which patients "prefer" to tolerate aloneness rather than expose themselves to the dangers they perceive as a consequence of being engulfed by emotional contagion.

Emotional contagion is a component of the universal process of scapegoating. Patients are frequently scapegoated for their monopolizing, help-rejecting, or noncollaborative behaviors. In the dynamics of scapegoating, the rapid spread of feeling or behavior through the group is frequently observable. In fact, many borderline patients are quite familiar with this process and may invite the response either to justify their position of safety outside of the group or as a rationale for quitting.

The fear of emotional contagion is a significant contributor to the defensive stance of many narcissistic individuals who protect themselves against exposing their needs for a selfobject. These patients have had prior experience with family or peer rejection, and only very carefully (and by no means consciously) do they expose themselves in group situations, where they fear being injured again as they were in childhood (Stone and Gustafson, 1982). The fear is magnified by an expectation that the other members will magically and universally join in harming them.

Scheidlinger (1982) nicely illustrates the process of emotional contagion in his description of a scapegoated child in an activity group: "as if on a signal, her response evoked more deliberate acts of throwing things in her direction amid a climate of laughter and derision" (p. 139). The almost simultaneous affective and behavioral response is characteristic of the emotional contagion associated with scapegoating.

Much of what has been described as "manic" behavior in groups is a result of emotional contagion. One group that included several borderline patients responded to the therapist's announcement of his vacation with an excited and detailed plan for a picnic to coincide with the time of the canceled meeting. These patients were expressing their wish to regain some sense of personal control in the face of an anticipated separation. The ever present vulnerability and sensitivity to separations and the fear of being helpless and alone touched off a manic response. The very nature of the reverberating stimulation precludes self-reflection. Generally these processes must run their course before members can regain their inner equilibrium and examine their affective and behavioral responses.

Contagion involves a regression in affect. No longer are affects used as signals; instead they lead to behavioral or other defensive affective responses. It is not unusual for members to experience somatic complaints (Krystal, 1974). Not infrequently the verbal content includes religious themes, an attempt to limit or contain the regression by invoking a higher authority.

Group Norms

Repetitive patterns of group interaction produce over time a series of norms and values generally serving the function of containing anxiety or at least keeping it within manageable bounds. This process results in an increased sense of safety which enables members to moderate affects and differentiate feelings more precisely. At times, however, the norms may reflect the lowest common denominator; i.e., the member least able to tolerate feelings becomes the controlling element. In this section I will examine norm setting in response to experiences of separation, exhibitionism, and competition. These processes are of particular significance to borderline and narcissistic patients.

Separation anxiety is more consistently activated in groups than in dyadic treatment. The very fact that six to eight individuals are included in the treatment means there will be a greater number of comings and goings. Commonly, patients will react with considerable affect, primarily anger, at the inability of the group or the therapist to control attendance. The essence of such a feeling state was succinctly stated by one borderline man who angrily told the others that they had to be present and on time each week. He stated that they did not have to speak (there was one very quiet member in the group), just be there in order for him to feel that the group could be helpful. In another group, a woman reported that her high school reunion was ruined for her because one class member was absent. This statement was an allusion to her wish for perfect attendance in the group. Without further elaboration, such statements may be understood as manifestations of separation anxiety—all members must be present. At another level these comments may reflect the need for the group to be complete and whole in order to provide a structure (a selfobject) that will prevent fragmentation of the disordered self. Similar dynamics are activated repeatedly in groups, and through careful attention to affects members can label and differentiate their feeling states and thus gain greater self-awareness and self-control.

Responses to the relatively porous boundaries of a psychotherapy

group often activate powerful defenses that prevent or delay exploration of the very behaviors that have stimulated the defenses—i.e.,
lateness, absences, or premature terminations. The man described
above, so exquisitely sensitive to separations, or to the loss of the
selfobject functions of the group, angrily attempted to institute a
norm of perfect attendance. In other circumstances members may
exhibit an empty withdrawn state as the overt affective response. In
dysfunctional groups, a norm minimizing or suppressing members'
responses to boundary disruptions protects against painful emptiness,
aloneness, or anger, and against secondary responses, internal or
external, to that affect. Yet only after a good deal of therapeutic work
has been accomplished do members become aware that they have
colluded to minimize their emotional responses.

Suppression or avoidance are not the only restrictive norms that
develop. In the illustration of emotional contagion, the members
excitedly planned a picnic in response to the therapist's planned
vacation, thereby protecting themselves from experiencing powerful
feelings of loss. Another behavioral norm is the implementation of a
party celebrating the successful termination of a member. Rutan and
Stone (1984) describe a group member who prepared a lavish spread
in honor of a termination. All of the members joyfully participated in
the celebration. The therapist's very sensitive exploration of this event
revealed that the "hostess" replicated in the group her behavior at her
mother's funeral and again was avoiding the experience of intense
grieving. More often, celebrations take place after the session; but,
either way, the result is that of replacing one affect with another.

Prominent among the dynamics of group membership are wishes
or needs for exhibitionistic (grandiose) or competitive gratification.
Grandiosity may be conceptualized along the developmental and
defensive continuum of normal need for mirroring, or the more
insistent exhibitionism and grandiosity characteristic of self disordered patients who are unable to maintain an inner sense of cohesion.
Alternatively, patients may defensively employ grandiosity to protect
against underlying feelings of envy and rage.

Group norms may prohibit or significantly interfere with showing off, or grabbing center stage. One manifestation of such a norm
is the nonrecognition or nonresponse to a member's report of
external success. Dynamically, such norms tend to reinforce defenses
against the emergence of exhibitionistic displays, and thereby limit
the therapeutic potential of the group. In the circumstance where

grandiosity is serving as a defense against underlying envy or rage, premature blocking or nonacceptance of the grandiosity via group norms also interferes with the exposure of the defensive structure involved in the transactions.

Illustrative of these processes was a session in which Jack cautiously revealed that he had secretly enjoyed putting down Jane in the prior meeting. Others initially ignored the comment, and only following an inquiry by the therapist did they respond, primarily by criticizing Jack—e.g., "You need to be kind to others here in the group." The groupwide response was not to a sadistic element in Jack's revelation (although his comment could have been construed to have that meaning) but rather had the intent of making his revelation seem merely exhibitionistic. The context of the revelation was the anticipated entry of a new male into the group, which was in the midst of a competitive exhibitionistic battle among the males who were already members. Jack's feelings were complex; he was embarrassed by the idea that he could feel pleasure in having power over women, but the entire response was also a surprise. He had not known that these feelings existed within himself. Jack appreciated the risk he had taken, but had felt reasonably secure in the setting, where usually the norm of openness and acceptance was operative. However, this time he was wrong. Anticipation of the new member altered the usual condition so that defensive grandiosity took precedence.

Unbridled grandiosity is often problematic in groups. It is experienced in a variety of ways, but generally the members try to suppress it in an effort to keep from exposing their own similar affective needs. Grandiosity does not occur in a vacuum; a responsive audience is necessary. The very nature of group therapy serves to stimulate these important affective configurations. Thus norms develop as a groupwide solution to the ever present concern that the exhibitionism will be contagious, in that all members will be stimulated to show off and demand center stage, or that they will not be appropriately mirrored. The precise dynamic understanding of any behavior becomes clearer during the treatment process, and this optimally occurs in an environment with open rather than constricting norms.

Group norms, once formed, become like character traits, neither particularly fluid nor easily alterable. The difficult process of altering established norms and tuning into the differing affective states of the members is illustrated in the following clinical example. In a well-established group, Paula, a narcissistic individual, was discussing her fears of trusting others. She began to describe Rhoda's positive attributes—her thoughtful, caring sensitivity to others' feelings—all in a glowing manner. Rhoda, however, became uncomfortable with this assessment. The other members were confused, in part because of the special "pairing" and in part because of the idealization. The therapist wondered if the confusion and Rhoda's discomfort might be caused by the fact that Paula was in effect limiting Rhoda—Rhoda could not be negative but had to respond in a sensitive, rational, and caring manner, never being able to express hostile or discordant feelings. He continued by saying that this might be understandable, as Paula was discussing trust and wanted to be certain she had one ally within the group. Paula vigorously protested, maintaining that the therapist did not understand her.

These transactions illustrate the confluence of Paula's efforts to establish an idealizing transference to Rhoda in order to assure herself that she would have one ally (Harwood, 1986; see also Chapter 8). At the same time, Paula was attempting to implement a restrictive norm of being nice. The therapist's intervention was designed to make the group's norms pliant, but was experienced by Paula as a narcissistic injury—she was not understood. Her experience was that she was simply praising (idealizing) Rhoda. The members' confusion may have resulted from the dissonance they felt in regard to the restrictive nature of the selfobject transference or from the group-wide affect related to an identification with the object of the idealization. Such idealization may be overstimulating, even stifling, and produce much dysphoria (Stone and Whitman, 1977). The hallmark of the transferential nature of the interaction was Paula's inability to step back and understand the impact of her adulation. She could not appreciate Rhoda as an autonomous individual with her own needs and responses.

THERAPEUTIC IMPLICATIONS

In 1934 Strachey introduced the phrase "mutative interpretation." He contended that the most therapeutically valuable interpretations should be made within the transference under optimal conditions of affective/cognitive balance. Such interpretations would be more likely to produce change than those made about extratransference situations. In a parallel fashion, the group therapist attempts to develop a norm that emphasizes the patients' freedom to experience affectively meaningful interactions within the meeting. In turn, these experiences are then available to understanding and explaining (interpretation), which are the essential ingredients for change and growth.

The dynamics of the group setting actively stimulate borderline and self disordered patients' affects. The problems associated with consistency in newly forming groups, the absence of a sense of basic trust, and the fear of aloneness increases the vulnerability to severe regression.

Le Bon's classic description of the crowd (1920) nicely captures the narcissistic or borderline patient's experience in participating in a small group: "the fact that they have been transformed into a group puts them in possession of a sort of collective mind which makes them feel, think, and act in a manner quite different from that in which each individual would feel, think, and act were he in a state of isolation" (p. 29). For patients who lack a firm sense of ego boundaries, or who have a deep-seated anxiety over fragmentation of the self, group membership may be a terrifying experience. Le Bon also makes note of the state of isolation, which is the other affective state stimulated by efforts to join a group. For the individual to remain outside is isolating and may be a reaction to the emotional pressure to join, but such a stance also evokes powerful and frightening feelings of aloneness.

In the process of joining and establishing an effective working environment, patients are attentive to both internal and external group boundaries. They hope to feel safe and not be traumatized again, as they had been in earlier periods (Stone and Gustafson, 1982). Group norms defining the limits of absences, lateness, and participation are of great significance, and are clear examples of the efforts to establish a cohesive group while simultaneously containing affects. However, fear of emotional contagion, which is almost invariably accompanied by affect regression and dedifferentiation, is equally important. The vitality and excitement evoked in scapegoating or in manic responses are but two examples of affect contagion and regression. The regressive state only adds to the difficulty in halting or reversing this process. Because of the centrality of these issues, they may require extended periods of therapeutic attention before a satisfactory resolution and strengthening of the self occurs.

Two common therapeutic considerations in managing affect

deserve brief comment. The first centers around patients' proneness
to regression, dedifferentiation of affects, and somatization. In the
regressed state, members may no longer be able to describe discrete
feelings. The therapist may attempt to reverse the regression through
both individual and group-as-a-whole interpretations (see chapter 6)
or may assist the patient by more precisely specifying the vague or
diffuse feelings. This latter tactic strengthens empathic connections
and enhances the selfobject functions of the group. In turn this
process helps reverse the regression.

The second consideration involves expression or containment of
anger, which is often of central concern for members and therapists
alike. Anger may be a defensive, distancing mechanism covering
other affect states, or may be a response to narcissistic injury.
Narcissistic rage is a response used by the vulnerable individual both
to gain revenge and to organize the vulnerable self. In patients with
greater self-cohesion and stability, anger disappears with removal of
an obstacle and achievement of a goal (Kohut, 1984). Ornstein (1985)
has added an additional dimension to understanding the expression
of anger. He contrasts the therapeutic situation with the original
traumatic childhood experience, when withdrawal and other self-
protective measures were felt to be necessary to maintain self-
cohesion. If the injury in the present is not too severe (as experienced
by the recipient, not as evaluated by the observer), the patient may be
able to express affect in a controlled manner rather than withdraw;
the experience is thereby utilized in the service of growth. The
therapist's task is to ensure that both he and the group-as-group serve
as a responsive selfobject that permits this process to occur.

The therapist needs to keep in mind that in many circumstances
the affective state appearing in one individual may be a response to a
group-as-a-whole pressure or the result of projective mechanisms. By
attending to interactive here-and-now patterns, the therapist can
appreciate the impact of an intervention on the total situation. This
perspective broadens the scope of the treatment to take into account
intrapsychic, interpersonal, and group-as-a-whole levels that may be
operating at any moment in the therapeutic process.

CONCLUSION

In general, the treatment goal in regard to affect is to use feelings
as a signal to the self rather than as a stimulus to direct expression.

Such an achievement indicates that affect tolerance has been accomplished. The patient is then in a position to decide on the value or impact of futher containment or expression of the feeling.

Within the group setting, affect contagion and the establishment of norms contribute to how affects are experienced and displayed. Awareness and knowledge of these dynamics inform and assist the therapist in sorting out individual elements from those stimulated by the setting. Affect contagion has not been thoroughly explored, and norm setting in relation to affects often receives insufficient attention. Knowledge regarding these dynamics is especially valuable in work with borderline and self disordered individuals.

Much more needs to be done in evolving our understanding of affects in group psychotherapy. This contribution has been an attempt to sharpen our focus on some of the important issues.

REFERENCES

Adler, G. (1985), *Borderline Psychopathology and Its Treatment.* New York: Aronson.

Blanck, G., & Blanck, R. (1974), *Ego Psychology: Theory and Practice.* New York: Columbia University Press.

Engel, G. L. (1962), Anxiety and depression—withdrawal: The primary affects of unpleasure. *Internat. J. Psycho-Anal.*, 43:89–97.

Freud, A. (1936), *The Ego and the Mechanisms of Defense.* New York: International Universities Press, 1966.

Freud, S. (1921), Group psychology and the analysis of the ego. *Standard Edition*, 18:65–143. London: Hogarth Press, 1955.

Harwood, I. (1986), The need for optimal, available caretakers: Moving towards extended selfobject experience. *Group Analysis*, 19:291–302.

Horner, A. J. (1979), *Object Relations and the Developing Ego in Therapy.* New York: Aronson.

Kernberg, O. F. (1975), *Borderline Conditions and Pathological Narcissism.* New York: Aronson.

———(1976), *Object Relations Theory and Clinical Psychoanalysis.* New York: Aronson.

Knapp, P. H. (1987), Some contemporary contributions to the study of emotions. *J. Amer. Psychoanal. Assn.*, 35:205–248.

Kohut, H. (1971), *The Analysis of the Self.* New York: International Universities Press.

———(1977), *The Restoration of the Self.* New York: International Universities Press.

———(1984), *How Does Analysis Cure?* Chicago: University of Chicago Press.

Krystal, H. (1974), The genetic development of affect and affect regression. *The Annual of Psychoanalysis*, 2:98–126. New York: International Universities Press.

————(1975), Affect tolerance. *The Annual of Psychoanalysis*, 3:179–219. New York: International Universities Press.

————(1978), Trauma and affects. *The Psychoanalytic Study of the Child*, 33:81–116. New Haven, CT: Yale University Press.

Lane, R. D., & Schwartz, G. E. (1987), Levels of emotional awareness: A cognitive-developmental theory and its application to psychopathology. *Amer. J. Psychiat.*, 144:133–143.

LeBon, G. (1920), *The Crowd: A Study of the Popular Mind.* New York: Fisher Unwin.

Novey, S. (1959), A clinical view of affect theory in psycho-analysis. *Internat. J. Psycho-Anal.*, 40:94–104.

————(1961), Further considerations on affect theory in psycho-analysis. *Internat. J. Psycho-Anal.*, 42:21–32.

Ornstein, P. H. (1985), The thwarted need to grow: Clinical-theoretical issues in the selfobject transferences. In: *The Transference in Psychotherapy.* ed. E. A. Schwaber. New York: International Universities Press, pp. 33–49.

Rioch, M. J. (1970), The work of Wilfred Bion on groups. *Psychiat.*, 33:55–66.

Rutan, J. S., & Stone, W. N. (1984), *Psychodynamic Group Psychotherapy.* New York: Macmillan.

Rycroft, C. (1956), The nature and function of the analyst's communication to the patient. *Internat. J. Psycho-Anal.*, 37:469–472.

Scheidlinger, S. (1982), On scapegoating in group psychotherapy. *Internat. J. Group Psychother.*, 32:131–143.

Schmale, A. N. (1964), A genetic view of affects. *The Psychoanalytic Study of the Child*, 19:287–310. New York: International Universities Press.

Schur, M. (1969), Affect and cognition. *Internat. J. Psycho-Anal.*, 50:647–653.

Socarides, D. D., & Stolorow, R. D. (1984), Affects and selfobjects. *The Annual of Psychoanalysis*, 12/13:105–119. New York: International Universities Press.

Stern, D. N. (1985), *The Interpersonal World of the Infant.* New York: Basic Books.

Stone, W. N., & Gustafson, J. P. (1982), Technique in group psychotherapy of narcissistic and borderline patients. *Internat. J. Group Psychother.*, 32:29–47.

————Whitman, R. M. (1977), Contributions of the psychology of the self to group process and group therapy. *Internat. J. Group Psychother.*, 27:343–359.

Strachey, J. (1934), The nature of the therapeutic action in psycho-analysis. In: *Psychoanalytic Clinical Interpretation*, ed. L. Paul. New York: Free Press, 1963, pp. 1–41.

Whitaker, D. S., & Lieberman, M. A. (1964), *Psychotherapy through the Group Process.* New York: Atherton.

Wolf, E. S. (1980), On the developmental line of selfobject relations. In: *Advances in Self Psychology*, ed. A. Goldberg. New York: International Universities Press, pp. 117–130.

Yalom, I. D. (1985), *The Theory and Practice of Group Psychotherapy.* New York: Basic Books.

Part III
Inpatient Groups

Introduction

The hospital setting provides an opportunity to refine and test our theories and strategies regarding the group treatment of very ill patients. In long-term inpatient settings the impact of the hospital social system on treatment groups is often considerable, for patients and leaders alike.

In Chapter 11, Klein, Hunter, and Brown carefully describe the multitude of factors that affect the successful conduct of small groups in a specialized hospital setting in which patients remain, on average, for over a year. The authors focus on the social systems of the hospital in order to understand events in the group. They note that boundary management, in its various aspects, is of vital importance. In the setting they present, the group therapists do not have control of the membership boundary, an arrangement whose impact is discussed in relation to the boundary issues of time and space, over which they exercise far greater control. Another factor studied at length is the group leader's dual role as both administrator and therapist, a situation whose effects in the group setting are manifold.

The authors propose the family as a useful model for conceptualizing their work. The family has two tasks: (1) helping its members learn about their inner world, a task framed primarily in object relations terms, and (2) adaptation to the external world (i.e., living in the hospital), a task framed in terms of adaptive ego functions. The model enables the therapist to integrate these seemingly disparate tasks.

Countertransference—properly the subject of Part IV—is of necessity discussed here at some length. The authors highlight its

211

complexity with inpatient groups by pointing to the intensive atmosphere of the hospital and the multiple sources of countertransference responses found there: the patients, who present a difficult
enough problem considering their early developmental pathology;
the staff, who are affiliated with various disciplines, exercise different
degrees of power and authority, and have different amounts of
experience; and the hospital itself, with its administrative demands, in
part arising from insurance companies and the need to justify a
patient's length of stay.

Kibel (Chapter 12), working in a similar setting, uses the hospital
group to raise significant unresolved questions regarding the place of
theory in small group work with this patient population. In presenting a vignette of an inpatient group, he carefully outlines how the
group context and recent administrative and leadership changes
impact a particular session. The analysis of this session, like Bacal's
analysis in Chapter 8, is presented from differing theoretical perspectives: that of object relations theory, with its emphasis on conflict
resolution, and that of self psychology, with its focus on the reparation
of structural deficits. Kibel finds self psychology insufficient to
explain the broad range of pathological phenomena found in these
long-term groups.

Youcha's contribution (Chapter 13) turns our attention to short-
term treatment groups in an acute hospital setting and presents a
three-tiered model. After careful diagnostic assessment, patients are
placed in a group for severely impaired patients whose ego functions
have been overwhelmed, generally by psychosis; in an intermediate
group for patients whose psychosis has undermined but not obliter-
ated their reality testing; or in a high-level group for patients, usually
nonpsychotic, whose defenses have temporarily disintegrated.

The most dysfunctional patients are placed in activity groups
which promote interaction without exploration of personal data.
Active and enthusiastic participation by the staff is essential if these
groups are to be successful. The intermediate group format is that of
topical discussion. Groups are structured to encourage patients to
listen to one another. Responses to the topic do not have to be
personal, and global or general statements are considered quite
acceptable. The most advanced group is conceptualized as focal
therapy concentrating on the precipitants of hospitalization and on
current behavior, both in and out of group.

Youcha stresses that optimally these groups are nonthreatening.

Designed to reintegrate patients, they are part of an overall treatment plan that often includes the use of psychopharmacological medication. The ultimate goal of these groups, which meet at least three times weekly in order to establish useful continuity, is "to make the experience one the patient will want to continue after discharge."

11

Long-Term Inpatient Group Psychotherapy

ROBERT H. KLEIN, Ph.D.,

DAVID E. K. HUNTER, Ph.D., A.C.S.W.,

and

SERENA-LYNN BROWN, M.D., Ph.D.

The use of small group therapy as an important aspect of hospital treatment has been steadily increasing. In a recent review, Kibel (1981) maintains that the key observations of early workers who utilized inpatient group psychotherapy—the central role of the therapist, the experiential benefits of the group and the relationship to the milieu—were not widely applied to inpatient groups because of limitations in the available conceptual models. Nevertheless, a number of approaches have continued to develop which primarily emphasize limited treatment goals, overcoming social isolation, training in social skills, reinforcing reality-centered behavior, modifying maladaptive symptoms, encouraging ventilation and catharsis, and prompt intervention. Models have appeared in the literature that involve adaptations of such varied approaches as the psychoanalytic (Battegay, 1966), the ego-supportive (Kibel, 1978, 1981), the educative (Maxmen, 1978), and didactic (Druck, 1978). Recommended techniques have ranged from nonverbal exercises (Cory and Page, 1978) through psychodrama and related experiential techniques (Farrell, 1976) to education regarding symptoms, precipitants, and the value of accepting help from others (Maxmen, 1978). Further, the importance of examining the inpatient group in relation to the social context in which patients undergo treatment has begun to receive considerable attention (Klein, 1977, 1981, 1983; Klein and Kugel,

1981). There is a growing appreciation of the reciprocal influences exerted by the therapy group and the inpatient unit on which it is located.

While these developments have added to our understanding of the relevance of inpatient group therapy, the primary focus of much of the recent work has been in the area of short-term inpatient group therapy (Gunderson, Will, and Mosher, 1983). Many converging social forces have contributed to the growing demand for short-term intervention strategies, including the escalating costs of inpatient care, the growing use of the hospital as a transient refuge, and the proliferation of day treatment and other transitional facilities. One important consequence of these developments, however, is that the use of inpatient small group therapy in conjunction with comprehensive long-term hospital treatment has received relatively little attention since the seminal contributions of Edelson (1964, 1970a, b).

The present chapter describes the ward group, a modified version of traditional group therapy, designed for use in conjunction with comprehensive long-term treatment for severely ill adolescents and young adults. From a developmental perspective, this small group closely resembles a family in that it simultaneously pursues diverse, complex, and at times what may appear to be contradictory tasks. Both administrative decision making and traditional group psychotherapy tasks are conducted by the same leader in the context of the group. The special functions of the group in relation to the ward and the hospital, and its composition, structure, and dynamics, will be considered. In particular, we will focus on the countertransference issues inherent in the role of group leader, since the integration of therapeutic and administrative functions by clinicians who conduct inpatient treatment is often confused, complicated, and undisciplined. Through a careful examination of our model for long-term inpatient group psychotherapy, we hope to elucidate some of the generic countertransference pressures faced by all administrators who also perform psychotherapeutic functions.

THE CONTEXT

The hospital context of the ward group we describe is a sixty-bed university hospital setting, the Yale Psychiatric Institute (YPI), devoted to long-term psychoanalytically oriented treatment. This hospital serves as a tertiary care facility providing treatment for severely ill, treatment-refractory patients who range in age from their early teens to their mid-thirties. The diagnostic mix is heterogeneous and primarily includes patients who are diagnosed as having schizophrenic disturbances, major affective disorders, and a variety of severe personality disorders (e.g., borderline, narcissistic, and antisocial). These relatively young (mostly teenage), severely disturbed patients remain in the hospital for an average length of stay of over four hundred days. A multimodal milieu treatment approach is used, which includes intensive individual psychotherapy, family and group psychotherapy, ward activities and community meetings, recreational and occupational therapy, a therapeutic school program (where applicable), and medication.

THE WARD GROUP: STRUCTURAL FEATURES

The hospital inpatient service is administratively subdivided into three units, each of which comprises three ward groups to which both patients and staff are assigned by unit leadership. Thus, each patient belongs to a unit and, within that unit, to a ward group—a small, open-ended group typically consisting of five to eight patients, three to five nurses or psychiatric aides, a co-leader, and a designated leader who serves as ward group administrator. Patients are assigned to their ward group immediately upon admission. As a rule, the assignment is made simply in terms of open patient slots within the unit's groups, although considerations of patient mix (e.g., gender and diagnosis), group needs, and group leadership characteristics may at times influence the placement of a patient in a ward group. Most ward groups, therefore, tend to be heterogeneous as regards patients' levels of functioning and may be thought of as "team" rather than "level" groups (Yalom, 1983).

Once assigned to a ward group, a patient is rarely moved to another one except in the event of a transfer to another unit. Groups are co-led. The ward group administrator, usually a fourth-year psychiatric resident or a postdoctoral psychology fellow, is expected to serve as group leader for one year. The group co-leader, who is a member of either the nursing or the social work staff, generally remains in the group for as long as he or she works on the unit. Similarly, the other staff assigned to a ward group remain quite constant over time, especially the nursing staff.

Ward groups meet for fifty-minute sessions three times a week.

Attendance for patients is mandatory; nursing staff attend whenever they are on duty. Both the co-leader and the administrator are expected to attend all group sessions. At times, this can mean that no nursing staff will be present.

In general, clinical leaders and nursing staff meet briefly before a session to highlight what might be expected to arise during the meeting in view of ongoing events on the unit or in the hospital (e.g., elopements, acts of violence, program or personnel changes) and to make more or less explicit plans for how to deal with such issues. For most groups, too, there is a brief wrap-up session for staff immediately after each meeting. In addition, all ward group staffs review their patients systematically in a variety of clinical settings, including biweekly floor staff meetings, monthly roundings, and semiannual treatment reviews. Moreover, three types of supervision occur. (1) Administrative supervision is provided by unit chiefs for ward group administrators; these half-hour supervisory sessions may include the chief resident and head nurse or some other leadership constellation. (2) Clinical supervision is conducted by faculty members in senior hospital positions during weekly unit-based hour-long group supervision sessions for all ward group administrators and co-leaders. (3) Team supervision, led by the ward group administrator during which the nursing staff and clinical leadership of the group address issues affecting their working relationships (e.g., reviewing disagreements over the handling of specific patients or situations).

THE WARD GROUP IN RELATION TO THE UNIT AND THE HOSPITAL

One way to examine the systemic relationships among the ward group, the unit, and the hospital is to consider the group boundaries. While various boundaries in outpatient group therapy can more easily be maintained by the leaders as relatively distinct and well-defined, inpatient group boundaries inevitably are less clear and more difficult for leaders to manage (Klein, 1981, 1983; Rice and Rutan, 1981; Yalom, 1983). It may be useful, therefore, to look at how ward group boundaries are drawn and maintained, and how transactions across these boundaries are regulated. We will begin with an examination of membership, confidentiality, questions of space and time and ward group identity. The complex issues involving considerations of task boundaries will then be addressed in greater detail.

Membership

As noted earlier, each group is assigned its team of patients, staff, and leaders by the leadership of the unit. Just as the Unit Chief is obliged to accept whichever patients the Director of Admissions and the Director of Inpatient Services assign to the unit, so too the group must accept those patients and staff assigned to it. The groups themselves have little or no control over who becomes a member (except through informal lobbying efforts with the unit leadership). When there are especially marked discrepancies between patients' levels of functioning, groups struggle with the problem of finding a way of working that does not exclude members for prolonged periods. Thus, although the membership boundary is quite clearly defined, the authority to regulate transactions across this important boundary does not reside with the group leadership.

Confidentiality

The management of information is a very complex matter. As a psychodynamically oriented therapy group focused on the here and now, the ward group asks of its members, both patients and staff, that what is said during meetings remains confidential. However, unlike the members of an outpatient group who disperse until the next meeting, hospitalized patients live together virtually twenty-four hours a day. What happens on the unit often is brought into the group (e.g., when a member has been bullying other patients, or when patients have a grievance against a staff member); conversely, what happens in the group frequently is brought out into the unit (e.g., when drug use or a plan to elope is exposed during a meeting). Further, as noted above, patients know that staff regularly report to each other salient issues that arise in groups, that relevant themes are charted for each patient, and, on one unit, that patients themselves regularly present notes on group meetings to the patient-run floor council.

Clearly, the concept of confidentiality applicable to typical outpatient groups applies to the ward group only in a very relative sense. Since patients are aware of all these exchanges of information, it is fair to say that, in accord with hospital policy, privileged information is shared in the service of providing sound integrated clinical care. Further, the authority for determining this policy does not reside with the group leadership but with the hospital administration. Leaders, however, are responsible for monitoring transactions across the group boundary that involve confidential information.

Space and Time

By contrast, the boundary defining the where and when of ward group meetings is rather tightly drawn and well-protected. The unit leadership assigns to each group the time and location of its meeting. The unit rarely will schedule an event that competes with ward group meetings or request that a group move from its customary assigned space. Further, staff usually attempt to make group meeting times their highest scheduling priority. Individuals' scheduling conflicts generally appear to be resolved in favor of group attendance—this with the explicit support of the hospital administration and unit leadership. Patients' activities and even home passes quite typically are planned with the group schedule in mind, and great pressure is brought to bear on patients when they resist attending a given meeting. It has happened, for instance, that patients who refuse to get out of bed find the entire group ensconced on their bedroom floor. Also, failure to attend group may lead to loss of status and privileges. Finally, staff who are not assigned to group are generally quite circumspect and apologetic about interrupting or intruding into meetings and will do so only for serious reasons. Thus, the authority for regulating transactions across this boundary resides with the unit leadership and is largely delegated to the group leaders.

The ward group, then, is very clearly demarcated in terms of membership and space and time boundaries, and somewhat less so regarding confidentiality. These boundaries are supported at all levels of organization within the hospital. Authority for boundary management, however, is vested not only in group leaders but in other members of the unit and hospital leadership. Further, breaches of any of those boundaries usually signify the existence of serious issues disturbing an individual patient, the ward group, or the unit. For example, a female borderline patient who was tied to a bed after seriously injuring herself screamed incessantly with the intention, clearly articulated, of preventing the group meeting from occurring. Significantly, she had just lost her individual therapist, the ward group's previous administrator had just stepped aside (this was the new administrator's first ward group meeting), and the unit had just been assigned a new chief resident. An issue of concern for her, as well as for other patients, was whether they were going to be taken care of adequately. This concern was addressed both verbally and nonverbally; it was interpreted, and then the group was moved to another setting, well away from the disruptive patient.

Ward Group Identity

Each ward group is identified by its administrator's surname, which is used by staff to give the locus of a patient's treatment on the unit ("Let's see, Tom is in Dr. B.'s group. Check with her about his privileges"). This label becomes a facet of each patient's social identity (new patients quickly will be categorized by other patients according to their group assignment). Ward groups have histories in the hospital culture, and events of note are located in the rich lore of collective memory in terms of who the group administrator was at the time of their occurrence.

Like the healthy family, the group provides a rather consistent, somewhat predictable organized context within which patients may learn about and change their social identities. The group serves initially as a means for engaging patients in the overall treatment process, and functions as a kind of home base from which patients can begin to explore issues of attachment, separation, and the experience of belonging.

Task Boundaries

Ward group task boundaries are complex and difficult to define. In an effort to clarify matters, we will first consider the group as an administrative unit and then as a therapeutic enterprise.

The ward group as administrative unit. The ward group administrator is responsible for the day-to-day case management and for integrating the efforts of all staff who are working with any of the patients in his or her group. The group serves as the primary vehicle through which the hospital's treatment approach is implemented. Patients' treatment plans are developed by their ward group staff and administrator under the direction of the unit chief (and often the chief resident, in consultation with the head nurse), who in turn take direction from the Director of the Inpatient Service and the Clinical Director of the hospital. In effect, then, the ward group administrator is at the base of a pyramidal hierarchy of clinical and medical responsibility for the patients, and is identified both on the unit and hospital-wide as the individual most immediately commissioned to govern the conditions of the patient's treatment.

On the most practical, often pressing level of clinical management, the administrator is called upon during group sessions to make decisions involving such matters as patients' statuses and privileges, passes, medications, school attendance, participation in special events, and so on. The authority to perform this work is institutionally conferred. This also provides an opportunity for the administrator to learn about the dilemmas associated with assuming and exercising clinical and administrative authority. Regularly scheduled meetings between group administrators and unit chiefs maintain the line of authority and serve as a vehicle through which the unit chief can provide administrative supervision.

The ward group as therapy group. The ward group is explicitly assigned the task of providing patients group therapy three times weekly. To promote this task, leaders are encouraged to adopt a support-oriented psychoanalytic approach that emphasizes the here-and-now and promotes increased coping, growth, and mastery (Klein, 1979, 1983; Yalom, 1983). This approach reflects the integration of a general systems perspective as well as a developmental approach rooted in object relations theory. The general systems perspective holds that the dynamics of the psychiatric unit bear directly on the small-group process, and that a total treatment approach must consider three dynamic levels of experience: the intrapsychic level of each individual patient, the processes of interaction within the small group at the interpersonal and group-as-a-whole levels, and corresponding relationships vis-à-vis the dynamics of the unit and the hospital (Klein, 1977, 1981; Kibel, 1981; Klein and Kugel, 1981). From this perspective, the small therapy group is usefully regarded as a subgroup of the larger psychiatric unit, which reflects all the tensions within the total unit system. Important interactions involving staff and patients ultimately are mirrored in transactions within the small group. Similarly, unresolved dynamic and structural issues within the unit as a whole and its relation to the hospital also find expression within this small group. From an object relations perspective, the small ward group provides an opportunity for patients to test out fears, wishes, and expectations (however distorted or realistic) regarding the staff and other patients that are based on severely distorted self- and object representations and on primitive mental mechanisms which patients (and sometimes staff, especially under conditions of heightened stress) rely on to protect themselves (Kernberg, 1976). The reenactment of pathologically distorted as well as healthy and adaptive interpersonal relationships becomes a major focus for examination. To promote this task, leaders attempt to establish a group climate that will enable members to examine who is doing what to whom, for what reasons, and with what consequences.

One factor that considerably complicates the phenomenon of the group is that it is an internally differentiated, multifunctional enterprise whose tasks are defined both implicitly and explicitly, and at times appear to be in conflict. To this complex picture we now turn our thoughts.

THE SIMULTANEOUS PURSUIT OF MULTIPLE TASKS IN THE WARD GROUP

In the context of a university hospital setting, the ward group, like other therapeutic modalities, is often caught up in the simultaneous pursuit of multiple tasks (Newton and Levinson, 1973). Thus, the hospital is engaged in patient care activities, teaching and training, research, and maintaining its financial viability. Clearly, each task may be assigned different priorities by the hospital staff, and these priorities may change as a function of time and circumstance. Periodically, conflicting and even incompatible demands may be placed on those responsible for accomplishing these tasks and can be important factors influencing the emergence of countertransference.

With regard to the ward group, experience dictates that leaders find the greatest difficulty in the simultaneous pursuit of two interrelated aspects of patient care: administrative decision making and reflective-exploratory work, both of which are to be implemented within the same small-group context. Thus, the traditional therapy subtask (i.e., examination of individual patients' deployment of primitive object relations and associated modes of defense in the social field of the hospital) might best be accomplished by the leaders systematically examining with patients their interpersonal experiences within the small group. Exploratory examination of patients' impacts on the immediate social system works best with a "neutral" leader, a supportive group atmosphere, and an appropriate level of group structure. A group that is too restrictive or rigid interferes with the full development and examination of patients' pathological object relations. Conversely, one that is too unstructured and amorphous may make complete examination of the patients' interpersonal field impossible. The leadership style, the structural format, and the group climate should promote free and open communication and interaction among all staff and patient participants, and should encourage staff members to use their psychological understanding, technical skills, and personalities to maximize the patients' opportunities for meaningful human relations (Kernberg, 1976). Exploring patients' interactions serves as a means for integrating their experiences in the total social field of the hospital, on the unit, in the small-group setting, and even in their individual psychotherapy sessions.

However, from the viewpoint of hospital treatment, the ward group does not conveniently fit into this "therapy group" category. It is neither exclusively a task group organized to carry out tasks involving interchange with the environment, nor a traditional psychotherapy group in which the only task is the examination of psychological developments within the group for the purpose of treating the psychopathology of the members. While the very nature of any small group contributes to the activation within it of primitive object relations and related defenses, the ward group is also geared to task performance. It is vitally concerned with the negotiation of individual and group needs within the hospital, and with the intergroup relationships involved, especially those between patients and staff. This focus clearly involves an examination of the control functions of the patients' egos.

Further, the group administrator carries out a particular boundary function between the hospital as a social system and the individual patient as an open system. Insofar as the group administrator is called on to make decisions concerning patients' lives, he or she is no longer in a neutral role. In formulating and implementing treatment plans, the administrator and the staff assume management functions for the patients. While this clearly implies the abandonment of neutrality in a technical sense, we believe that this shift (from neutral consultant to manager) is necessary when dealing with severely disturbed patients such as those seen in a typical tertiary care setting. As observed by Kernberg (1976), "It is an aspect of the medical—indeed humanitarian—ethic that we 'take over' for a patient whose control function has broken down and who would, psychologically (and sometimes physically), die if we did not move in" (p. 262). In such circumstances, the group administrator becomes a hospital administrator for severely regressed, not infrequently psychotic patients, including many whose primary diagnosis is severe personality disturbance.

To meet this challenge, the YPI maintains a therapist/administrator (T/A) split with regard to the role of the individual therapist, but not to that of the group leader. The individual therapist's role in this system is a "neutral" one, without authority to make or to implement administrative decisions, whereas the ward group leader's role combines both administrative and psychotherapeutic functions. Many clinicians who conduct inpatient treatment assume roles similar to YPI's ward group leaders. Typically, the psychiatrist (or psychiatric resident) must manage patients and attend to the milieu while also performing certain therapeutic functions. This is what the A of the T/A split does in our setting. In other settings, decision making usually is done in staff meetings where patients are not present. Yet similar pressures are felt by such staff and, more particularly, by the team leader.

It is important to note two critical consequences that result from this alteration of the therapist's "neutral" role. First, locating the authority to make clinical administrative decisions in the role of the group leader invariably heightens the attention members ordinarily devote to the exercise of the leader's authority. This consequence provides certain additional opportunities for treatment, since many of these patients have histories of chronic difficulty in dealing with people in positions of authority and/or serious problems in assuming responsibility and exercising authority over themselves. In either case, the opportunity to closely observe, interact with, and learn from (as well as identify with) a person capable of assuming and exercising decision making authority in a rational manner can be enormously helpful.

A second consequence of the deviation from a purely neutral role by the group leader is that it becomes much more difficult to distinguish transference phenomena from reality-based responses to the leader when in fact the leader makes decisions that tangibly affect the patients' lives. In turn, this complicates the leader's task of teasing out countertransference issues from reality-based emotional responses to individual patients and group phenomena.

Thus, group leaders (and staff) simultaneously are involved in diagnosing and treating patients' difficulties with control (ego) functions, as well as their problems with the internal world of object relations. This includes the ways in which these distorted relations and the defenses associated with them are manifested in the course of the patients' interpersonal interactions in the group.

Faced with the ward group as a vehicle for treatment, patients often feel confronted by a difficult dilemma with regard to how much of their thoughts, feelings, and behavior to reveal and discuss in the group. After all, the leaders are empowered with administrative decision making functions that have direct, immediate consequences for patients' care and status. For example, openly discussing violations of hospital rules involving the use of illicit drugs or alcohol may give rise to important opportunities to explore attitudes held toward people in authority, but may well result in unwelcome changes in clinical status and privileges.

In an effort to deal with these complexities, group leaders and their patients typically resort to a variety of strategies. Many groups, for example, designate one of their three weekly meetings as "status day," during which administrative decisions are negotiated, and reserve the remaining two sessions primarily for more traditional therapy tasks. Of course, the same people participate in all sessions, and consequently such task boundaries, like many others in working with severely disturbed patients, are difficult to preserve. The peremptory, urgent nature of patients' needs, coupled with their faulty ego controls, often serve to blur the task focus. Further, group administrators frequently are required to make immediate management decisions regardless of the schedule for group sessions.

Another solution often involves an attempt to split clinical-administrative from traditional therapy tasks. This solution typically takes one of two forms: (1) the group administrator consciously decides to meet individually with patients outside the group in order to arrive at management decisions, thereby enabling the group to devote all its sessions to "therapy" tasks; or (2) patients persistently seek out available administrators to negotiate their individual requests and demands in private, away from the scrutiny of other patients and staff. Of course, the content of these individual sessions, whether planned by the administrator or initiated by the patient, may also be devoted to personal (therapeutic) concerns, with the group sessions then used exclusively for clinical administration. In either case, however, careful examination often reveals the presence of unconscious transferential and countertransferential feelings motivating such tactics. Frequently it becomes clear that the family dynamics of individuals (whether patients, staff, or leaders) are stimulated by interactions within the ward group and are being unconsciously enacted. These include conflicts about the exercise of authority; concerns about one's personal role or status; anxiety regarding the nature of the relationships which are formed; the desire to be the "good parent" or "favorite child"; rivalries and dissension among staff members; and difficulties in sharing or trusting. It is useful, therefore, to urge both patients and staff to bring significant extragroup contacts back into the ward group for examination. This is especially important since it preserves the group as a container that can collect, hold, and process data that might otherwise escape attention.

For the group administrator, learning to effectively manage the complex interplay between these two subtasks is to a significant extent linked with learning to use available resources, particularly the staff members assigned to the ward group. Staff members can be employed by the leader to serve as additional eyes and ears both in the group and on the unit, to facilitate boundary maintenance and limit setting, to sort out complicated transference-countertransference reactions, and to work with the continual undercurrents of potential chaos, fragmentation, and despair that threaten to disrupt or overwhelm groups of severely disturbed patients. The group administrator must determine the extent to which authority in various areas will be delegated to team members, including the co-leader. The specific role of the co-leader may involve anything from presiding in the group administrator's absence, to having limited administrative or leadership authority. Team meetings can be used to clarify task and role definitions, to resolve differences, to teach, to provide mutual supervision, and to attend to and to gratify felt needs. All these issues require examination in order to insure collaborative working relationships. Thus, the group leader needs to learn the unique assets and liabilities of the staff, how best to deploy these individuals, and how to work effectively with both the ward group as a whole and the staff as a subgroup within it.

In addition, the leader must learn how to represent the ward group to other staff on the unit. Adequate lines of authority and communication must be maintained between the ward group and the unit, a requirement that is particularly necessary when a patient group member is behaving disruptively on the unit and other staff are insisting that the ward group administrator "do something" immediately to remedy the situation. Like the head of a family, the administrator may be held accountable (at times unwittingly and unreasonably) for the behavior of a patient in his or her group. Other staff must be properly informed about the treatment plan for that particular patient and assisted in formulating responses consistent with that plan.

TREATMENT FUNCTIONS IN WARD GROUPS

We believe it useful to think of the ward group as the hospital-based functional counterpart of the family when trying to understand crucial factors in long-term inpatient treatment of individuals with severe personality disorders. Thus, in the group, patients are faced with the task of learning to function effectively in the presence of "siblings" (other patients and perhaps some students or psychiatric aides) and "parents" (principally the co-leaders but sometimes other staff members). The group serves as the context within which, among other things, patients are able to review and negotiate individual statuses and limits, plan activities and outings, examine the nature and quality of intragroup interpersonal relationships, and begin to comprehend the implications of being a citizen of the group, the unit, and the hospital. Such work requires that patients be able to delay immediate gratification, acquire the verbal skills necessary for participation, maintain frustration tolerance, and learn to exercise appropriate planning and social judgment. They must try to engage with others, share their experiences, develop their capacities for observation and introspection, develop their abilities to represent themselves and to present their requests in a convincing fashion, and learn to live within established norms and rules.

Many of these tasks closely resemble those of enculturation and socialization accomplished within the context of a normal family. Most patients, however, have histories of family disengagement, rigidity, fragmentation, or enmeshment, and of severe disruptions of socially adaptive boundary maintenance. Exposing patients to the more rational and constructive exercise of authority aimed at maintaining boundaries that enable the group to work effectively serves to relieve and stabilize internal states of confusion, disorganization, and chaos engendered initially in the contexts of patients' families. It also presents patients with a series of models (other patients and staff) who can be imitated, identified with, and eventually internalized. Thus, provided that a climate of openness, tolerance, support, adaptive flexibility, and exploration can be established, the group may begin, along with the ward and the hospital itself, to promote the development of some of the fundamental executive ego and superego controls that patients failed to acquire within their own families. Further, the development in the group of a stable holding environment, one that permits and contains the expression of the split-off unacceptable parts of its members, sets the stage for the eventual (re)assembly and (re)integration of the self. Under such conditions, where the self can be defined in relational terms, patients can begin to explore, in relation to both peers and to persons in authority, their distorted self- and object introjects and their chronically poor interpersonal relationships.

Viewed from this perspective, although the "neutral" role of the group administrator is clearly altered, rigorous distinctions between the subtasks of clinical administrative "management" and more traditional reflective-exploratory "therapy" become somewhat artificial. Addressing management issues involves the simultaneous performance of supportive therapy. Exercising authority or control in collaboration with and on behalf of these patients—to assist them in effectively identifying their needs, negotiating with others, and maintaining more adaptive boundary regulation—is inextricably linked to bolstering their faltering ego and superego functions. This is an integral part of their hospital treatment. Provided that patients are invited and encouraged to become active participants and that attention is devoted to the processes affecting the exercise of this clinical administrative authority (i.e., the patient's intrapsychic condition plus the interpersonal, group, unit, and hospital dynamics involved in the decision), this work clearly falls within the domain of "therapy."

Similarly, in conducting any form of "therapy" one is immediately and intimately involved in "management" considerations. Decisions must be made from the instant one sees the patient about what will be treated, how, when, where, etc. In the ward group, staff members focus on certain issues and not on others, adopt a particular format, deploy their resources, define their roles, and develop various lines of authority and communication. All of these "management" decisions involving articulation and maintenance of boundaries enable "therapy" to be conducted and, in fact, are central to the process itself. Indeed, the very act of choosing to examine a particular aspect of what a patient may be expressing during a group session, and then attempting to negotiate a shared focus of attention, clearly involves the exercise of managerial authority.

Further, we believe that successful treatment of severely disturbed adolescents and young adults hinges on helping them gradually assume increasing responsibility for managing their own lives. Over the course of treatment, managerial authority for regulating

patients' lives, assumed initially by the staff at the outset of hospitalization, must be gradually returned or transferred on an interpersonal level. Thus, the ward group, with its dual focus, is the
cornerstone of our approach to hospital treatment.

However, while the ward group may serve a crucial treatment
integration function and may derive much of its therapeutic benefit
from providing something equivalent to a corrective family experience, it also presents extremely perplexing problems for both leaders
and members. A fundamental aspect of these problems involves
countertransference reactions, to which we will now turn our attention.

COUNTERTRANSFERENCE ISSUES

To begin with, some definition of countertransference is in
order. Specifically, we adopt a "holistic" definition whereby countertransference is regarded as the total emotional reaction of the
therapist to the patient in the treatment situation (Kernberg, 1975).
This view holds that certain strong emotional "objective reactions"
(Winnicott, 1947) can indeed be elicited in the therapist on a relatively
universal basis; these appear to follow from the extreme manifestations of patients' behavior toward the therapist. Further, we believe
that such countertransference reactions can inform the therapeutic
work by providing important clues as to the nature of patients'
pathological internal object relations and their characteristic ways of
relating to others in the world around them.

The countertransference issues routinely encountered by inpatient group therapists are often deeply disturbing, prolonged, and not
subject to easy resolution (Hannah, 1984). Many of these issues,
difficult to verbalize and to admit into consciousness, are preoedipal
in nature. Generally they represent our warts, not our beautiful parts.
Though the variations are infinite, four major preoedipal countertransference themes are frequently in evidence: (1) fears of being
attacked, injured, or killed by a patient or a group of patients, or (as
a result of their use of forceful projective modes of defense or the
collapse of one's own defensive resolutions) wishes and fears regarding the expression or enactment of an unacceptable level of aggression toward a patient; (2) fears that one will become the object of
patients' intense oral needs and in the process be drained, devoured,
and eventually discarded; (3) fears that one will succumb to patients'

madness and primitive modes of defense, resulting in the loss of one's boundaries, allegiance to reality, adaptive function, and personal and professional identity; and (4) fears that the patients' situation is utterly hopeless or, conversely, wishes that although parents and other mental health professionals have repeatedly failed, one will nonetheless succeed in understanding, rescuing, and even curing the patient, and that one will gain the recognition and gratitude one so richly deserves. Obviously, these four themes are related to the major dynamic issues mobilized in both patients and staff during the intensive treatment process: enormous rage; intense struggles for control; primitive orality; fears of attachment and closeness; threats to boundary maintenance and self-preservation; and narcissistic needs for omnipotence, omniscience, and fame. Further, as a result of the failure of patients' reality-oriented ego functions, the therapist/administrator, in particular, is often called on to provide these missing adaptive ego functions. In the YPI, he or she must explain reality, set limits, and, especially for hospitalized adolescents and young adults, act *in loco parentis* without being drawn into the patient's internal drama and unwittingly becoming the patient's "loco" parent.

Our aim in this section, however, is not to provide an exhaustive catalogue of commonly encountered countertransference issues and the defenses typically used to cope with them; many admirable efforts in this direction have already appeared in the literature, with regard to work with both schizophrenics (e.g., Winnicott, 1947; Searles, 1966) and borderline and narcissistically disturbed patients (e.g., Kernberg, 1976; Roth, 1980; Kibel, 1981; Meissner, 1984). Instead we will try to identify the sources of countertransference issues to the ward group, a mode of treatment intervention that combines administrative decision making with psychotherapeutic functions.

Staff-Induced Countertransference

In order to address these concerns, it is important to emphasize that in ward groups, as in systems generally, the old adage well applies: the whole is greater than the sum of its parts. The full range of concerns of individual members is often amplified and augmented in the group. Individuals often feel stimulated and provoked in the presence of others. Encouragement, both overt and covert, to act out one's concerns often leads to lapses in control and to transient regressive episodes. The unpredictable nature of the group and the prospect of facing angry, needy patients without adequate support from the rest of the staff often arouses in group leaders fantasies about Christians and lions, and the prospect of some primitive cannibalistic catastrophe.

Despite the fact that the group has a consistent, long-term membership and is not routinely disrupted by the comings and goings of patients and staff members, it is nevertheless subject to continuous regressive shifts and unpredictable alternations in adaptive level of functioning. Hence, the development of the group and the establishment of constructive norms proceeds very slowly, indeed at times imperceptibly. Leading such a group is like participating in a marathon, with all the perils, loneliness, and exhaustion experienced by the long-distance runner. Staff working with such severely disturbed patients often work in an atmosphere of depression, in which they feel hopeless, negative, and starved for affection and recognition (Cooper, 1978). The notion of "staff burnout" is relevant here. In this setting particularly, to rely on one's patients for gratification is risky business; it is likely to result in countertransference problems that are very difficult to resolve. In large measure this reflects the fact that these patients have so little capacity to give much back emotionally. Treaters are often left to wonder whether anything they are doing in the group is beneficial or, for that matter, has any meaning at all for many of the patients.

Although the hospital is offered as a means toward psychological integration for patients, it frequently stimulates their already helpless or fearful attitudes toward authority, attitudes based on internalized object images of parental origin (Kibel, 1978; Rice and Rutan, 1981; Klein, 1983). Patients in such a regressed dependent state express not only intense oral longings but enormous aggression and threats of violence. Under continuous emotional assault from their patients, staff are required to provide patients' missing ego functions despite the fact that they may themselves feel vulnerable and deprived. Small wonder that frequently they find themselves caught up in patient concerns about trust, abandonment, and retaliation; these mirror their own concerns about compromised autonomy and the inadequate support, recognition, and gratification they receive from their superiors.

Precisely what patients attribute to staff in the way of deprivation, anticipated punishment, and reprisals, staff often attribute to the administration. This process is augmented by the misuse of empathy, resulting in the arousal of concordant identifications (Racker, 1968) among staff members; these frequently can be understood as a consequence of staff efforts to defend against and to deflect the full force of their patients' rage. In effect, staff members seem to say: "We are in this together; but it is not staff who are depriving and punishing; it is 'them,' the administration!" Thus, staff too frequently feel abandoned, enraged, helpless, and overwhelmed in the face of intensely needy and severely disturbed patients. Feeling thrown to the wolves is not uncommon. Working in these conditions, it is tempting indeed for staff to "side with" patients.

Factors Affecting Staff-Induced Countertransference

Two major factors can be implicated in staff-induced stimulation of countertransferential feelings in the leader through interactions with other staff in the group context: (a) the multiplicity of professional and paraprofessional disciplines, and (b) formal and informal authority relationships. Naturally, these are intimately interrelated and amplify each other's impact on the leader.

The multiplicity of professional and paraprofessional disciplines. In outlining the structural features of the ward group, we described the diverse professional and paraprofessional positions typically represented on the staff; these include psychiatric resident or psychology postdoctoral fellow (leader), social worker or social work student (co-leader), nurses, psychiatric aides, and (in some groups) recreation staff. Differential status based on membership in a particular professional discipline is a fact of life. Individual staff bring with them societally endorsed differences in power, prestige, prerogatives, and pay. Such differences can stimulate competition, greed, envy, and jealousy, as well as defensive efforts to conceal, contain, distort, and deny such reactions. To the extent that these matters are experienced but not examined during the course of the staff's work together, they tend to be enacted, often in unconscious and disruptive ways.

Further, the specific roles occupied by individual staff members within the group are institutionally defined in accord with professional discipline, not necessarily clinical talent or suitability. Nominally, the staff is under the direction of the designated leader (a psychiatric resident or psychology fellow), who is held administratively accountable for what happens in the group and for individual patient members outside the group. However, it is the nurses and aides who have the most frequent contact with the patients, and who normally have the best sense of a patient's daily functioning and state of mind. Typically, frontline nursing staff are very highly stressed and often feel put upon and unappreciated (especially when they become containers for the unacceptable split off feelings of severely disturbed patients). Within the group they can subtly communicate to the leader their aggrieved feelings through such devices as speaking for patients, withholding critical information that would affect a decision, nonverbally undercutting the leader's spoken statements, subtly distancing themselves from decisions made by the group or the leader, acting confused or as if they did not have information or were not privy to decision making processes outside the group, and so on. When this happens the individuals involved are usually minimally aware of what they are doing; nevertheless, these maneuvers involving projective identification (Ogden, 1979) induce in the leader very unpleasant feelings, whose source is at times very difficult to identify, especially if the leader seeks their origins exclusively in patient-generated dynamics. In one group for example, nursing staff repeatedly failed fully to implement treatment plans that seemed "too complicated" to them, even when they had helped in their design. Hence, the plans repeatedly failed, and the leader felt demoralized and helpless—until finally the dynamic was identified and discussed. After this the nursing staff was able to identify other contributory stressors, such as the recent departure of the head nurse, which had left them feeling demoralized.

The social worker or social work student who acts as co-leader may also cause countertransferential difficulties for the leader. First of all, ambiguity in the terminology of leadership labels ("leader" and "co-leader") suggests an institutionally sanctioned evasion of forthright acknowledgment of a hierarchical aspect to the relationship (why not "leader" and "assistant leader"?). Thus, a false, "as-if" egalitarianism is promoted that is discredited constantly by the daily administrative decisions of the leader. This structurally induced cognitive dissonance (Festinger, Rieken, and Schacter, 1956) tends to be ignored, rationalized, denied, or affectively split off—giving both leaders and co-leaders countless opportunities to act out unconscious resentments, devaluations, or jealousies.

To the degree that these staff issues are clearly identified and explicitly discussed, staff-induced countertransference issues in the leader are minimized and the staff functions in relative harmony.

However, when this is not the case, the leader can become overwhelmed with powerful thoughts and feelings that disturb ego functioning, assault self-esteem, and severely compromise task performance. Effective supervision then becomes essential to rectifying what can at times become a bewildering and terrifying process with a high likelihood that iatrogenic problems will erupt in patients.

Formal and informal authority relationships. Formally, in terms of the administrative delegation of responsibility and authority to make decisions, the ward group leader is "in charge." This means that he or she is expected to make decisions regarding the treatment of patients, decisions that often have consequences for other staff. For instance, a decision to withhold cigarettes or permission to go on an outing may subject the nursing staff to barrages of rage from a nicotine-deprived patient or force them to tackle and restrain an eloping patient who wishes to go on a field trip. Hence, staff are wont to reserve judgment on decisions made by the leader, and to feel critical when things go wrong.

The situation is complicated when the leader is a trainee (a resident or postdoctoral fellow) who quite possibly has had less clinical experience (particularly on a long-term inpatient unit) than the co-leader and many of the nursing staff. The leader is quite obviously dependent on the accumulated clinical knowledge and wisdom of the nursing staff, and on the co-leader's experience with inpatient groups. Further, though formally they are beneath the ward group leader administratively, permanent staff members have often won well-deserved respect and informal authority from peers, ward leadership, and even high-level hospital administrators. In a real conflict of opinion, a trainee leader may lose or may win only a Pyrrhic victory.

Many indeed are the unconscious responses of leaders to this double-bind situation, from which, on an inpatient unit, there is literally no escape. Denial, splitting, projection, projective identification, and other notably primitive defenses are engendered in otherwise high functioning and mature leaders. Thus, for example, leaders have been known to foment conflict among staff by pitting members against each other through unconsciously slanting and selecting what to tell whom (and how to tell it); they may convince themselves that they had not been privy to critical information that in fact had been communicated explicitly; and a very few, in the context of feeling persecuted by their staff or by ward leadership, have even called "secret" group meetings of patients without informing other staff. Such behavior almost always is explicable as regression in the face of the double bind in authority relationships, and when thus interpreted to a floundering leader, generally stops.

Factors Outside the Group: Role Strain within the Institutional Context

Within the context of the university hospital, issues of role strain are apparent in the form of conflicted internalized values among staff. We and others have explored elsewhere in greater detail the fact that the university hospital system is engaged in the simultaneous pursuit of multiple and at times incompatible tasks (e.g., Kernberg, 1976; Klein, 1977). These include the teaching, clinical care, research, and financial tasks, all of which are critical to our existence. Although most organizations attempt to protect individual members from being caught up in the pursuit of conflicting tasks by carefully defining their particular roles and insuring appropriate layering within the organizational context, it is not unusual for a single individual to occupy several different roles within a single organization. Individual members often experience role strain arising from the ways in which different roles, and the values implicitly associated with them, are socially endorsed and maintained (Brown and Klein, 1985). Here we wish to focus on four specific aspects of the role of ward group leader that are likely to arouse countertransference reactions.

Identifying and settling for small gains. What is critical to remember here is that we are talking about leading a group composed of severely impaired patients, most of whom are likely to remain in the YPI for about one year. Almost without exception these patients come from chaotic and disorganized families to which many of the younger patients are likely to return following discharge. In addition, by the time most patients and families get to the YPI, they have already been through several prior hospitalizations and various outpatient treatments, all of which have proven more or less ineffective. Thus, patients and families come to regard the YPI as their last hope. It is a tertiary care institution from which the unsuccessfully treated patient is likely to be transferred into a state hospital facility. In the minds of many (both patients and staff), the YPI offers a last-ditch attempt to promote growth and change.

Nevertheless, since the YPI is oriented to long-term intensive treatment, it is regarded by most insurance carriers as something of an anachronism. Thus, the treatment of virtually every patient in the hospital is under constant review by these third-party payers. Justification for this treatment must be provided in terms of the time, energy, and cost involved. There is, therefore, a strong pull to identify suitably lofty and comprehensive goals.

All those involved in the treatment process, including patients, families, and staff, must eventually come to terms with their wishes, hopes, and dreams on the one hand, and certain, at times harsh, realities on the other. Patients need considerable support in their efforts to comprehend realistically the nature and extent of their illnesses and impairments, as do their families, and the implications these will have for their futures. Powerful expressions of grief, despair, and dashed hopes emerge when shared denial begins to give way. Staff must be available to help contain and work through these issues without themselves feeling overwhelmed and burnt out. Given the enormous investment of time, resources, and emotional energy on the part of all those involved in the treatment process, and their needs, wishes, fears, and hopes, plus the external demands for accountability and justification for continuing treatment, it is not surprising that group leaders often find it difficult indeed to identify modest, attainable, realistic goals for treatment. Being able to settle for small gains in their work with patients and families can become linked, because of unresolved countertransference, with a sense of failure and hopelessness.

Confining group business to group. Group leaders, as noted earlier, are responsible for coordinating their patients' treatment plans. They are, of course, faced with the pressing and peremptory nature of the needs experienced by severely disturbed patients whose allegiance to reality, capacity to tolerate frustration and delay of gratification, and ability to plan ahead is severely curtailed. Thus, leaders often feel "under the gun," facing a continuous barrage of patient demands. Further, leaders must deal with the fact that patients have access to them outside of group sessions. For example, patients may pursue leaders going in and out of their offices, talk with them in the cafeteria, etc. Leaders frequently are accosted during an unguarded moment or feel manipulated by higher-functioning patients as these individuals attempt to have their needs met. Faced with insistent demands, leaders may feel reluctant to take on the entire group in a session, for example, that has been set aside to discuss privileges. Instead they may find it easier to give in to various patients who attempt to plead their cases outside the group. Such giving in, of course, may well work against the maintenance of appropriate treatment boundaries, and may involve the violation of implicit or explicit contracts with other staff assigned to the group.

The prospect of the staff being split and pitted against one another readily emerges and often is quite consistent with patients' disturbed object relations. Patients are often in competition with each other for what they perceive to be limited supplies, and each wishes to somehow get on the inside track with the leader and thereby earn the status of "special patient." Attempts to do this inside the group may be quite frightening, whereas more subtle overtures outside the group are often a much safer route for patients to pursue. Leaders, for their part, must struggle with wishes to gratify or punish in ways that can be privately enacted outside the group. To do so publicly inside the group might well risk exposure, cause anxiety, and lead to heightened staff conflict.

Sharing patients. Closely related to these issues is the complicated matter of sharing patients. In dealing with the shared patient, the leader may welcome the support, encouragement, and collaboration of other staff but find it difficult to share either the credit for small therapeutic gains or the attachment and loyalties generated in the course of working with the patient. It is not unusual, for example, for staff members to entertain privately the belief that their work has been especially valuable for a particular patient, that only they truly understand this person, and that other team members are guilty of acting out countertransferences. When dealing with a borderline patient well versed in the use of splitting, it is difficult indeed for the leader to be the "bad object." Like the blind men encountering the elephant, each of whom has direct experience with only a single part of the object, however, the entire staff needs to work together in order to form a more accurate view of patients and the nature of their object relationships.

Sharing responsibility and authority. As described earlier, the ward group leader is held administratively responsible for patient care and is identified as the person who has the authority to make day-to-day decisions governing the provision of care. This aspect of the leader's role often engenders considerable internal conflict around how to remain democratic, fair, and thoughtful. This set of concerns is relevant not only for leaders' relationships with patients and their families, but also for their relationships with staff. In the former instance, leaders act *in loco parentis;* i.e., they are entrusted to exercise significant control over their patients' lives without getting caught up in pathological object relations. Leaders are also asked to remain objective and not fall into the often tempting position of blaming parents and families for the patients' difficulties. Of course patients, ever vigilant, seem uniquely sensitive to any lapses in a fair, thoughtful, and democratic mode of functioning on the part of the leader. They are eager to point out such inconsistencies and to endow them projectively with enormous meaning, often at the expense of the leader's sense of self-esteem.

Leaders must find some way to share responsibility, delegate authority, and communicate to staff that they are important and valued members of a collaborative team approach. Staff members' needs for recognition, appreciation, and narcissistic stroking are often just as important as those of the patients. Nevertheless, leaders often feel pressured to make rapid-fire decisions in the heat of the moment, particularly when one or another crisis is about to unfold. Thus, they are often caught on the horns of a difficult dilemma involving the need to get things done in a timely fashion and the awareness that democracy in action takes time and is not always the most efficient means of resolving problems. Not unlike our own children, patients and staff members are quite observant in circumstances such as these, and most often wind up doing what we do rather than what we say.

In addition, the special training, competence, and experience of the physician leader qualifies that person to take full responsibility for medical management of certain emergency situations. Thus, at one moment the leader may be called on to behave in a rather controlling, autocratic manner, while at the next moment a more democratic orientation may be called for. The leader is likely to experience pressure, however, from patients, from staff, and not least from the superego, to remain absolutely and consistently fair, thoughtful, and democratic. A leader must become neither an absent, passive, or seemingly unconcerned parent-leader, nor an intrusive, controlling, and unpredictable one. These problems are not unlike those faced by others in leadership roles, but the emotional stakes are particularly high here because so much of how leaders implement their roles is open to public scrutiny and evaluation, both inside and outside the group.

Factors Outside the Group: Role Conflict within the Institutional Context

In most institutional contexts, individuals normally will occupy multiple roles and hence organize their behavior in terms of the attendant multiplicity of conventionalized role expectations (norms of behavior associated with each role and status in the prevailing culture). When role expectations conflict too severely, individuals adopt strategies to diminish the attendant internal conflict (Brown and Klein, 1985). Among the well recognized maneuvers described in the literature are procrastination in taking action, conventionalization of behavior, and role segmentation (Merton, 1968). Ward group leaders, who occupy at least two distinct and highly cathected statuses— "therapist" and "administrator"—frequently apply these maneuvers and are minimally conscious of doing so.

In the culture of the hospital, much is made of the Therapist/Administrator (T/A) split. Expectable differences in feelings, perceptions, and attitudes emerge toward patients from their individual therapist, and their group leader. It is widely (but, we believe, naively) held that the former has a deeper understanding of a patient's inner life than has the latter, and hence is likely to have a more well-rounded understanding of the patient. As a result, the individual therapist may be resistant to what seem to be simplistic attempts at behavioral controls put in place by a group leader (who at YPI is also an administrator).

Here we wish to sidestep that argument, rich in clinical import as it is, and point to another T/A split—i.e., the one inside the ward group leader. Every leader we have known has explicitly and inconclusively wrestled with the problem of the conflicting role expectations attached to the simultaneously held dual roles of "group therapist" and "patient administrator." In the former role, the leader is expected to work toward achieving an intimate and facilitative relationship with the patients in the group; in the latter role the leader explicitly occupies a position of social control. How can these two stances be reconciled?

As we have indicated above, if one uses the family as a metaphor for the ward group, this role conflict becomes both comprehensible (it is not inherently "crazy-making," as new leaders are apt to charge) and masterable—in the ways in which similar role conflicts of parenthood are. In the pressurized context of a psychiatric hospital where decisions are public, fast-paced, and reviewed from many different perspectives, and where mistakes may have extremely serious consequences (self-mutilation, elopement, suicide, assaults on other patients or staff), the stakes seem inordinately high, and notable anxiety is a chronic feature of the leader's existence. In this context, then, we would expect defensive maneuvers aimed at diminishing this chronic, institutionally induced role conflict.

Often such maneuvers are misconstrued as simply patient-induced countertransferences—for instance, when a leader procrastinates in putting a treatment plan into place. Supervision that focuses exclusively on the ways in which such inactivity may reflect the leader's painful feelings (hatred, helplessness, despair) toward the patient is likely to be wide of the mark; the procrastination may also be unconsciously intended to punish nursing staff who have been pressing the leader to take quick (and perhaps punitive) action without due deliberation, or it may be expressive of unconscious passive aggression toward the unit chief (possibly for failing to adequately appreciate the difficult task).

Often leaders under severe pressure will conventionalize their behavior; they streamline their actions into a shallow repertoire of well-rehearsed responses to patients, nursing staff, group co-leaders, and unit leadership. They split off affect and resist inner voices and the suggestions of others urging reflection and an acknowledgment of the inherent complexities of the tasks at hand, complexities which, unfortunately, can never be attended to more than partially.

Similarly, role segmentation offers the beleaguered leader temporary refuge from pain. A task can be defined simply in terms of one of the conflicting role demands: "I am not interested in what it means to Robert to search him when he comes back from pass—this is simply an administrative tactic to prevent him from smuggling in drugs." Or: "I will not stop Cheryl from yelling at staff in the ward group by invoking so-called 'responses' (behavioral consequences); this is, after all, group *therapy*." Such stances should erode in the face of constructively critical responses from other staff members or in clinical supervision. Nevertheless, as transient responses to role conflict, they represent severe disturbances of perception, cognition, and affect. Here, too, if these responses are interpreted solely in terms of patient-induced countertransference, the leader will be led to an incomplete understanding of the problem and hence will be severely handicapped in taking corrective measures.

At supervisory and administrative levels, then, serious consideration must be given not only to the level of stress associated with the clinical role we ask our trainees and staff to perform, but also to the nature of the institutional and personal support, protection, and reward systems available. Since continuity of care is so vitally important in the long-term intensive treatment of severely disturbed patients, we must try to screen out unduly self-serving, self-sacrificing, or self-destructive staff members.

Moreover, careful attention must be devoted to the proper education of staff and trainees. This is especially true for those for whom this is but a brief stop in their professional careers, a time-limited subterranean journey into a deep psychic forest where wild and dangerous creatures reside—a journey which, when successfully completed, prepares one for any hazard one might later encounter.

CONCLUDING REMARKS

This chapter describes the ward group, a unique clinical entity that requires a great deal from its leaders. Among other things, its leaders must develop a general systems perspective, an understanding of object relations theory, and a clear conceptualization of their administrative role and the implications it has for the "neutral" therapeutic role. Conducting a ward group requires effective team collaboration and an ability on the part of the leadership to continuously and rapidly assess task priorities, and to shift these in accord with patient needs and levels of functioning. Above all, the ward group requires considerable intellectual and personal flexibility from its clinical leaders, and an ability to understand the awesome diversity of factors operating to induce countertransference feelings, which must be contained, worked through, and used to good clinical effect. For these same reasons the ward group provides a wonderfully rich context for the long-term treatment of severely disturbed psychiatric patients.

Yet, despite the inherent potential and power of the group as a form of treatment intervention, several intriguing questions remain to be resolved. For example, given the complexity of the ward group and the nature of the demands placed upon the participants, how should group administrators and their staffs be selected, prepared, and supervised to implement their roles effectively? Indeed, how well suited are senior psychiatric residents or postdoctoral fellows in psychology, many of whom are in their late twenties or early thirties, unmarried and childless, to act *in loco parentis* for severely disturbed adolescents and young adults? Further, does it make sense for these trainees, who are transient members of the unit, to be trained by more experienced members of the staff and faculty, to assume leadership roles and to be held accountable as the titular heads of ward group families? And, to the extent that various intrastaff tensions exist around status and recognition, plus unresolved problems in authority relations reflected at the institutional level in the "co-leader" designation, are ward groups able to work therapeutically with patients' difficulties in these same areas? Finally, has our sophisticated systems analysis of ward groups far outstripped the technical and theoretical competence of those who are asked to conduct them? Ought we to reconsider the prospect of separating the two major task systems (group therapy and patient administration) pursued by ward groups, or perhaps find some other creative solution whereby they may be implemented together?

Clearly, these and other equally important questions require continuing assessment and evaluation.

REFERENCES

Battegay, R. (1966), Group psychotherapy in the hospital. *Internat. J. Group Psychother.,* 16:270–278.

Brown, S. L., & Klein, R. H. (1985), Role boundary dilemmas: Special problems for women. *J. Amer. Med. Women's Assn.,* 40:181–185

Cooper, E. J. (1978), The pre-group: The narcissistic phase of group development with the severely disturbed patient. In: *Group Therapy,* ed. L. R. Wolberg & M. L. Aronson. New York: Stratton Intercontinental, pp. 60–71.

Cory, T. L., & Page, D. (1978), Group techniques for effecting changes in the more disturbed patient. *Group,* 2:144–155.

Druck, A. B. (1978), The role of didactic group psychotherapy in short-term psychiatric settings. *Group,* 2:98–109.

Edelson, M. (1964), *Ego Psychology, Group Dynamics, and the Therapeutic Community.* New York: Grune & Stratton.

———(1970a), *The Practice of Sociotherapy.* New Haven, CT: Yale University Press.

———(1970b), *Sociotherapy and Psychotherapy.* Chicago: University of Chicago Press.

Farrell, D. (1976), The use of active experiential group techniques with hospitalized patients. In: *Group Therapy,* ed. L. R. Wolberg & M. L. Aronson. New York: Stratton Intercontinental, 1978, pp. 133–141.

Festinger, L., Rieken, H. W., & Schacter, S. (1956), *When Prophesy Fails.* New York: Harper Torch.

Gunderson, J. G., Will, O. A., Jr., & Mosher, L. R. (1983), *Principles and Practice of Milieu Therapy*. New York: Aronson.

Hannah, S. (1984), Countertransference in inpatient group psychotherapy: Implications for technique. *J. Group Psychother.*, 34:257–272.

Kernberg, O. F. (1975), *Borderline Conditions and Pathological Narcissism*. New York: Aronson.

———(1976), *Object Relations Theory and Clinical Psychoanalysis*. New York: Aronson.

Kibel, H. D. (1978), The rationale for the use of group psychotherapy for borderline patients in a short-term unit. *Internat. J. Group Psychother.*, 28:339–358.

———(1981), A conceptual model for short-term inpatient group psychotherapy. *Amer. J. Psychiat.*, 138:74–80.

Klein, R. H. (1977), Inpatient group psychotherapy: Practical considerations and special problems. *Internat. J. Group Psychother.*, 27:201–214.

———(1981), The patient-staff community meeting: A tea party with the Mad Hatter. *Internat. J. Group Psychother.*, 31:205–222.

———(1983), A therapy group for adult inpatients on a psychiatric ward. In: *Handbook of Short-Term Therapy Groups*, ed. M. Rosenbaum. New York: McGraw-Hill, pp. 291–320.

———Kugel, B. (1981), Inpatient group psychotherapy from a systems perspective: Reflections through a glass darkly. *Internat. J. Group Psychother.*, 31:311–328.

Maxmen, J. S. (1978), An educative model for inpatient group therapy. *Internat. J. Group Psychother.*, 28:321–338.

Meissner, W. W. (1984), *The Borderline Spectrum*. New York: Aronson.

Merton R. K. (1968), *Social Theory and Social Structure*, rev. ed. New York: Free Press.

Newton, P. M., & Levinson, D. J. (1973), The work group within the organization: A sociopsychological approach. *Psychiat.*, 36:115–142.

Ogden, T. H. (1979), On projective identification. *Internat. J. Psycho-Anal.*, 60:357–373.

Racker, H. (1968), *Transference and Countertransference*. New York: International Universities Press.

Rice, C. A., & Rutan, J. S. (1981), Boundary maintenance in inpatient therapy groups. *Internat. J. Group Psychother.*, 31:297–309.

Roth, B. (1980), Understanding the development of a homogeneous, identity-impaired group through countertransference phenomena. *Internat. J. Group Psychother.*, 30:405–426.

Searles, H. (1966), Feelings of guilt in the psychoanalyst. In: *Countertransference and Related Subjects*. New York: International Universities Press, 1979, pp. 28–35.

Winnicott, D. W. (1947), Hate in the countertransference. In: *Collected Papers: Through Pediatrics to Psycho-Analysis*. New York: Basic Books, 1958, pp. 194–203.

Yalom, I. D. (1983), *Inpatient Group Psychotherapy*. New York: Basic Books.

12

The Inpatient Psychotherapy Group as a Testing Ground for Theory

HOWARD D. KIBEL, M.D.

Patients with severe character pathology have a wide range of symptomatic, personality, and behavioral disturbances. Descriptively, they may be diagnosed as suffering from certain affective disorders (major depression, dysthymia, or cyclothymia), many of the anxiety or somatoform disorders, some of the dissociative or impulse disorders, and certainly most personality disorders. They usually seek hospitalization only when the extent of their distress or dysfunction becomes excessive. This, in itself, attests to their having severe, often chronic ego weakness. In other words, from a psychoanalytic vantage point, these patients have poorly integrated ego structures.

Examination of severe psychopathology on an inpatient setting can provide unique opportunities for psychoanalytic investigation. It is well known that the full range of these patients' pathology will be evoked in the multifaceted milieu of the psychiatric unit. When conditions are sufficiently controlled, in-depth diagnosis is enriched. This chapter proposes using such findings to test the heuristic value of the newer psychoanalytic theories; namely, self psychology and object relations theory. Verification of hypothesis is important to scientific inquiry, as models of intrapsychic dysfunction dictate what is considered important in treatment. In other words, how therapy is conducted is very much the result of one's theoretical model (Tuttman, 1984a).

The inpatient psychotherapy group will be used here as the focus for inquiry. This is because, as noted elsewhere (Kibel, 1987) and below, this group functions as an interface between the intrapsychic experience of each member and the conflicts that are generated within the social system of the milieu.

INPATIENT REGRESSION

When in crisis, patients with severe character pathology may require hospitalization because of self-destructive acts, disabling anxiety, somatic incapacity, or impulsive actions. Under these circumstances, hospitalization can serve protective or nurturing functions, as well as comprehensive diagnostic ones. Beyond short-term hospitalization, longer-term inpatient treatment, of several months to two years, is indicated under certain specific conditions. Basically, these are the circumstances which preclude the effective use of outpatient psychotherapy. They include the presence of chronic, self-destructive tendencies, poor motivation for change, a diminished capacity for introspection, antisocial behavior (including lack of honesty with the therapist), negative therapeutic reactions, the presence of symptoms which provide significant secondary gain, and destructive family circumstances (Kernberg, 1980).

Once they are hospitalized, the clinical picture of these patients changes. The psychiatric unit, unless it is highly regimented, induces regression. This is because the unit as a whole functions as a large group, with all the attendant properties—enigmatic organization, communication distortions, and impersonal social relations. Moreover, this environment is replete with ambiguities that are inherent in the social roles of both patients and staff (Kibel, 1978). Such conditions have been demonstrated to produce, even in normal individuals, severe identity diffusion, with a concomitant dramatic decrease in the capacity to evaluate social reality (Turquet, 1975). In other words, in anyone—and more particularly in those with severe character pathology—when ordinary social structure is lost and usual social roles are abrogated, primitive levels of psychological functioning emerge (Kernberg, 1976). In a narrower sense, the staff and other patients serve as an array of multiple objects for potential gratification of intrapsychic needs, thereby evoking the social display of pristine ego structures. Because of all this, the interpersonal field of the inpatient milieu offers new opportunities for diagnosis.

The task of the inpatient unit, in some sense, runs counter to these regressive trends. The treatment team aims to influence these primitive object relations activated in the interpersonal sphere in order to enhance development of more adaptive ego functioning. On short-term units this is accomplished by the use of limit-setting, environmental structure, and activities. But on longer-term units, where psychotherapeutic approaches are emphasized, staff and therapists also use confrontation, explanation, clarification, and even interpretation. While the social system of the inpatient milieu may temporarily further ego disintegration, the task of the unit ultimately is to promote ego synthesis. The former process, by exposing the pristine ego to examination, can enrich the psychodynamic understanding of psychopathology. The latter, which forces us to intervene, tests the therapeutic constructs that emanate from analytic theory. Study of these processes is eminently easier on longer-term units, where time permits.

Between regression and reconstitution lies an arena, according to psychoanalytic thinking, that hearkens to preverbal experience. Propositions that are used to describe the mental apparatus of that state must, of necessity, rest upon high degrees of inference. Theories that are barely open to verification or refutation are still highly influential on technique (Friedman, 1975). For this reason, the analytic laboratory of the inpatient unit must examine and recheck its theories in several places. The small group is one such testing ground.

The two most influential psychoanalytic theories of severe character pathology are those of Kohut (1971) and Kernberg (1975). Each has arisen from the study of treatment with intensive, individual psychoanalytic psychotherapy. Transposition of these findings to the social system of the inpatient unit may be misleading. This is because inpatient psychotherapeutic investigation, compared to its outpatient counterpart, is conducted in a broader and less well-defined social field (Ogden, 1981). On the one hand, the psychotherapy is powerfully influenced by the social system of the hospital within which it takes place. On the other, any attempt to maintain an illusion of analytic purity is thwarted by the necessity of the hospital therapist to be actively involved in the milieu through participation in a number of meetings and a variety of patient, staff, and family contacts, and because the therapist has a very real effect on the management of the patient's overall treatment.

Given that these patients are overdependent on external objects, analytic investigation of their pathology should be conducted in a social context, as well as a dyadic one. The inpatient group can be suited to this task. Study of the inpatient group as a dynamic entity allows the investigator to evaluate the contemporaneous effects of the social system of the psychiatric unit along with the contributions of individual psychopathology. This group functions at the interface between the milieu at large and the intrapsychic experience of each of its members (Kibel, 1987). The small group is a nodal point at which the larger dynamics of the inpatient unit find expression, and it provides a controlled environment for the reenactment of internal object relations.[1]

This chapter will now examine the application of self psychology and object relations theory to the understanding of severe character pathology on a psychiatric unit and to its treatment within the inpatient psychotherapy group. The focus will be on how a therapist might use a theoretical base to organize the diverse material of the session in order to formulate interventions in accordance with its thesis.

SELF PSYCHOLOGY

In the last fifteen years, self psychology has expanded from its early narrow focus on clinical narcissism to encompass the treatment of all forms of psychopathology (Ornstein and Ornstein, 1980). Beginning with a limited focus on so-called narcissistic conditions, Kohut eventually viewed some degree of disorder in the self as universal in psychopathology (Chessick, 1985). The self has come to be defined as the core of personality, that is, the center of the individual's psychological universe. Psychopathology, in general, is thought to occur when the self is weakened or inherently defective. In severe character pathology, more specifically, the self has not been solidly established as a firm, cohesive entity, providing the individual with confidence, self-esteem, and the capacity for selflessness. Rather, a false sense of coherency, of inner stability, is attained by an enfeebled self through dependency on the presence of selfobjects. Mutuality in relationships is lacking; the disturbed person is self-involved to the detriment of mature object relations.

The concept of the selfobject is crucial to an understanding,

---

[1]The term "object relations" is used, at this point, in a general sense, not as indicating a preference for one theory over another. Remember, Kohut defined the self only in relation to selfobjects. For this reason, Bacal (chapter 8) states that "psychoanalytic self psychology [is] very much . . . an 'object-relations theory.'"

within self psychology, of psychopathological processes and their treatment. It is alternately defined as an external object (i.e., a person outside the individual's psyche) who is experienced as a part of the self and as an archaic structure clearly inside the psychic apparatus (Greene, 1984). Moreover, the term refers to an object that is experienced as incompletely distinguished from the self and that can serve to restore or maintain the sense of self, i.e., the sense of internal cohesion (Stolorow and Lachmann, 1980).

Earlier in life, selfobjects are necessary for the nurturance, growth, and development of the self. Mirroring and idealization are crucial functions of this process. Mirroring produces the developmentally necessary inflation of a wishful self, that is, an archaic omnipotent sense of oneself; merger with an idealized parental imago provides sustenance, nurturance, and gratification for the developing self. These processes are necessary underpinnings for the advent of transmuting internalization—Kohut's term for the consolidation of the self through the development of internal stability and the selective incorporation of parental attributes. However, if sufficient mirroring and idealization are lacking in childhood, then these early narcissistic configurations do not become integrated into the rest of the personality, or at least do so incompletely. Thus, the difference between normal and disturbed individuals as regards this process is only a matter of degree (Roth, 1982). In all people, both the healthy and the disturbed, some need for selfobjects remains throughout life. In short, self psychology is a development deficit theory in which the difference is rather subtle between what is normal and what is defensive.

Patients with severe character pathology may be identified by the distorted way they use others as selfobjects. They may be classified likewise. At one end of the spectrum are those who need to merge psychically with others. They experience others as they do their own selves, are exquisitely sensitive to separation, and expect, without question, the continuous presence of selfobjects. At the other end are those who avoid social contact and become isolated, not out of disinterest but because the need for a selfobject is so intense that they fear narcissistic injury at every turn (Kohut and Wolf, 1978). They have learned to distance themselves from others in order to avoid exposing themselves to narcissistic insult, i.e., to avoid the very situation that their counterparts inevitably meet.

Stability is attained in patients with severe character pathology through the maintenance of archaic narcissistic positions. This means that the developmentally normal "grandiose self" persists as delusional grandiosity, while the "idealized parental imago" becomes fixated on an object that gets invested with glorified attributes. This may occur either in fantasy (e.g., in a schizoid personality) or in reality (e.g., for many dependent and borderline personalities), or a combination of the two. In any case, decompensation is generally ushered in by some sort of narcissistic injury. By this is meant some actual rupture in a relationship that, in effect, produces loss of narcissistically cathected archaic objects (Kohut, 1971). Symptomatic behavior represents secondary, restitutive attempts to resurrect the archaic relationship and thereby restore a semblance of cohesion to the self.

The crucial variable in the regressive process is the experience of the surroundings as nonempathic (Kohut, 1977). This is true whether the patient has experienced narcissistic injury because of a perception of rejection (for the so-called merger-hungry personalities) or whether forceful events have intruded on the insulated world of the schizoid and paranoid individual (the so-called contact-shunning personalities). The reversibility of untoward changes from decompensation depends on the provision of soothing selfobjects, i.e., ones that permit, at the very least, restoration of archaic narcissistic positions. In other words, the conditions of treatment ought to allow for the establishment of selfobject transferences, either with the therapist or, in the case of this chapter, with the group entity itself (Stone and Whitman, 1977). This development should be encouraged and not interdicted by interpretation of postulated underlying aggression or conflict. Interventions should give substance to the need for defenses to protect the self against further frustration and provide understanding for the inevitable disruption of attempts to restore selfobject relations (see Chapter 8). The treatment environment, in general, and the inpatient psychotherapy group, in particular, should be containing and nurturing. Technically, this requires the use of procedures that create empathic connections to the self. Empathy is the key ingredient that makes interventions palliative.

Kohut (1975) described three components of empathy. First, there is the usually accepted use of the term as referring to the recognition of oneself in another. Second, there is a more subjective concept of an expansion of the self to include the other, so as to constitute a powerful psychological bond between individuals. Third, empathy refers to the acceptance, confirmation, and deep understanding of an individual. In this sense, another person can serve as a human echo for the self and thereby provide basic psychological nutriment. It is through empathy, particularly this third aspect, that relations with soothing selfobjects are reestablished. Practically, this means that development of working alliances within the group represents a goal rather than an intermediate step in the treatment of these patients (Stone and Gustafson, 1982).

OBJECT RELATIONS THEORY

Over the last twenty years, there has been within traditional psychoanalytic circles a growing interest in the treatment of patients with severe character pathology (e.g., Grinker, Werble, and Drye, 1968) and the parallel development of a theory of fundamental ego weakness. Beginning with the work of Jacobson (1964), borrowing from British psychoanalytic schools, and incorporating the work of several ego psychologists, Kernberg (1976) has synthesized a comprehensive formulation of object relations theory. It can be said to lie within the mainstream of traditional psychoanalytic thinking because of its adherence to the notion that psychological disturbance is a product of intrapsychic conflict—in this case, between core aspects of the personality that are established respectively under the influence of libidinal and aggressive drive derivatives. This theory employs analogues from its own postulates on the preoedipal development of intrapsychic structures and applies them in order to construct a dynamic model of the nature of severe character pathology.

Kernberg (1975), using object relations theory, defined a specific developmental defect for such patients. He postulated the existence of a fundamental fault in the integrative capacity of the ego. During an earlier phase of ego development, perceptions of oneself and others were coalesced into separate sets of mental representations of both self and object, each under the sway of divergent drive derivatives. Object constancy—a more mature and realistic appreciation of oneself and others—evolves through the blending and merger of these opposing sets of internal object relations. In those with severe character pathology, however, primitive division of the ego into libidinal and aggressive components is maintained defensively, by the mechanism of splitting, in order to protect that ego core built around positive internalizations. Splitting, with associated mutual denial, protects the ego from intrusion by aggressively linked introjects by means of dissociation. As long as separation of contradictory ego states can be maintained, a reasonable degree of internal equilibrium prevails. However, when splitting fails to accomplish this goal, the libidinally determined ego is flooded by its aggressive counterpart and the individual is overwhelmed by anxiety. The relative failure of the splitting mechanism results in varying degrees of decompensation and, along with secondary defensive operations of the ego, accounts for the wide variety of symptomatic pathologies (Kibel, 1978).

This theory, stated in another way, postulates that in the face of unmetabolized aggression, aggressively determined internal part objects are untethered and the ego core or central experience of the self is weakened. Once debilitated, the ego tries to rid itself of unwanted or endangering parts by employing projective mechanisms—specifically, projective identification. This permits the individual to maintain some degree of internal tranquility, albeit on a regressed level, by means of the unconscious fantasy that noxious images, particularly sadistic ones, have been deposited into another person or persons. The result is the adoption of a global paranoid-schizoid-like position (Kibel, 1987) that colors a multiplicity of relationships. Specifically, there are pervasive distortions in these patients' perception of authority as depriving, persecutory, or even sadistic.

Understanding this failure of splitting and the mechanism of projective identification is the key to developing a treatment approach based on object relations theory. In the short run, treatment must aim to dissociate aggressively determined internalizations from their libidinal counterparts, so that splitting can return as a prominent defense, adaptively protecting the central ego core from contamination by "bad" objects. Techniques must be used which help individuals manage their own aggression, while simultaneously bolstering their internal sense of self-worth. Accordingly, successful treatment produces a reorganization of internal representations in their relationship to one another, so that equilibrium between opposing forces is reestablished.

A variety of supportive maneuvers proves salutary, particularly those which aim to shore up a debilitated ego core. However, a pivotal technique in group psychotherapy is the use of interpretations that clarify the way in which group behavior is reactive to confluent environmental and transference influences (Kibel, 1978, 1981, 1987). This serves a variety of related goals. One effect is to demystify (Levinson, 1981) the patients' internal experiences, particularly aggressively linked ones, as these are reenacted within both the small group and the larger milieu of the psychiatric unit. Clarification conveys the idea that symptoms are basically distorted responses to realities in the immediate environment. This promulgates the notion that what seems frightening and incomprehensible can actually be explained and understood. In this way, the method offers patients hope for the development of mastery over their chaotic experiences. Technically, the leader not only provides understanding but also promotes the development of substantive cohesion, i.e., a quality of attachment within the group whereby members feel bound to one another, so that their enfeebled selves are strengthened through identification with a collective whole. A group-centered approach (Stein and Kibel, 1984; Kibel, 1987) is indispensable here.

Projective identification plays a central role in the pathological process but when managed properly can be turned to therapeutic advantage. Through this mechanism patients pressure others to think, feel, and behave in a manner that is congruent with the projector's ejected fantasy and its associated affects. Usually in these patients' lives, recipients of such projections react in unsalutary ways, which unfortunately confirm for them the original belief that their feelings and fantasies are dangerous and unbearable. However, in the therapeutic situation, the recipient-therapist demonstrates an ability to live with such feelings and manage them through, for example, mastery or integration. In this case, patients "can, via introjection or identification, internalize aspects of how the recipient handles the induced feelings" (Ogden, 1981, p. 319). For this reason, interpretations in a psychotherapy group must not merely clarify the aggressive component of the experience, they must also provide a recipient or container (Bion, 1962) for projected aggression. This occurs through the use of transference interpretations which sanction the development of a benign group paranoia by indicating how members of the treatment team in general, and the group therapist in particular, serve as persecutory objects (Kibel, 1987). In short, aggression gets attenuated in three ways: through the dissipating effect of group interactions, through clarifications that encourage mastery, and through containment by the therapist.

In the long run, however, definitive treatment, according to an object relations model, requires healing the split between so-called "good" and "bad" sets of internalized perceptions of oneself and others. This is a long and complicated process whereby integration of fragmented elements of the personality occurs. Interpretation and working through of disturbed object relations are necessary components, so that the patient can gradually but ultimately "own" the split-off or rejected, aggressively linked representations of oneself and others. The inpatient group, by its very nature, is not entirely suited to this task. However, it is very well suited for palliation, that is, so-called supportive psychotherapy, in contrast to the potentially curative benefits of explorative psychoanalytic psychotherapy.

CLINICAL ILLUSTRATION

Undoubtedly, the relative merits and clinical value of these two theoretical systems will be debated for decades to come. Both have made important contributions to the treatment of patients with severe character pathology. Examination of clinical material can sharpen our view of the salient differences between the two. But whether one system will prove to be of more heuristic value than the other only time will tell.

The example to be presented, it is hoped, will highlight the divergence between self psychology and object relations theory. Of course, like any clinical illustration, it suffers from the stated bias of this author and perhaps the unstated predilections of the group cotherapists involved. While the senior cotherapist had considerable clinical experience, she was not committed to a theoretical position. The junior cotherapist was a novice in every way. This example is chosen because it demonstrates an attempt by the more experienced therapist to establish empathic connections with the group members and because it shows how the vicissitudes of untethered aggression produced a noxious effect.

The example is drawn from a once-weekly psychotherapy group of eight months' duration. All its patients had severe character pathology. The group was conducted on a unit with an average length of stay of three to four months. During the previous few months this particular psychiatric unit had undergone changes in its administrative structure. In addition, there were some changes in personnel. As a consequence, the senior cotherapist had recently assumed temporary leadership of one of the unit's two treatment teams. This entire situation—particularly the change in the role of some staff—was confusing to both patients and staff.

The start of this session was marked by disorganization. Only one patient was on time, but in short order the others trickled in. The patients soon realized that one of their seven members, Miss X., was absent again. Another pass out of the hospital had been granted to her during the time of a scheduled session. (This reflected the administrative confusion of the staff.) The members were clearly irritated by what they perceived as a repeated devaluation of the group. In response, they began to discuss the possible institution of sanctions against Miss X. While one member was bold enough to suggest that she be terminated, there was clearly no consensus for action. This was not the first time such a discussion had occurred. One patient hinted that Miss X. was told, outside the session, of a similar proposal for sanctions that was made the previous week. When one therapist asked if this was told to her explicitly, the members agreed that not one of them would have dared to do so. They stood in fear of her allegedly wrathful nature.

Further consideration of the members' anger was curtailed when Mr. C. reported, apologetically, that he had to leave this session early to attend a job interview. He said that he had two job possibilities, either of which would help him prepare for discharge. Unfortunately, the work schedule of one conflicted with the time for the group. If he took that one, he would no longer be able to attend. The members responded with expressions of happiness for his apparent good fortune. They totally disregarded the potential conflict with the group sessions and his likely termination. Instead they discussed his work prospects supportively and enthusiastically. Yet Mr. C. could not ignore the conflict. He confessed to embarrassment in the face of a probable sudden and unexpected termination. He then expressed appreciation to the members for their help and thanked each and every one, acting as if this would be his final session.

At this point the therapists took divergent paths. The junior therapist tried to focus the members' attention toward their unresolved feelings for Miss X. and suggested that their enthusiasm for Mr. C. served to avoid their conflicts with her. The senior therapist joined the members in support of Mr. C.'s vocational efforts. She extracted a promise from him to return to at least one more session in order to terminate more smoothly. (His promise appeared to have been given reluctantly.) The members continued to applaud Mr. C.'s endeavors. Some indicated that they admired him; others revealed how they envied him; finally, as if comparing themselves to him, a few expressed doubts about their abilities to "make it on the outside."

Once this latter sentiment pervaded the atmosphere, the tone of the session changed. Suddenly, Miss S. began to cry vehemently, almost convulsively. She, more than any, expressed profound pessimism about her future. She cited several recent incidents to demonstrate that whenever she was off the hospital grounds she felt overwhelmed with anxiety. The others, in a rational manner, presented evidence to the contrary. Their arguments for her effectiveness seemed to outweigh hers. They were very supportive and encouraging. Yet they were unable to assuage her despair.

At this point, the senior therapist asked the patients how Miss S.'s crying affected them. They discounted any effect, but spoke with optimism about her discharge a month hence. The junior therapist asked how they imagined they would feel when she left. At once, all the patients seemed annoyed with both therapists and demeaned their observations as factitious psychologizing. Some claimed the therapists were overanalyzing them; others claimed they were simply wrong.

Next, very quickly, the tone changed again. The members began to joke with Miss S. The conversation became unusually jocular and seemingly irrelevant. The therapists gently but persistently interpreted their manner as avoidance of the feelings precipitated by Miss S.'s behavior. Yet even Miss S. defiantly stated that the therapists were inaccurate. The senior therapist conceded that perhaps the two of them were wrong. With this, the session ended.

DISCUSSION

From a self psychology perspective, we can speculate that the disorganization in the early phase of this session reflected the fragmentation of the self that these patients were experiencing. The administrative confusion within the staff only served to perpetuate their experience of the environment as nonnurturing. In other words, the psychiatric unit in general, and the group in particular, failed to function as a protective envelope (Day, 1981), to soothe their narcissistic wounds. Miss X. came to symbolize this failure. The attempt to institute sanctions against her would be seen as a manifestation of narcissistic rage. Specifically, empathic failure by the selfobject of the group, in a narrow sense, and the unit in a broader sense, produced further breakup, in each patient, of the self. The aggressive response, therefore, would be said to be a disintegration product of this nuclear psychic structure.

Mr. C. appeared to have facilitated, for the members, reestablishment of an archaic narcissistic position. He provided some of the qualities of an idealized selfobject. More specifically, he represented the success for which each of them longed. Through his competence, each shared in the triumph, because of their empathic connection to him. The self-esteem of all was inflated. Yet this state of contentment was short-lived. Mr. C. told them that he would be leaving soon. Anticipation of further loss threatened to disrupt these patients' narcissistic equilibrium, especially since it was immediately and fragilely tied to his presence. The senior therapist tried to soften the blow by supporting his accomplishment and also encouraging him to return. But when his promise to do so was given reluctantly, the tenuous tie to Mr. C. as a selfobject was broken. Very quickly, their admiration for him turned into envy and self-doubt. Once again narcissistic rage erupted. Miss S. came to embody their struggle to restore a semblance of cohesion to the self. The members tried to resurrect the soothing image of union with the selfobject by being supportive and exhorting her to persevere. In this instance, by virtue of their tie to the group-as-group (Stone and Whitman, 1977), they functioned as the idealized selfobject in relation to her. Then, through identification with her, they could relate to the group imago, thereby accomplishing the same for themselves.

This state of affairs was tenuous at best. The members' relationship to the soothing selfobject of the group-as-group soon collapsed, perhaps because of some empathic failure by the therapists, perhaps because Miss S. was intractable in her despair and therefore was no longer experienced as part of the group, or perhaps because nothing could compensate for the loss which, by virtue of the members' inner connection to Mr. C. and Miss X., was destined to be experienced as a rejection. In any case, the image of the group as a selfobject dissolved. Anger again erupted and the session became disorganized. Within this morass of confusion, the therapists were experienced as nonempathic, despite the senior one's admission of error.

This explanation seems comprehensive but does not explain all that happened. It fails to account for the perception of Miss X. as having a wrathful nature (assuming this to be a distortion, or at least an exaggeration). Likewise, it does not account sufficiently for the members' willingness to impose sanctions on her in contrast to their benign treatment of Mr. C. To put this another way, it does not explain why the anticipation of rejection by Mr. C. did not produce the same angry reaction toward him.

As this account stands, it postulates the presence of an identification, at one point, of the group members with themselves (as a group) in order to fulfill their need for a selfobject. It is as if the patients had internalized, for the moment, the functions of an idealized object. Within a self psychology framework, this would be akin to a transmuting internalization. For this to be, one needs to suppose that the members, as part of a group, were employing a maturationally advanced intrapsychic mechanism. This is hardly what one would expect of patients with primitive self structures. On the other hand, their shifting identification to the group, first as subject and then as object, could be explained by the object relations concept of projective identification (and its concomitant mechanism of introjection).

From the perspective of object relations theory, this session would be understood differently, at least in part. The administrative confusion within the staff would still be seen as impairing the protective and nurturing functions of both the psychiatric unit and the small group. However, in the absence of appropriate environmental structure, it would be postulated, the central ego core, for which it serves as support, would be weakened. This in turn would cause aggressive drive derivatives to be activated. In this example, aggressively linked introjects initially caused members to withdraw to a schizoid position, as evidenced by their lateness, but these images soon converged on Miss X. She served as a focus for projected aggression. Through the mechanism of projective identification, Miss X. became the object onto whom aggression was projected. Identification with her allowed for the persistence of an empathic tie[2] to this object. These processes account for the members' perception of her as potentially awesome and for their affective link to her—specifically, their fear of her. Because the members were in agreement with this view, they developed a sense of unity.

In such a state a group functions well internally, but with total disregard for outside reality. Because the group atmosphere creates a sense of cohesion, members feel safe inside its borders. But in this

[2]In object relations theory, the term "empathic" means something different than it does for Kohut. It is less specific here, referring to a strong sense of kinship.

case, the group's stability soon was disrupted by Mr. C.'s announcements. No longer could aggression be projected outward. The patients were forced to contend with the stark reality of the fragmentation of the group as an entity—its members were leaving. Manic defenses with primitive denial functioned temporarily, as they joined Mr. C. in a brief period of congratulatory activity. He could have been the object of the same complex of images and affects that earlier were associated directly with Miss X. However, the members could not put these into operation since, at this point, his presence and apparent competence made it seem too risky. After Mr. C. left the group, the members were to retrospectively deprecated him, claiming that they had been demonstrably angry with him at this session. Their support during his departure was to be underplayed. Such is the action of splitting and primitive denial.

The pervasive zest for Mr. C. served to deny their aggression, while they did not have a container for it. But without an object for projection, such defenses prove unstable. As admiration (i.e., idealization) emerged, it was juxtaposed with its counterpart, envy. As the aggressive component of the latter threatened to surface to consciousness, it was turned against themselves. This too was barely tolerable. Primitive denial crumbled and a container was sought.

Generally, once aggression is unbridled within a group, it has to be contained. In typical fashion, it was projected into its most vulnerable member, Miss S. She became the scapegoat (Scheidlinger, 1982). The collective origins of her affect accounted for its intensity. She became overwhelmed with aggressive images, and this devastated her central ego core. Consequently, she experienced herself as incapable, defective, and worthless. Only when the therapists suggested that members might be reacting to her did she feel better, because this intervention activated her linkage to the group. This tie may have also served to bolster her self-esteem.

These postulates would explain how she was catapulted into despair, and only moments later suddenly emerged to join the members in the banter (a manic defense) of the terminal phase of the session. The therapists' persistent focus on the members' reactions to her helped them turn from her as an object to complain about them. Given the intensity of affect generated by collective projective identification, it is no wonder the senior therapist was ultimately engulfed in self-doubt. Like Miss S., the therapist was caught in its web. The group process had moved the aggression from Miss S. to this therapist, albeit in an unsalutary way.

CONCLUSION

The differences between the two theoretical perspectives are clear in this example. At first glance, object relations theory appears to provide a more comprehensive explanation of the material and of the shifts of content. It provides an in-depth description of the relationship between sequential segments of the session, so as to give the material a dynamic unity. It explains the therapist's self-doubt as a reaction to a powerful group process. In contrast, self psychology would see that as a simple technical error, that is, as a result of a failure to understand and empathize with the patients. More important, what is seen as restitutive in self psychology is viewed as defensive in object relations theory. Such is the case with the group's adoration of Mr. C. This difference has technical consequences.

Object relations theory, and for that matter traditional psychoanalysis, tends to view many clinical phenomena as defensive in character, specifically as constituting attempts to ward off awareness of unacceptable wishes, affects, and internal images. In contrast, self psychology views behavior mainly as the expression of selfobject needs, but sometimes as an effort to protect the individual from narcissistic trauma. Thus, the group's encouragement and support for Mr. C was understood differently from the two theoretical vantage points. In one it was seen to serve the denial of aggression, but in the other it was seen to facilitate the establishment of a therapeutically beneficial narcissistic position.

The technical consequences of these differences are important. According to object relations theory, support for defenses comes at a price. Functioning may improve, but change does not occur. For treatment to be mutative, resistances must be overcome and underlying anxieties worked out. Within traditional psychoanalytic concepts, the difference between one approach and the other is the difference between supportive and explorative psychotherapy. In contrast, self psychology makes no such distinction. Rather, technique is viewed on a continuum. The first step is to make emotional contact through empathy and, thereby, to restabilize a fragmented or disruptive self. Then, through interpretation of the narcissistically traumatic process, the patient is provided with understanding. Here, both nurturance of phase-legitimate emotional needs and cognitive appreciation of what has happened are necessary for structure building, that is, for transmuting internalization.

Each of these psychologies will dictate, in some instances, divergent interventions.[3] Yet there will be similarities between the two. Both view the experiential aspects of the group process as palliative. Both advocate the use of support, empathy, and the development of a working alliance. A therapeutic group is particularly useful, in this regard, with either approach (Tuttman, 1984b). Object relations theory views the alliance as a means toward an end. Self psychology sees it as an end in itself (Stone and Gustafson, 1982). This is because self psychology considers empathy, in a profoundly substantive way (Kohut, 1975), to be the essential nutriment for psychological growth, whereas object relations theory views aggression to be the main obstacle to ego development.

On the inpatient unit (and sometimes with outpatients) therapists of one persuasion or another will use similar techniques. However, they would view the function of these differently. For example, a benign explanation of the members' response to Mr. C., in terms of their reaction to Miss X., would be deemed an interpretation by a self psychologist. But it would be labeled a clarification by an object relations theorist, with the term "interpretation" being reserved for the exposure of the destructive aspects of motivation. Here, the explanation would be considered to be ego-supportive, in that it would be viewed as promoting mastery of experience.

SUMMARY

Object relations theory has expanded the scope of psychoanalytic thinking with its investigation of early ego pathology. In this sense, it remains part of a traditional psychology of human behavior. It leaves open the question of whether ego weakness is the product of constitutional or environmental failures.[4] In contrast, self psychology

[3]The particulars of interventions for those working within a self psychology framework have been described by others. The recommendations of this author have been elaborated elsewhere (Kibel, 1978, 1981, 1987).

[4]Object relations theorists have taken divergent views on causality. Melanie Klein placed a heavy emphasis on the influence of the instinctual drives, particularly the death instinct, as the foundation of intrapsychic conflict. Thus her ideological position was constitutionalist (Kernberg, 1980), as opposed to that of culturalists such as Masterson (Masterson and Rinsley, 1975), who stress psychosocial determinants.

began as a means to explain limited facets of psychopathology. However, Kohut was unable to reshape the framework of psychoanalysis to include the clinical phenomena he had observed with regard to the self. He therefore formulated a new psychology (Greene, 1984), one that views the self as the fulcrum of ego development. Certainly Kohut added to our clinical knowledge. But to extrapolate from one kind of psychopathology, narcissistic disorders to be specific, to all patients is a dubious practice. Again, to assume, as self psychology does, that developmental psychology is primarily the consequence of what parents are unduly narrows investigation into etiology.

Object relations theory is based on a particular notion of conflict, namely, that the individual is unable to manage opposing parts of the personality. The existence of libidinal and aggressive drives is a given. Disability occurs because the central core of personality is impaired in the presence of unmodulated aggression. The emphasis appears to be on the secondary consequences of pathological aggressive drive derivatives. In contrast, self psychology considers the destructive derivatives of aggression to be secondary phenomena, a consequence of the failure of the environment to provide optimal need-gratification. More specifically, in the adult it is a disintegration product of the fragmentation of a feeble self. The latter is deficient to begin with, in the sense that its early development was arrested. This presumed stunting of the central core of personality is linked to self psychology's emphasis on the therapeutic use of nurturance and, more specifically, empathy. In short, treatment is designed to provide patients with a second chance to develop personality structures which the earlier environment had precluded.

Within the framework of self psychology there appears to be a continuum from what is traditionally called supportive psychotherapy to its expressive counterpart. In both, empathy is the essential ingredient for the establishment of a therapeutic attachment to a selfobject. This serves, on the one hand, to soothe narcissistic wounds and, on the other, to provide the necessary condition for the eventual development of a more stable self. In short, the difference between supportive and definitive treatment appears to be a matter of degree.

According to object relations theory, supportive therapy produces a realignment of the relationships that internal structures have to one another. Specifically, it fosters a partial dissociation of aggressively linked structures from their libidinal counterparts, while the central core of the personality is bolstered. Techniques are designed to enhance self-regard and to diminish the sense that internal aggression is unbridled (Kibel, 1987). As with self psychology, the development of the working alliance is central. However, an object relations model presupposes that more definitive treatment has a further task. Its goal is to integrate fragmented aspects of personality so that the individual becomes capable of appreciating the realistic aspects of oneself and others, specifically the inherent nature of ambivalence. The road toward integration is a tortuous and arduous one.

In summary, object relations theory is one of conflict, whereas self psychology is one of psychic deficit (Kernberg, 1982). Their goals in short-term treatment may be similar. But for one, the aim of reconstructive therapy is the resolution of conflict, whereas for the other it is the filling in of structural defects (Chapter 8). The relative merits of the two, particularly with respect to the treatment of a broad range of severe character pathology, will be determined ultimately by their relative heuristic value.

REFERENCES

Bion, W. R. (1962), *Learning from Experience*. New York: Basic Books.

Chessick, R. D. (1985), Book review of *How Does Analysis Cure?* Contributions to the *Psychology of the Self*, by Heinz Kohut. *Amer. J. Psychiat.*, 142:255–256.

Day, M. (1981), Process in classical psychodynamic groups. *Internat. J. Group Psychother.*, 31:153–174.

Friedman, H. J. (1975), Psychotherapy of borderline patients: The influence of theory on technique. *Amer. J. Psychiat.*, 132:1048–1052.

Greene, M. A. (1984), The self psychology of Heinz Kohut: A synopsis and critique. *Bull. Menn. Clin.*, 48:37–53.

Grinker, R. R., Werble, B., & Drye, R. (1968), *The Borderline Syndrome: A Behavioral Study of Ego Functions.* New York: Basic Books.

Jacobson, E. (1964), *The Self and the Object World.* New York: International Universities Press.

Kernberg, O. F. (1975), *Borderline Conditions and Pathological Narcissism.* New York: Aronson.

———(1976), *Object Relations Theory and Clinical Psychoanalysis.* New York: Aronson.

———(1980), *Internal World and External Reality.* New York: Aronson.

———(1982), Book review of *Advances in Self Psychology*, edited by Arnold Goldberg. *Amer. J. Psychiat.*, 139:374–375.

Kibel, H. D. (1978), The rationale for the use of group psychotherapy for borderline patients on a short-term unit. *Internat. J. Group Psychother.*, 28:339–358.

———(1981), A conceptual model for short-term inpatient group psychotherapy. *Amer. J. Psychiat.*, 138:74–80.

————(1987), Inpatient group psychotherapy—where treatment philosophies converge. In: *Yearbook of Psychoanalysis and Psychotherapy*, Vol. 2, ed. R. Langs. New York: Gardner Press, pp. 94–116.

Kohut, H. (1971), *The Analysis of the Self*. New York: International Universities Press.

————(1975), The psychoanalyst in the community of scholars. *Annual of Psychoanalysis*, 3:341–370.

————(1977), *The Restoration of the Self*. New York: International Universities Press.

————Wolf, E. S. (1978), The disorders of the self and their treatment: An outline. *Internat. J. Psycho-Anal.*, 59:413–425.

Levinson, E. A. (1981), The rhetoric of intimacy, *Group*, 5(4):3–11.

Masterson, J., & Rinsley, D. B. (1975), The borderline syndrome: The role of the mother in the genesis and structure of the borderline personality. *Internat. J. Psycho-Anal.*, 56:163–177.

Ogden, T. H. (1981), Projective identification in psychiatric hospital treatment. *Bull. Menn. Clin.*, 45:317–333.

Ornstein, P. H., & Ornstein, A. (1980), Formulating interpretations in clinical psychoanalysis. *Internat. J. Psycho-Anal.*, 61:203–211.

Roth, B. E. (1982), Six types of borderline and narcissistic patients: An initial typology. *Internat. J. Group Psychother.*, 32:9–27.

Scheidlinger, S. (1982), On scapegoating in group psychotherapy. *Internat. J. Group Psychother.*, 32:131–143.

Stein, A., & Kibel, H. D. (1984), A group dynamic—peer interaction approach to group psychotherapy. *Internat. J. Group Psychother.*, 34:315–333.

Stolorow, R. D., & Lachmann, F. M. (1980), *Psychoanalysis of Developmental Arrests: Theory and Treatment*. New York: International Universities Press.

Stone, W. N., & Gustafson, J. P. (1982), Technique in group psychotherapy of narcissistic and borderline patients. *Internat. J. Group Psychother.*, 32:29–47.

————Whitman, R. M. (1977), Contributions of the psychology of the self to group therapy. *Internat. J. Group Psychother.*, 27:343–359.

Turquet, P. (1975), Threats to identity in the large group. In: *The Large Group: Dynamics and Therapy*, ed. L. Kreeger. London: Constable, pp. 87–144.

Tuttman, S. (1984a), The impact of psychoanalytic theories of conflict upon treatment. *J. Acad. Psychoanal.*, 12:491–509.

————(1984b), Applications of object relations theory and self-psychology in current group therapy. *Group*, 8(4):41–48.

13

The Short-Term Inpatient Group: Formation and Beginnings

ISAAC ZEKE YOUCHA, C.S.W.

On most dynamic inpatient psychiatric services there is a constant effort made to offer effective treatment in the shortest possible time. Due to high costs, insurance companies' policies, governmental pressure, and modern psychopharmacology, the length of an average hospital stay has been drastically reduced. On many units four weeks is considered an extended stay.

This reality has forced therapists into the position of attempting very short-term psychotherapy with severely disturbed people, yet group therapy has had little opportunity and time to develop a body of theory, method, and techniques to meet the challenge.

For most of the last decade I have had the opportunity to work as a group consultant in a state mental hospital as well as on a psychiatric unit within a general hospital. I will attempt to present some of the theory, methods, and techniques which have evolved from this experience.

PATIENT CATEGORIES

In the main we tend to see three broad categories of patients: (a) those whose psychosis has overwhelmed all ego functions; (b) patients who are psychotic or acutely depressed but who have enough ego

This chapter was first published in *Group Process* (1976), 7:119–137, and is reprinted with permission.

functions operating to which the therapist can ally himself; and (c) Patients who are not psychotic but have (1) overdosed, (2) are on nonopiate drugs, (3) are alcoholics or heroin addicts, (4) have made suicide attempts, (5) have severe somatic disturbances of unknown origin, or (6) are crippled by conversion hysteria. The major differentiating factor among the three categories is the degree of ego strength and functioning.

Category A

In this category the psychotic process dominates the ego. For example, one patient was hearing voices yelling at her and could not accept that idea that they were coming from within. Those voices were real and would not leave her alone. They told her to put her baby in the oven and that she was the worst creature on earth. She accused the therapist of being one of "them" when he suggested that the voices were really coming from within herself. A large part of this group is composed of chronic patients with process schizophrenia whose illness overwhelmed or stunted ego development early in life. Many patients on admission fit into category A but in time, with drug treatment, rest, support, good meals, and activity group approaches, move into category B.

Category B

In this category a similar process is at work, but some of the ego remains unaffected, especially the function of reality testing. For example, a second woman heard voices screaming at her and was sure they were coming from the next room. She ran to the nearest police station for protection. On admission, an experienced clinician was able to discuss with her the possibility that the voices were emanating from within herself. She replied, "You know, that may be true, because when I'm talking to you or am closing my eyes, I don't hear them. I'd rather talk to you. Wow, what the hell is happening to me anyway?"

The therapist was able to appeal to and ally himself with the observing ego in the patient, which could still reflect upon herself and realize that something was happening to her. This group is composed of people with a psychotic underlay but strong enough repressive defenses and coping mechanisms to enable them to function when not under excessive stress.

Category C

In this group we see people whose reality testing is relatively intact and who often have the capacity for self-reflection and insight into the immediate causes of their stress and anxiety. With therapeutic help they can understand intellectually some of the precipitating causes of their disturbances. This is no way means that they can do anything to remedy their situation, but the problem can be outlined and defined in a relatively short period of time. Their behavior often represents a desperate appeal for help. One woman stopped her car on a busy bridge, lifted up the hood of her car, and blocked traffic for miles. She was really flagging for help.

This last category includes those with severe neurotic and characterological disturbances whose adaptive mechanisms have crumbled under continuous internal and external stress.

EVALUATION

It is incumbent upon the therapist to evaluate the degree of pathology and ego condition as quickly as possible. This will determine the choice of treatment methods and goals. It will be necessary for the entire ward staff to accumulate as much data as they can get in the shortest possible time, and this requires *total* staff involvement and cooperation.

Each category of patient requires a different group approach, though often it is not possible to adhere strictly to this approach or to evaluate each patient so precisely. A broad outline of theory, methods, and techniques, however, does offer the group therapist a conceptual framework. This may eliminate the confusion, indecision, and lack of purposefulness often seen in a ward staff when it comes time to decide which patients should be put into what kind of group and why.

Regardless of the group approach utilized, all require at least three to five meetings a week, of one to two hours' duration. Once-a-week meetings during a hospitalization of one to four weeks are almost valueless.

A thorough dynamic understanding of each patient's problems, conflicts, ego condition, psychodynamics, present life situation, and interpersonal relationships is essential.

GOALS

Clear-cut and realistic treatment goals must be established as quickly as possible. These are arrived at through discussion between staff and patients, individually or within the group therapy situation.

Minimal goals might be to (1) reduce the acute psychotic manifestations of the disturbance so that the patient can participate in ward activities and (2) help the patient (through the use of drugs, rest, reassurance, and support) to seal over the eruption of the unbearable psychic pain and anxiety that necessitated the use of regressive psychotic mechanisms of defense. This implies an attempt to substitute and encourage repressive defensive mechanisms—i.e., obsessive-compulsive or denial devices—in place of the psychotic ones the patient had resorted to. This is done when the goal is not to uncover and resolve the sources and nature of the anxiety-producing conflicts, but instead to enable the patient to reestablish previous nonpsychotic levels of functioning. For example, a twenty-six-year-old mother of two, employed as a schoolteacher, believed that her family was under surveillance by enemy powers and was going to be murdered at any moment. After four days of drug therapy and exposure to a benign therapeutic community and activity group approach (to be described below), the delusion ceased to be active. It was replaced by an obsessive-compulsive concern with performing all of her chores perfectly. Any attempt to deal with her rage at her husband, her early deprivation as a child, or her displacement of rage at her mother onto her husband was met with agitation, confusion, and an acute exacerbation of the psychotic delusion.

No one could establish an alliance with an intact portion of her ego. (She obviously would fit into category A.) Thus, our minimal goals were to accept and support severe compulsive-obsessive repressive defenses in place of regressive psychotic ones.

Intermediate goals with such a patient might have been to help her recognize that she was unhappy in her marriage and her job, that her husband frequently hurt and enraged her, and that this rage was attributed to others. These could have been approached on a behavioral level by helping her to express anger to fellow patients and ward staff, which she never did, even when sharply provoked. In a group situation we could have dealt with why she was unaware of feelings of irritation even at a most provocative group member.

Maximal goals would have included couple, group, and individual therapy with the aim of working on her transferential distortion of her husband, her fear of homicidal rage, its sources, etc. The group would have been utilized to examine how she dealt with her major affects and to help her discover less destructive modes of expressing affect.

We chose not to select these as our goals, as the length of hospitalization permitted her by her insurance policy prevented the kind of extensive work that would exacerbate and extend the psychotic state. The whole point of discussing goals is to emphasize the importance of establishing them as soon as possible in cooperation with staff and patients. Many therapists are accustomed to working with an extended or even unlimited time, a luxury that is denied the therapeutic staff of most inpatient services. In order to avoid an amorphous, nonspecific, and unclear treatment experience, the therapist must have clear-cut treatment goals, however tentative, from very early on.

The ultimate goal for all hospital groups is to make the experience one the patient will want to continue after discharge. Too many therapists are unaware of how traumatic certain group experiences can be for hypersensitive schizophrenic patients. Upon discharge, it is often impossible to get a large number of them back into an aftercare therapy group. They refer back to certain hospital group experiences with terror and to others as a complete and boring waste of time.

The aim is to get patients involved in a therapeutic process while still in the hospital, a process they will be willing and even desirous of continuing on an outpatient basis. This assumes that for most patients only a part of the job can be done while they are in the hospital.

It is important for the therapist to identify the nature of the conflicts and stresses that have produced the psychotic process and to help the patient contain that process. The therapist cannot, however, expect to resolve lifelong problems in the short time allotted. For most patients an extended aftercare program, with extensive use of groups, is essential.

A different group approach is used for each category of patient. None of them are new and all have been used elsewhere.

For category A (patients with completely overwhelmed egos) an activity method is used; for category B (partially overwhelmed ego) a discussion technique, and for category C (more intact patients) a focal therapeutic approach.

ACTIVITY GROUP

The activity group session is divided into three parts: (1) individual activity; (2) dyadic activity (pairs); and (3) group activity.

The purpose is to get the patients involved and interacting with each other. Neither exploration nor insight is sought. The aim is to help them know the staff and each other through engaging in an activity that is nonthreatening and enjoyable. I call it a noninsight–supportive relationship activity group. An activity is exploited to get everyone involved in a common group endeavor.

The group may start by working with finger painting or clay. (At Good Samaritan Hospital in Suffern, N.Y., at least twenty activities have been devised by the staff.) The group is told, "We would like to know you better and understand how you relate to yourselves and to each other. This is an exercise which increases self-awareness and by engaging in it you can help yourself and others." The first part engages the patient in a solo but parallel activity.

Typed instructions clearly explain the equipment that everyone is going to work with. All therapists participate fully in every phase of the work. The instructions for finger painting read, "The jars are on the table, along with newspaper, paper cups, spatulas, wet paper, etc. Go up to the table and fill up several paper cups with the different colors you wish to use. Bring newspaper, cups, and the wet paper back to your place. Spread out the newspaper, put your wet paper down on top of it, etc." Before starting, one of the patients usually reads the instructions aloud.

Why written instructions? The aim is to exercise as many ego functions as possible. Some of these patients are still hallucinating; others are delusional or acutely depressed. Reading forces them to come into touch with an outside reality. (Patients often report that they have their most bizarre symptoms when they are alone and inactive.)

No one is coerced into participating, although almost all do. Occasionally a particularly paranoid delusional person or an extremely terrified and fastidious patient will refuse. But when they see the others walking up to the table, getting their paints, sitting down, and engaging in the activity, most grudgingly get involved. It is difficult for them to resist the flow of the group, although they may not do exactly what the others are doing and may remain isolated on the periphery. Those who will not engage at all are told that that is fine. They can sit and watch and are free to join in whenever they wish. (If a patient leaves the room, a staff member goes out and encourages him to return. Later, when a minimal degree of group cohesiveness is established, the group is asked to handle the situation.) The nonactive but observing patient is engaged by watching the others. Participation as a spectator is acceptable during this first part of the activity session.

This solo phase is dedicated to getting the patient out of himself and engaged in a simple, nonthreatening task, all by himself but near others. Patients usually start engaging in simple interactions—e.g., "pass me a cup" or "I'll get that for you." They look at what their neighbor is doing and smile or frown. Parallel activity inevitably fosters this type of process.

After patients and staff complete their pictures, a minute is taken to explain what was painted and what it meant. (Sometimes everyone paints to music and relates the painting to what is heard.) Members often comment on each other's work, and all words of praise and encouragement by patients are rewarded by the leaders. This reenforcement of positive feelings between members is consciously used to foster group closeness (Liberman, 1971). The reward for positive patient interaction may consist of a simple, "That was nice of you to say that to Mary."

After the individual phase is completed, the patients are asked to return to their instruction sheets. Here they are told to select a partner and to paint a picture with that person. This is often an easier operation if minimal interaction has occurred during the solo phase. This dyadic activity forces patients to engage with another person in a structured, nonthreatening, and enjoyable activity. He has the opportunity to learn that simple interrelatedness and interaction can be fun and not full of pain and humiliation. This may enable him to take another step in relating to others.

The pair discusses and decides upon their common project, and after they carry it through the group discusses each pair's endeavors. Once again the aim is to encourage interaction and to generate group cohesiveness.

In the last portion of the activity session the entire group is instructed to engage in a common joint effort. They must all decide what they want to do. They have to determine who does what part of the project and then produce their masterpiece.

By this time the feeling emerges that these separate, isolated people belong to a group. There is usually a lot of laughter, encouragement, self-criticism, praise, and disappointment, but it is a shared experience. There is discussion about how different people reacted and behaved and how they felt about the project and each other. Nothing profound is sought, and everyone's contribution is highly appreciated. The staff's full and even joyous participation is the key to success. When the staff sits by, professionally detached and merely observing, the spontaneity and joy are noticeably diminished, or even entirely absent, in the group.

This approach leads people into talking with each other and to discussing nonthreatening areas. After a session or two, with most groups, the discussion has not been completed by the end of the session; at this point the therapist suggests that they continue it at the next session.

At the following session the group follows through on the topic they had ended on. This follow-through from activity to discussion is not forced and usually comes about easily and naturally. At times, with a very regressed group, activity has to be resorted to again once the discussion is exhausted. This occurs more often on units in a mental hospital serving chronic long-term patients. The choice of what part of the activity (individual, dyadic, or group) to return to depends on the particular group.

With chronic patients who have been hospitalized for several years, it may be necessary to stay with an activity approach for several weeks, even months. With less damaged patients, the ego exercise received through the activity, together with the enormous decrease in anxiety due to drug therapy and removal from the external stress of (family) situations, as well as rest, hot meals, and sleep, enable flooded ego capacities to emerge rather quickly. This frequently occurs due to a significant decrease in the secondary anxiety level. Patients who experience bizarre symptoms for the first time are terrified by the realization that something strange is happening to them, something they cannot control or comprehend. One patient who began seeing the devil one morning reported thinking at the time that he must be going crazy. "I went into a total panic, which made it even worse." The anxiety and terror generated by the person's awareness that a sick process is occurring tend to completely overwhelm any remaining ego functions. On admission, such patients fit into category A. In a relatively short period of time, often two days to one week, they are again able to reflect on the psychotic process. This happens because the overall anxiety level is decreased by drugs and a supportive and understanding treatment approach. At this point they fit into category B.

The group approach during this anxiety-decreasing period should do nothing to increase anxiety. With this in mind, the nature and sequence of the chosen activity should be explored.

Certain activities arouse more anxiety in patients than do others. Dancing, for example, arouses more overt fear and resistance in patients than does working with clay or blocks. Any activity that requires people to touch each other should come later in the group's life. This is true also for activities that require the patients to make up stories or to reveal personal life experiences.

Thus the purpose of the activity group is to enable terrified, suspicious, and psychotic people to approach each other and then, through a structured method, to start interacting. This will help some to seal over their psychotic symptoms and permit early discharge and maintenance therapy. Most will move on in the discussion group.

DISCUSSION GROUP TECHNIQUES

For those who have moved from category A into category B or who entered with some nonpsychotic ego capacity, a discussion group technique has evolved.

Ten to twelve patients sit around a table and are free to choose their own discussion topics. The table is used to avoid immediate intimacy, which usually raises the anxiety level. Topics are broad and general, and people are allowed to be nonspecific and nonpersonal. The therapist may suggest certain themes to start things off, e.g., What usually annoys people about others? How does it feel to be a patient? How do we usually deal with angry feelings? What usually stops people from expressing strong emotions?

These themes are clearly related to the kinds of problems that brought most of these patients into the hospital, yet no one is forced to be personal or intimate or even to speak in the first person. General global statements are accepted and any participation is encouraged and rewarded.

What frequently happens is that people do not listen to each other and bring up totally unrelated material. Non sequiturs abound, eight people talk at once, and all statements are directed at the therapist. People want to know about medication, discharge, and visits; patients try to have one-to-one sessions with the staff leader;

and, if more than one therapist is present, each may be approached separately, with three separate interviews going on at the same time. People want to leave. Comments are made only to the nearest neighbors, and the leaders keep trying heroically to keep everyone on the agreed-upon topic. At times it makes a three-ring circus seem a quiet and pleasant affair. This happens most frequently during the beginning phase of the discussion group or when category A patients are mistakenly placed in it.

I prefer to preface the meeting by outlining its purpose and methods very clearly. I may open the session with, "We are here today to talk about topics which are of interest and concern to all of us. Everyone should make a serious attempt to contribute his thoughts. You may be scared or think that your ideas are unimportant. They are not. They may be useful to someone in the group. At the same time, try to give your fellow group members a chance to speak, too. One thing we have all learned from life is that people seldom *really* listen to each other. They either interrupt or else are thinking about what they are going to say while the other person is still talking. Let us try to be different and really try to listen. Then try and honestly respond to what you heard. This is the least we can do for each other and it often turns out to be very helpful."

A group may spend a week or even two on general discussions. The leader sums up the general ideas and themes and conceptualizes broad mental health concepts. After the first week the leader may encourage people to speak in the first person and directly to others. He may also ask for specific examples which underlie the generalization, e.g., "Could you tell the group how this actually applies to your life?"

This cannot be pressed too hard nor too soon. The leader must take his cues from the group. One or two members usually start it off on their own, and the leader then helps others do the same.

An interesting phenomenon occurs after a period of speaking in general terms. Certain members know that they are soon leaving the hospital. They also know that they have not been discussing their personal problems. Such sentiments as, "I don't feel this group is getting down to the real source or core of our problems" or "We never get down to the nitty gritty" or "This is all very nice, but it isn't really going to help me when I leave."

It is at this point that the group is asking for and is ready for a different group therapy approach. Groups give their cues, and a sensitive leader can hear them and respond accordingly. A major advantage of the first two approaches is that skillful clinicians are not necessary. Outside of large cities and teaching hospitals, few experienced therapists are available to conduct these groups several times a week. The work can be done by beginning social workers, experienced nurses, and occupational and recreational therapists. Trained aides and other mature paraprofessionals have conducted these groups with great success and with minimal supervision.

FOCAL THERAPY

Membership is open to those from category C and those from category B whose ego resources have strengthened and recuperated during their stay and who are now ready for a more insightful approach to their problems. Quite often, a discussion group which had evolved from an activity group progresses into a focal therapy group. This does not tend to occur rapidly with chronic long-term patients but most frequently happens on a short-term unit of a general hospital or in a short-term private hospital. Needless to say, a state hospital serves a very different patient population than does a small unit in a suburban or rural community. Our society still sends its poorest and most damaged members to its out-of-sight-out-of-mind institutions.

Focal therapy is limited to (1) what precipitated the acute pathological response that necessitated hospitalization; (2) what the immediate conflicts were that produced the pathological reaction; (3) how they dealt with it; (4) how their maladaptive patterns emerge on the ward and especially in the group in the here and now; and (5) the discovery of alternate modes of behavior which they can practice and which can be rewarded and reinforced while still in the hospital.

It is not the therapist's intention to resolve these conflicts completely but rather to identify them and to engage the patient in working on them. The aim is to involve the patient in a therapeutic process he will be willing if not eager to continue upon discharge.

When the past is explored, it is only in relation to specific present-day conflicts and care is taken not to uncover at random past conflicts, pains, traumas, and anxieties. When the past is discussed it is directly linked, in a clear way, to how it is influencing present-day functioning.

If possible, the focus remains on the factors precipitating the maladaptive response. John, 41, married with three children, was admitted because of a depression. He had been on the surgical ward for major surgery a few weeks earlier, and a few weeks after discharge had become depressed. He was constantly concerned about his wife, who he feared could not manage while he was away. He had suffered a depression eight years before. It soon became clear that his wife had been telling him her problems and fears, both while he was awaiting surgery and during his recuperation. She had expected *him* to look after *her* needs, even though he very much needed to be taken care of himself. Her blindness to his realistic needs was obvious to everyone but him.

Instead of asserting his own needs, he kept worrying about her and began to feel guilty about being sick. "What is she going to do without me? Her mother is going home in a few days and she will be alone."

In the group, members pointed out how unrealistic he was about himself. He was the one that needed to be cared for and his wife was quite able to manage by herself. In fact, after all these years, if they had a real partnership, she ought to be looking after him. Other members expressed great anger at his wife. John, protective of her, was able to admit a slight annoyance with her.

The patient was unaware of the degree of his rage at his infantile and demanding mate. His reactive depression was due to a general weakening of ego strength due to the recent major surgery. The surgery affected his self and body image and also deprived him of the compulsive work activities that had served as an adequate defense against rage. Deprived of this, his rage was turned against himself and emerged as depression. We judged the rage to be homicidal in nature, especially after surgery. We speculated that his wife was similar to his mother, whom he had looked after until her death. We were not interested in making that connection, however, and instead stayed in the present and supported his right to be annoyed. On the floor and in the group we highlighted again and again how he could not express anger at anyone. We questioned the reasons for this, since it was clear to the entire group that this was a problem. On the floor we attempted to help him assert himself and rewarded any slight sign of it. Gradually and tentatively, he began to speak up.

We wanted to make the connection between his depression and sense of being burdened with his feelings about the constant demands made on him by his wife. We considered in the group why he felt he had to do everything for her. That was not required, nor was it good for her. She had to use and exercise her own strengths and assets. His babying her made her weaker, not stronger. In eight days his depression lifted. He felt stronger, asked for couples therapy on an outpatient basis, and wanted to continue in group therapy.

In this instance, the goals were quite limited and focused. We identified the immediate noxious source; focused in on it; helped him see how unexpressed affects can boomerang; and encouraged and reinforced an alternative form of behavior which he then practiced both on the floor and in the group.

Whether or not patients tell us what they think their problems are, they invariably demonstrate, in the group, the pathological behavior patterns that underlie their disturbance. The experienced therapist is bombarded by these communications, which the patient can express in no other way than by enacting them for the therapist in relation to group members. The therapist, if he can, points out these maladaptive patterns and shows how they work against the patient, both in the group and in everyday life.

These focal therapy groups are smaller in size than the activity and discussion groups—usually from six to eight patients. A senior member of the staff, with more extensive clinical experience, usually conducts them. It is hard to keep goals in view and to work only in selected areas; untrained therapists tend to wander, allow for too much uncovering, and find it difficult to detect repetitive maladaptive patterns.

The experience has to be crisp and exciting. The therapist identifies the problem and gets the patients involved in working on them. In the final phase, outpatient treatment plans are discussed and arranged; if possible, the patient starts attending an outpatient group while still in the hospital. It is important that the inpatient group help the patient become involved in outpatient treatment.

As one young woman stated, "At least I know now what the hell is bothering me and I know what I have to work on. Although I'm going to be afraid to start, I'm going to." Since she was going to return to another city, the staff could not follow through completely, but did find a therapist for her and spoke to him. If she did not contact him they were to be informed. They never heard from him and assumed she did follow through.

Over all, groups are used to make the hospital stay pleasant, exciting, and rewarding. A therapeutic milieu is provided that gives the drug therapy a chance to work. People often think it is the other way around, but it is not. Some staffs immobilize their patients on high dosages in order to manage them. I find that the therapeutic group approach helps to manage the patient so that he can be treated with reasonable dosage levels that do not make him a walking zombie. Groups can be used to bring the patient out of his emotional isolation and withdrawal and into contact and relation with other human beings.

A medium is offered in which he can learn and practice different modes of relating and get some idea of how he affects other people. The therapist focuses on how the patient unwittingly alienates and antagonizes others and how he deals with his major emotions, such as anger, tenderness, and hurt.

This is started during the end phase of the discussion group and centered on in focal therapy. The entire staff is used, all through the day and night, to help the patient practice less self-destructive ways of expressing affects. This is discussed in the group, and the patient's cooperation is enlisted in determining what behavior he wishes to alter. Therapy is thus an all-day process that is formulated in the group and carried on by every staff member through all the shifts. Fellow group members are even more important as they are involved in helping each other alter the maladaptive patterns revealed in group sessions; they encourage each other throughout the day to practice the new patterns that are suggested in the group.

A deep sense of community begins to develop, with warmth, support, and camaraderie much in evidence. One very withdrawn and suspicious man, George, age 46, could say after ten days, "You know, this is the first time in my life that I have ever spoken like this in front of a group. I had to bring myself up since I was a little boy. My father died when I was three and I was the oldest. I never let anybody help me. It was always, 'George could always do it for himself. George knows how.' Shit, George didn't know beans and I am only beginning to realize that now. It's the first time I've expressed anything about myself to anybody. You know what? It feels great!"

For the therapist, the approaches discussed above are rewarding and difficult. Often patients remain in the activity or discussion phase of the work. Sometimes there are not enough people to form a focal therapy group. With very damaged patients there is little opportunity during a short hospitalization to work with them in focal therapy—by the time they are ready for it, they are also ready for discharge.

On many psychiatric wards therapists immediately attempt to use focal insight therapy with acutely psychotic patients (category A). The therapist then finds himself coping with all kinds of management problems, as this approach can stimulate levels of anxiety this category of patient cannot tolerate without resorting to extreme fight-flight reactions and bizarre psychotic behavior.

The patient who is still struggling with an active psychosis does not want to talk about the causes of his problems. This patient might say, "I don't want to talk about my real problem because it upsets me too much and it doesn't help me. I can't deal with it." This is told verbally to a therapist the patient knows and trusts. But when the therapist is a stranger, the patient will say it through behavior. He will run out of the room, not be on the ward for the next meeting, become agitated and violent during and after the group session, withdraw into sleep or bizarre behavior, "go awol," or, as a last resort, commit suicide.

The therapist who insists in working in an uncovering way with such patients finds himself dealing with these problems. He has to decide such questions as: Should we lock and bar the door? Should we prohibit (using physical force if necessary) any patient from leaving the session? Should we lock up the ward so as to prevent patients from leaving before sessions? How are we going to deal with a resentful staff that has to live with the agitated and violent reactions? Should we use high levels of medication to restrain violent and agitated behavior during and after the sessions?

If the above approach is to be used successfully, the therapist must have a considerable body of experience and skill and thoroughly train and involve his staff so that they can tolerate and actively support this approach. In many cases this is unfeasible, as most hospitals have undermanned and undertrained staffs.

An approach that is more acceptable to me is one that recognizes the enormous anxiety and pain the schizophrenic patient is struggling with. The schizophrenic must be approached at a pace he can tolerate, one that does not threaten him with complete loss of control. A healthy respect for his defenses and the reasons for them is essential.

Therapists may become impatient in their desire to help as much as possible in the short time allotted them and may therefore use methods that unintentionally may be hurtful. Unfortunately a myth exists in the field that the only "real therapy" is insight therapy, that anything else (such as activity or discussion) is for those who are low on the hierarchical totem pole. This has proven disastrous for the severely disturbed patient, as the more experienced and trained professional will not deign to engage in a treatment approach which, though considered to be beneath his dignity, may nevertheless be best for the patient. The experienced therapist often has little experience or skill in activity or theme-centered approaches, and so does not use them. He instead attempts to do what he is most familiar and comfortable with, which often proves unhelpful and even hurtful to the still psychotic patient.

The therapist in the very short-term group psychotherapy approach I have presented can never reach the working through stage of treatment. He is always in the formation and first stage of group therapy, and gets patients prepared for ongoing therapy with someone else. It can be frustrating for those who like to see things through to the end. It is a repetitive and endless job. The complete turnover of patients almost every two weeks keeps the staff at the beginning of the process. If they are to be successful, they must become involved, committed, and deeply concerned. They then have to separate from the people they have come to care about. This chronic separation makes short-term inpatient group psychotherapy a painful job, especially for the neophyte therapist.

CONCLUDING REMARKS

This approach attempts to establish a therapeutic regimen with acutely ill patients. Group methods are used to diminish the anxiety associated with self-exposure before others. Structured situations are used to control the anxiety level of the group. Since confrontation and nondirective approaches stimulate high degrees of tension and anxiety, they should be avoided in the short-term setting. This does not rule out eventual forms of confrontation or nondirective approaches. My approach aims to establish a treatment relationship that can tolerate and fully utilize these approaches when they are indicated with particular patients. My major concern is that we take care not to alienate patients from the treatment process that many of them need to continue when they leave hospital care. The fight against a psychotic process is often a lifetime battle, and group approaches are proving very valuable in helping people to remain free of psychosis for longer periods of time.

REFERENCE

Liberman, R. (1971), Reinforcement of cohesiveness in group therapy. *Arch. Gen. Psychiat.*, 25:168–177.

Part IV
Countertransference

Introduction

The complex and important dynamics of countertransference in relation to group psychotherapy is a neglected area of investigation. This is particularly so as regards the treatment of hospitalized patients. The sympathetic listening that all patients are entitled to in psychoanalytic treatment is a psychic stance not easily arrived at within the psychotherapy group, particularly when one is confronted with a group of severely disturbed patients.

There are many reasons for the neglect of this important area. Not so long ago, countertransference was an exclusively pejorative term; it was not supposed to happen. Over time, however, a growing recognition of the ubiquity of countertransference reactions has developed, as well as of the ongoing need for the therapist to analyze these reactions as a source of important information concerning both therapist and patient.

In Chapter 14, an updated version of an earlier paper with the same title, Roth provides a general introduction to the area. Hannah Hull's comprehensive review of group countertransference with inpatient groups (Chapter 15) originally appeared in 1984 and is considered one of the outstanding contributions in this area. Finally, Chapter 16, in which Liebenberg very courageously and candidly relates her experience of a group failure, offers a sensitive portrait that conveys the clinical importance of countertransference in the conduct of analytic group psychotherapy.

14

Countertransference and the Group Therapist's State of Mind

BENNETT E. ROTH, Ph.D.

Countertransference, considered as an interference in the group psychotherapist's state of mind, can occur either while in the group or when thinking about the group or its individual members. This interference has psychic origins. In a group composed of patients with narcissistic and borderline defenses, the presence of oscillating demands made on the group by patients, of special attention being paid to a particular member, or of the need for the therapist to take safe psychological distance from patients often indicates an underlying countertransference. If the patient in a group can be successfully treated only on the basis of the development of group transferences, then the group therapist can analyze the group only through his ability to analyze the complex individual and group countertransference dynamics.

To accomplish the therapeutic analysis within any ongoing psychotherapy group, the therapist is required to make a series of empathic trial identifications with each member. Empathy toward the patient is a natural occurrence and not a technique. Among the problems that occur because of group members' wide range of regressive conflicts is the strain on the therapist's empathic capacity.

The appearance of what is called countertransference is a common occurrence with therapists who work closely with the manifest level of material and is particularly important when dealing with the so-called narcissistic defenses. When dealing with countertransference, many variables must be considered: source, function, psychological valence (whether countertransference or empathic failure), and clinical management. But most of all what has to be considered is the following: once you have isolated it as countertransference, what is to be done?

Freud (1910, 1915) originated the term "countertransference" to denote a neurosis that deprived the therapist or psychoanalyst of the required analytic neutrality and could lead to the analyst's acting out and psychologically contaminating the operational field in which psychoanalytic treatment takes place. As psychoanalytic theory has become more sophisticated and complex, so too has our understanding of the transference-countertransference situation. The recent theoretical foundations of contemporary ego psychology, object relations theory, and self psychology have required a reexamination of the operational field of both psychoanalysis and psychotherapy, and a closer look at the complex psychic forces at work between the persons in that field.

It is possible to summarize the important theoretical positions regarding countertransference as follows. The *totalistic* position considers all feelings and attitudes of the therapist toward the patient as countertransference; that is, they are, totally and exclusively, reactions to the patient. The *classical* position defines countertransference as the unconscious reaction of the therapist to the patient's transference; these responses may be neurotic, psychotic, or nonpathological. The *interactive* position views countertransference as the counterpart or complement to the transference of the patient; in other words a transference-transference situation.

Before going further into this subject, I would like to sound some cautionary notes. Whenever I think of countertransference, I am mindful of remarks Bion made in a private seminar in New York some years ago. When asked how he managed his countertransference reactions to schizophrenic patients, he replied to the effect, "When I am aware of it, I try and use it somehow." Bion's reply did not please the questioner, who persisted and wanted to know more. Bion tried again and said, "After all, countertransference is unconscious by definition. Like everyone else, the practitioner can only get a 'good enough analysis'. . . . If countertransference remains a problem, he should go back to treatment."

I have chosen to start with Freud and Bion because they represent the awareness that all forms of psychoanalytic treatment are composed of a field of experience involving at least two persons, a field that holds the interactive potential to interfere in each partici-

pant's mental life. Likely this is true of any interpersonal arrangement, but what is unique about psychoanalytic treatment is that we
arrange this interference on a regular basis with some therapeutic
hope and expectancy.

It is not possible to think of countertransference as isolated from
other complex human parameters. Countertransference in a particular group therapy situation is a function of the particular group
therapist, the mix of patients in the group, their particular state at the
moment, and the therapist's theory of technique and style of leadership, and what he or she may actually be doing in the group setting.

When a phenomenological eye is cast on the operational field of
group psychotherapy, we are confronted with a more complex
arrangement than in the bipersonal field of psychoanalysis. Let me set
the operational stage of a psychotherapy group: let us imagine a
number of unrelated adults, say eight or nine, convened in a room,
seated, all in various states of interpersonal distress and intrapsychic
discomfort, with different self states or ego states at any given
moment. Located in this field is another person, a designated group
psychotherapist, armed with understanding, knowledge, training,
and a fund of group experience. The group therapist's covert role
may be generally understood as being the offering of equal protection
and interpretive help to each member of the group, to encourage
interaction, and to offer and maintain a nonabrasive boundary of
permissible verbal behavior. Add to this field of interaction each
individual's mythic and real transferences to the other group members, to the group as a psychic entity, and to the therapist as the leader
of the group.

The group psychotherapist, secure in role and function, presides
over this complex, dynamic, and conflicted situation. The group
psychotherapist maintains a balance of inner- and outer-directed
attention: inwardly to his or her own thoughts and feelings, memory
and intuition, and outwardly to the individual members, their manifest conflicts, and the intuited group as a whole. When attentive to the
members of the group, the psychotherapist is closest to the raw
phenomena of the group and most likely to act out—or more
precisely to act in—and become a member of the group. When
outside the group and more inner-directed, the psychotherapist is
absorbed in the role of therapist and reliant on the ego functions
appropriate to that role: namely, listening, remembering, synthesiz-
ing, intuiting, and interpreting. When attentive to the intuited group

as a whole, to the unconscious contribution of each member, and to an unconscious group purpose, the therapist is receptive to the mythic purposes in all groups and mentally far away from the individuals in the group.

It is my experience that individuals and groups have different requirements and tolerances as regards the mental state of the group psychotherapist. In time there develops an awareness of the interactive balance between being inside or outside the group that is most comfortable and most effective for a particular psychotherapist. It is within this interactive equation that the unspoken dynamics of separation and individuation are often revealed. Both individual and group tolerances, as well as demands for the closeness or distance of the psychotherapist, operate to move the therapist to the required interpersonal and interactive distance. Needless to say, these operations on the part of the group or the individual also affect the available ego functions of the therapist.

Let us look at the group psychotherapy situation, with its various levels of interfering transferences. Since patients come to the group psychotherapy situation with a number of conscious and unconscious expectations, they attempt to change the nature of the group and the function of the group therapist in line with these. Most of the expectations are unconscious and can be understood as originating in the patient's childhood in the form and structure of a childhood neurosis or, in some cases, a childhood trauma and psychosis. A commonly held expectation by patients is that nothing will happen, that no change will occur, or that something bad will happen. Resistive expectations of this sort are far from neutral in their power and force and require collaborative individual and group effort if they are to be overcome.

If patients have an expectation based on the structure and dynamics of their conflicts, group therapists must be alert to their own expectation, for while it is similar in origin to that of their patients, the therapist is better able to use it analytically. In general, any expectation on the part of the therapist interferes with the receptor function of the therapist, much as a colored filter interferes with the light that enters a camera lens. It is possible, though not always certain, that expectations in a well-analyzed psychotherapist are induced by the group or by a patient. It is also possible that, as Reich (1966) pointed out, a particular patient or a particular conflict situation in the group may recall an unanalyzed infantile object for the psychotherapist.

I have continued to have problems with the concepts, originally introduced by Racker (1968), of induced and reactive countertransference. This remains so despite my efforts to track and trace these reactions in my paper on identity-impaired persons (Roth, 1980). My confusion with these concepts is that they seem to overlap in the inductive crucible of the psychoanalytic group situation. I also have serious doubts concerning the object relations position that induced reactions are an exact replica of an infantile situation; or, more clearly, that either the group or the psychotherapist can become identical with a patient's infantile object or selfobject without a collaborative willingness on the part of the psychotherapist. It is my experience that induced reactions are simply not generated simply by the therapist's failure to accurately understand an important resistance, but are either attempts to closely replicate a narcissistic fault in a two-person experience or to generate proof of a regressively returned inconsistent infantile object relationship. Borderline and narcissistic patients in particular, although it is possible in all patients, maintain a constant pressure to establish between psychotherapist and patient, patient and group, or between patient and patient, an emotionally charged empathic fault or trauma that has the potential to destroy, disrupt, or divert the treatment. The therapist's countertransference reactions to these events are not as specific as the original relationship, particularly when they occur in a group.

Since I believe there is an interaction between transference and countertransference, this two-person fault can be overcome only through the combined interactive effort of the therapist and the patients involved. This usually requires a long working through of multidetermined events. Otherwise, a negative therapeutic reaction, a transference-countertransference stalemate, or a false self or "as if" group organization will occur.

To return again to the group psychotherapy situation: the shared intimacy of the group situation has a distinct dynamic all its own and sets before the presiding group psychotherapist a veritable array of psychological events and data. Sources of the data are the content of communications, the various modes of verbal and nonverbal communication, verbal nuances, gestures, facial expressions, silence, and the contiguity of group events. This manifest material reveals the underlying structures and forces that give the group events their multiple analytic meaning. It is the therapist's organization of the meaning of group and individual events, for both participants and observers, that leads to the core analytic understandings. To drink from this deep well, the group therapist must sort out fragments of group action and reaction, defense and desire, ego form and substance, and self and infantile objects. In actual practice this is no easy task, for the subject of our understanding is not the utterances of a single person but the shifting, often turbulent patterns of regressive reactions and reactive potentials in a group of persons.

Each, and perhaps every, group event, were we able to put it in stop action, is the product of the multi-person transferences of the group situation and the original conflict situation, with all of the relevant regressive self- and infantile objects. For example, the expression of a wish by a member of a group may simultaneously elicit defenses against such a wish in other group members, a breaking of the group rules of behavior, the silent wish of some other group member, vicarious support in another, and a complex transference process, combining the here and now and the regressive past, for all the members. This multifunctional and multipurpose group event is the basis of the countertransference reactions inherent in group psychotherapy. That is, the group offers to the presiding group psychotherapist a smorgasbord of psychic events with which to identify. The presentation of this chaotic array is enough to generate confusion in the inexperienced. In groups that are liable to function on a primitive level, the psychic cacophony is even more disjunctive and is punctuated by conflictual material from even earlier nonverbal sources. Some group therapists are unable psychically to hold this confusion and seek to stifle or prematurely interpret it: they cannot discern what is important for the individuals and the group.

The psychic array of desire and defense, narcissistic objects, real objects, and infantile part objects sets up another problem for the group therapist. Since empathic identification or trial identification allows the empathic closeness between therapist and patient and forms the empathic link that is essential to interpretive understanding and acceptance, the group therapist is faced with the formidable task of multiple empathic identifications. Put another way, the group psychotherapist must identify with both wishes and their defenses, with healthy ego functions, and with infantile and reality-based object relationships, in a number of persons. In order to accomplish this multiple identification, a particular form of bifurcation on the part of the group therapist is required, an oscillation among all these that allows the therapist to maintain an analytic balance. Failure to maintain this introspective balance and bifurcation results in a one-sided understanding that leads to technical errors, misinterpretations, and countertransference reactions. While I have not finished thinking through this oscillation process, it seems clear that the failure to maintain this introspective stance in the face of the constant array of group psychological events prevents both recall and reconstruction of the genetic roots of the patient's conflicts and induces an array of transference cures or transference subjugations. For me, at least, certainty or the complete absence of doubt is an indication that I have failed to maintain an introspective balance.

The group therapy situation described in operational terms in this chapter is fraught with various levels of interference for each of the participants. Here we are concerned in particular with the interferences that occur for the group therapist. The therapist's state of mind is not a tabula rasa; rather, the therapist enters the group with a set of attitudes toward people in general and toward groups in general. With this assumption, we are already into a process of interferences. The who, the what, and the how of countertransference can be discerned only when we can enumerate further the components of our state of mind when we are at work. A working model of the therapeutic stance that I have found useful is as follows: (1) intellectual understanding, based on the knowledge possessed by the therapist and on the intellectual, informational aspects of the clinical data; (2) emotional availability, the dynamics of the emotional range of the therapist as they relate to the particular conflicts and defenses of his or her own life at any particular time; (3) the real response to the patient or group, the counterpart of what Greenson (1971) calls the real response to the analyst; (4) the therapist's transference to the patient or the group, the reliving of infantile object, part-object, or infantile urges elicited by certain features in the group or patient; (5) the therapist's countertransference proper, the reaction of the therapist's unconscious, to the role or object assignment of the patient's or the group's transferences; (6) the therapist's capacity to tune empathically into the psychological state of the-patient-in-the-group (here I find myself frequently using the word "strain"); (7) the therapist's theoretical understanding of complex group and individual dynamics, including ideas about healthy functioning.

It is important to remember that "tuning in" also exists in "creative patients" and in certain narcissistic and borderline patients who have learned to tune in quickly to aspects of the therapist's personality, thereby creating a complex transference-counter-transference reaction.

While I have been able to divide these mental states and to give them clarity, I have also rendered them harm by making them separate: it is obvious that they are related to one another. Their separate significance becomes apparent only through self-analysis of the interferences that patients effect on their therapists.

Intensive psychoanalytic work with borderline and narcissistic patients, in both group and individual psychotherapy, has repeatedly demonstrated how vulnerable each of these therapist functions is to the projective defenses of these patients. In this brief presentation, clinical examples of these interferences cannot be given, but such instances will be found in the chapters to follow.

I trust that I have nowhere implied any agreement with the idea that the therapist is the single analyzing instrument, in either individual or group psychotherapy, and is simply played upon by psychological events. Such a notion, aside from its casting the therapist in a totally receptive or passive role, makes treatment too one-sided and atheoretical. There is a difference, as Winnicott (1971) has suggested, between being played upon and being played with. At the other extreme, I have not the narcissistic conviction that my countertransference can be an exact replica of the patient's experience. Such a position denies the difference between patient and therapist, as well as the dynamic complexity of patients' transference and the multitude of infantile objects and part-objects in which the group and the therapist can simultaneously be cast.

REFERENCES

Freud, S. (1910), The future prospects of psycho-analytic therapy. *Standard Edition*, 11:141–151. London: Hogarth Press, 1957.
———— (1915), Observations on transference-love. *Standard Edition*, 12:159–171. London: Hogarth Press, 1958.
Greenson, R. R. (1971), The "real" relationship between the patient and the psychoanalyst. In: *The Unconscious Today: Essays in Honor of Max Schur*, ed. M. Kanzer. New York: International Universities Press, pp. 213–232.
Racker, H. (1968), *Transference and Countertransference*. New York: International Universities Press.
Reich, A. (1966), Empathy and countertransference. In: *Psychoanalytic Contributions*. New York: International Universities Press, 1973, pp. 344–360.
Roth, B. (1980), Understanding the development of a homogeneous, identity-impaired group through countertransference phenomena. *Internat. J. Group Psychother.*, 30:405–426.
Winnicott, D. W. (1971), *Playing and Reality*. New York: Basic Books.

15

Countertransference in Inpatient Group Psychotherapy: Implications for Technique

SUSAN HANNAH HULL, Ph.D.

Countertransference and technique are subjects seldom discussed in the group psychotherapy literature. Countertransference, fortunately, has finally taken its place beside transference and resistance as a major dimension of the therapeutic relationship that can significantly affect treatment outcome; as a result, therapists have become more willing to share countertransference experiences (see Roth, 1980). A further benefit derived from the emergence of countertransference as a legitimate focus for the therapist's attention has been the increasing emphasis on what has been termed the "creative" use of countertransference, i.e., the use of the therapist's emotional responses to the patient as valuable clues to possible latent or clouded aspects of the therapeutic relationship that may have been impeding progress in the treatment. In other words, countertransference responses can affect a therapist's technical decisions for better or worse.

Discussions of technique, as I have suggested, have been infrequent in the literature on group psychotherapy. This is partly because theoretical principles must be clearly defined if decisions regarding technique are to carry real meaning, and in the field of group psychotherapy a distinct theoretical base is still lacking. It is also difficult to be specific about technical issues when they are so closely

This chapter was first published in the *International Journal of Group Psychotherapy* (1984), 34(2):257–272, and is reprinted with permission.

tied to the personal style and characteristics of particular group therapists. Nevertheless, questions and concerns about technique are often uppermost in the minds of even experienced group therapists. Given the multitude of stimuli and choices of intervention in the group setting, it is likely that the active, conscious thinking process of the therapist will be focused on technical issues at least as often as on theoretical issues.

On the short-term hospital unit, questions regarding countertransference and technique take on an added intensity. Technique may become just another word for management, and factors unique to the inpatient setting can seem to be conspiring to elicit strong countertransference reactions in even the most skilled and well-intentioned therapists.

The present discussion will first address some of the unique aspects of the setting, including the inpatient milieu and the patients who are found there. This will lead to a complex and multidimensional view of the small psychotherapy group, a view that is essential if countertransference reactions are to be examined and understood. I will discuss types of countertransference reactions that frequently occur in the inpatient group therapist, with emphasis on reactions pertaining to confrontational and supportive attitudes toward the group and its members. It is a major premise of this chapter that techniques used in working with inpatient groups are often in fact derived from countertransference reactions that have been rationalized as being therapeutically necessary responses to patients. The role of group supervision as a particularly appropriate means of facilitating the therapist's awareness and use of countertransference in the group will be described.

THE HOSPITAL MILIEU

The most striking contrast between the short-term inpatient unit and the typical private practice setting is in the degree of autonomy enjoyed by the therapist. Decisions about the boundaries of the group, on the most overt level of who shall enter or leave the group, who shall observe the group, and where and when the group shall meet, are rarely left to the inpatient group therapist. Often such decisions are made completely on the basis of administrative concerns and may even run counter to the therapist's wishes and to the requirements of good treatment.

The hospital setting also maximizes the amount of contact between members of the group and between patients and staff, not all of whom will behave consistently with the therapist's treatment plan. One might imagine each member of the group having an array of other professionals, the treatment team, accompanying him or her to the group session. In fact, countertransference reactions can form distinct patterns within the treatment team that reflect the various splitting and projective processes in the patient (Harty, 1979). This notion is similar to that to be discussed in this chapter, but it operates on another level of the complex hospital system.

Finally, the group therapist is usually on the unit at times other than when the group meets and may interact with the patients in a capacity totally different from that of therapy group leader. Thus, not only do the patients bring an array of other experiences with other hospital staff with them to the group, but the therapist may also bring an array of experiences with each patient, such as having been the patient's primary nurse, social worker, occupational therapist, individual therapist, or medicating psychiatrist. Needless to say, given these external complexities of the hospital environment, the therapy group takes on added, and potentially confusing, dimensions.

THE HOSPITALIZED PATIENT

In addition to environmental factors, the process in the therapy group will be affected by each individual patient and his or her internalized object world. The impact of the variety of persons with whom the patient comes into contact while in the hospital will be further complicated by the fact that decompensated patients' perceptions are frequently dominated by primitive paranoid and narcissistic identifications (Kibel, 1978) and by the effects of primitive mental processes that may be largely unchecked by reality-oriented defenses. Volkan (1976) used the term "emotional flooding" and described the changes in perceptions of self, object, and environment that can occur under such conditions in psychotic patients.

The prehospital state of such patients is usually one in which some degree of self-object differentiation has been maintained and in which splitting as a defense mechanism has been relatively intact and successful at keeping a core, however small, of "good" self- and object representations safe from contamination by aggressive impulses (Kernberg, 1975). One of the assumptions that has been made about

these patients is that they require hospitalization when the splitting
mechanism fails and the "good" self- and object representations are
overrun by aggression; self-object differentiation may then break
down, possibly as a last resort to ward off total destruction (Kibel,
1978).

Once patients are hospitalized, it would be expected that projective identifications would abound, as attempts to expel bad self- and
object images and to reestablish splitting in some reliable manner are
continued. Modell (1963) points out that it is important to accept the
aggression of these patients, as it is primarily a defense stemming
from the fear that their love is destructive. It thus becomes the task of
the therapist to permit what can sometimes feel like a literal assault of
demands and anger from these patients; the therapist must serve as a
"container" for their negative projections (Grinberg, Sor, and de
Bianchedi, 1977) while maintaining a differentiation from them and
avoiding what has been called projective counteridentification (Grinberg, 1979).

As a further complication, the fact that hospitalization has been
required suggests that, regardless of the diagnosis or particular
dynamics of a patient, a failure of some (perhaps all) reality-related
ego functions has occurred. This requires that the therapist provide
some of the necessary ego functioning for the patient, explaining
reality and setting limits without being drawn into the patient's
internal drama through overgratification or overfrustration.

Confusion regarding appropriate responses to patients is understandable given the fact that the role of the hospital and of the
inpatient therapist is a paradoxical one. The hospital is offered as a
means to reintegration, yet it also has the potential to foster a
dependent regression by further stimulating the patient's helpless,
omnipotent, or fearful attitudes toward authority; these are associated with internalized object images of parental origin (Kibel, 1978).
Serious problems can arise, particularly with borderline patients,
when an intensive treatment milieu does not include clearly defined
and consistent limits on the gratification of the patients' wishes
(Friedman, 1969).

Group psychotherapy with these patients presents the added
complication of a range of psychopathology and available ego resources within the group. The group therapist must not only assess
and respond to the needs of one patient but must find a way to
"orchestrate" the variety of needs and defenses of all members of the

group so that some coherent process results. Because each interaction in the group, whether between therapist and group member or between the members themselves, will have an impact on the entire group as well as on the direct participants in the exchange, the potential for countertransference reactions seems geometrically increased over that of the individual treatment situation (Roth, 1980).

COUNTERTRANSFERENCE AND EMPATHY IN THE GROUP

For the purpose of this discussion, countertransference is taken to include all emotional responses that the therapist has toward the patient and the group. This definition allows such responses to be seen as either interfering with or facilitating the therapeutic interaction, depending upon the manner in which they are understood and utilized by the therapist. Such a definition also facilitates discussion in the supervisory group, since it is not necessary to presuppose the presence of unresolved infantile conflicts in order to talk about the therapist's feelings while in the group. In fact, it is preferable to heighten therapists' and observers' awareness of the universality of many of their responses to patients.

One reason that a supervisory group is an effective means of learning about group therapy is that there are many parallels that can be drawn between the experience of the inpatient group therapist and that of the hospitalized patient in the group. These parallels will often emerge spontaneously in the supervisory group and can be important ways of identifying and exploring countertransference reactions.

For example, it is not uncommon for the supervisory group to be struggling with the same fundamental issues that emerge in the patient group, including concerns about trust, aggressive impulses, and responses to the leader. The staff group is part of the same hospital system as are the patients and thus are subject to similar problems regarding frustration, dependency, and loss of autonomy. These parallels make the supervisory group a valuable opportunity for exploring some of the defensive barriers that can be constructed in the group therapist's attempts at self-preservation. The ultimate goal is to facilitate the making or repairing of empathic connections between staff and patients in the group.

In the approach described here, empathy is a particular type of countertransference, used in a facilitative way. On an individual level, Racker (1968) makes this distinction in his use of the terms "con-

cordant" and "complementary" identifications. A concordant identification is one between the ego of the therapist, or an aspect of the
therapist's ego, and the same aspect of the patient's ego; this identification forms the basis for empathy. A complementary identification
is one formed with an object in the patient's internal world, which, if
not recognized by the therapist, can induce the therapist to behave
toward the patient as that object has behaved. Thus in the therapist is
found a parallel to projective identification in the patient.

In the group, a failure in the empathic connection is more likely
to be obscured than in the individual setting, as there is a larger cast
of characters, of whom some will be particularly suited as vehicles for
the projective identifications of others, including those of the therapist. Further, the therapist may feel especially vulnerable in the group
to certain interferences with the necessary empathic regression (Roth,
1980) and thus is more likely to resort to relatively primitive defenses.

It is important to note, however, that whereas the group setting
increases the demands on the therapist, in that empathic identifications are required for not one but many patients, with a wide range of
disturbances, the group can also offer assistance to both its members
and its leader which is not available in the individual setting.

For example, in one group a patient had arrived for the session
after an extremely destructive outburst the night before, during
which she had destroyed the Christmas tree that had been decorated
by patients and staff. The entire unit had been shaken by this event;
most group members had seen its aftermath in the morning, but
many did not know who was responsible. The group leader, having
weathered many aggressive and sarcastic assaults from this patient in
the group, felt too overcome with rage at the patient to make any
objective judgment as to whether the incident should be brought up
and how it should be pursued, if at all. She decided, based on the
intensity of her feelings, to wait, more out of a feeling of helplessness
than out of any sense that it was the appropriate response.

The group proceeded to express a variety of reactions to the
incident, with a predominant affect of sadness, rather than anger.
The patient was able to admit having destroyed the tree, and was
helped by the group's questions to discuss the possible precipitating
factors. One group member took on a protective, explanatory role,
another was more disapproving, whereas a third expressed anger at
the staff. The therapist was able to direct her attention to the process
in the group without having to restore the empathic connection to the

patient immediately. In fact, after the group the therapist reported that her rage toward the patient had diminished considerably.

Similarly, the presence of other group members as targets for projections may permit an adaptive type of splitting that can facilitate the expression of complex feelings. In the group just described, an older Catholic policeman often became involved in discussions about relationships to authority figures, expressing opinions that allowed other members to react to and project aspects of their own attitudes and aggressions. Unverbalized, these might otherwise have contributed to the acting out of a group resistance.

As demonstrated in the first example, aggressive impulses in the group therapist, as well as in the group members, can often be the cause of a breakdown in the therapeutic process. In the absence of inhibiting defenses in the patients, the threat of violence on an inpatient unit is a very real one. Certainly emotional violence is a central part of the inpatient experience, both within individual patients and in interaction with others on the unit. Because of the necessity of providing missing ego functions, and the strong emotions that can be evoked, issues of control are as prominent in the hospital staff as in the patients. Though realistic controls are needed, tendencies in the staff toward restriction and suppression of all aggressive impulses in the patients can lead to what has been termed an "erosion of mature personality" on the hospital unit (Gustafson, 1979). Disturbances in either the awareness or the management of aggression can result in the misuse or misunderstanding of the supportive and confrontational attitudes that are essential for the most effective use of the group.

Obviously, therapists' relative comfort with their own aggression will influence the handling of aggression in the group. This can be seen in the overcontrolling, restrictive methods previously mentioned, but can also interfere in the opposite direction. Therapists may gloss over or deny aggression in the group so that their own aggression will not be stimulated. For example, in one group an extremely provocative and aggressive young woman was taunting the men in the group with sexual innuendos and was becoming increasingly agitated. The therapist, defending against strong punitive impulses, attempted to reason with the young woman rather than eject her from the group, thus forgetting that the group therapist's primary task is to guard the boundaries of the group against violation, from within as well as from without. The patient's provocations escalated to the point where she began to undress in the group, whereupon the therapist had to call for assistance from a nurse, whom the patient physically assaulted. The discussion in the supervisory group afterward focused on the confusion that can occur when a group therapist must weigh group and individual needs as well as sorting out countertransference and realistic responses to events in the group.

Group psychotherapy can require different interventions than might be indicated in an individual setting. It is not enough for the group therapist to respond to individual members with individualized comments, however appropriate or accurate the remarks might be. Any event, whether it occurs in the group or on the unit, has an impact on every member of the group, regardless of how peripheral a member might seem. The group therapist who values the goal of group cohesiveness, even in the face of extreme diversity of members, will select material and focus interventions differently than in a dyadic relationship. In fact, reminding oneself that one is treating a *group* can prove to be a valuable aid in resolving countertransference dilemmas triggered by responses to individual patients.

Another clinical example may help to illustrate some of the points made thus far. This group, as is often the case, was frequently dominated by one verbal, angry member, and in one session the therapist found herself quite angry as this patient continually berated her for numerous failures to help him; he imagined rebuffs, lack of warmth, and so on. In fact, the therapist's countertransference had already led to her going out of her way to be helpful to this patient, who had sabotaged each attempt. In the group she became pulled into a debate with the patient, defending herself and feeling simultaneously enraged and out of control. After having ignored the rest of the group, all of whom had remained silent and some of whom had left the room, the therapist abruptly turned the discussion around to the other patients and refused to reply to the complaining patient at all, thereby enacting the very rejection of which he complained. The patient left the room while the therapist attempted in vain to get other group members to talk about subjects unrelated to the incident that had just occurred.

In the supervisory group following the session, the therapist said that she had been aware of her feelings but had felt totally unable to control them, particularly the final rejection of the patient. As the supervisory group had shared their own feelings of frustration in observing the interaction, I asked them to imagine how frustrated the patient must feel, and how sad it was that someone could be so compelled to make people hate him. The therapist became able to identify with the patient's frustrated wishes for contact as well as with the fears that caused him to push her away. She also realized that her overly helpful stance with the patient was derived more from her guilt than from a clear sense of what the patient could actually use. The supervisory group helped to remind her that she had forgotten the rest of the patients in the group, and that in fact she was not facilitating the difficult patient's integration into the group but rather felt personally responsible for handling all his complaints.

In the next group session, when the patient again began to complain, the therapist said, "It hurts you to feel so disappointed in me." The patient's demeanor became markedly softer and, for a moment experiencing the contact he had thwarted thus far, he brought up material about his relationship with his disturbed mother which to that point had been kept out of the group. Other group members then became more directly involved with this patient by bringing up associations about mothers. One woman, a mother herself, defended an idealized view of her mother. The therapist did not interpret the first patient's aggression, the second patient's denial, or the group's earlier silence, as it was clear that the silence had been a fearful one for some but an identification with the angry patient for others. Instead, she remarked, "It is often hard to say how we feel about people who are important to us. Mr. Smith gets angry, and Mrs. Jones feels she shouldn't complain." The intervention recognized the individual contributions while also linking them together, at the same time empathizing with the anxiety of the silent members and encouraging the group to share differing points of view.

Related to problems concerning aggression are countertransference reactions involving guilt. Despite the realities of severely ill patients and severely limited time and resources, the inpatient group therapist often feels pressure to have tangible evidence of a job well done, especially when the group is being observed by peers and supervisors. This can lead to the group's having the power to defeat and shame the therapist, which can then lead to a cycle of resentment and guilt in the therapist's countertransference reactions. Possible manifestations of this process include the formation of an indulgent, pursuing, all-giving attitude on the one hand (Searles, 1979) or to a denial of responsibility through a defensively minimized participation in the therapeutic relationship on the other.

Most psychotherapy training does not explicitly attend to or encourage the expression of feelings of hatred, disgust, or exasperation toward patients. Yet the suppression of these feelings is a major source of the empathic failures that so frequently occur in the inpatient setting. The concept of therapeutic neutrality should not include the omnipotent expectation that the therapist remain unperturbed and undaunted at all times.

Searles (1979), who has made a major contribution toward the open discussion of countertransference feelings, suggests that realistic and realizable goals for oneself and the group are the most important means of avoiding the need for guilt-induced defenses. Goals will of necessity be dependent on the particular structure and dynamics of each hospital unit, but three fundamental goals can be suggested: first, that the group members feel that their communications will be accepted and understood; second, that they feel *to some degree* a part of, or connected to, the group; and third, that they begin to see that actions or behavior are related to their feelings.

Such goals can bring the needs of the therapist and of the group members into closer harmony. For example, a silent member may be addressed by name in each session, and perhaps linked to other group members who are reluctant to speak, without the therapist feeling the burden of having to "get" the patient to talk. Patients who walk out of the group session may be described as anxious or uncomfortable, and as needing some distance from the group, without the therapist having to "keep" the patient in the session. As is always the case, the "shoulds" in the therapist's mind will usually interfere with the capacity to be fully "with" the group and to respond to its needs and communications in the immediate moment.

CONFRONTATION AND SUPPORT

Confrontation and support are generally considered to be important elements in the treatment of disturbed patients, and specifically so in group treatment (Horwitz, 1977). However, technical questions about confrontation and support are often clouded, for a number of reasons. First, there exists no clear-cut and incontrovertible theory upon which an equally clear-cut technique can be based. Second, decisions about confrontation and support are very directly related to the therapist's emotional responses to the patient or group, and thus are open to a wide range of interpretations and misinterpretations. Third, and perhaps most fundamental, confrontation and support are areas in which drive derivatives of the patients in the group can encounter a particular resonance or disharmony with those of the group therapist.

More specifically, confrontation might be viewed as a derivative of aggression, as it certainly is in the popular use of the word. In the treatment situation we speak of confronting the defenses, confronting the patient's resistant behavior, confronting the patient's acting out, and so on. These phrases all refer to something, usually behavior, that might be considered to be interfering with the treatment. The next step might be to consider confrontation to be indicated when the patient is doing something "wrong" or something the therapist does not like. One would not speak of confronting the working alliance or confronting the patient with evidence of improved behavior.

In a group of hospitalized patients together in a room with a group therapist, there is usually the potential for a great deal of disruptive behavior. Fragmented, or at best weakened, egos are only minimally available for active cooperation in the group. The potential for greater anxiety and less control in the group is likely to necessitate the use of more primitive, regressive defenses, so that it can become easy for the group therapist to experience such a group, or certain members of it, as doing the wrong thing or behaving badly, particularly if the group is being observed by other staff members. Even if the therapist's response is not so clearly judgmental, it is nevertheless possible in the face of the group's regression to blur the awareness of the group's purpose and to think that the therapist's job is to change problematic behavior in some way, with confrontation often playing a significant role in carrying out that task.

An example of the way in which negative countertransference reactions can be rationalized as therapeutic might be a situation in which a provocative or unpleasant patient is "confronted" about frequent verbal interruptions and is eventually expelled from the group, whereas an inoffensive or engaging "weaker" patient might interrupt as frequently but receive a very different response from the therapist. The therapist might then justify the rejecting, controlling response by citing the need for "limit setting" with psychotic patients.

This is not to say that limit setting is not a relevant concept, or that it might not even have been useful in this example, but rather to point out the relative ease with which countertransference reactions can be incorporated into technical decisions. Real use of confrontation has to do with clarifying reality, refusing to join the patient's denial, and demonstrating the courage to talk about disturbing issues. However, refusal to join denial does not mean aggressively assaulting it. This is where the therapist's anger can be rationalized as confrontation but is obviously not in the service of the patient (see Greenson, 1974).

As noted above, the group situation is uniquely suited to provide assistance to the group therapist who loses perspective as a result of a countertransference reaction. For example, in one group the therapist had been drawn into what began to sound like a cross-examination of a particularly provocative patient who had arrived late and announced that he did not feel like talking that day. In the midst of an increasingly tense one-to-one interaction between therapist and patient, another patient, who had been completely silent and who was generally considered to be too psychotic to understand what was going on, made her only contribution to the group: a loud, sighing yawn. She was unable to say anything about what she was feeling and returned immediately to her silent status, but her interruption of the transference-countertransference struggle served to alert the therapist that perhaps he had lost touch with the rest of the group.

The same argument just made regarding confrontation applies also to the use of support. Perhaps even more errors can be masked by what are called "supportive" techniques, as they overtly reflect libidinal drive derivatives that often are more consciously acceptable to us as rationales for therapeutic activity—e.g., "caring for" the members of the group, being "accepting," and other apparently positive activities. I say "apparently" positive because of the likelihood of unconscious aggression behind pursuing and overly giving attitudes toward patients (Searles, 1979).

Support is often misunderstood to mean a passive acceptance of anything expressed in the group, including expressions of resistance such as lateness or disruptions, in the belief that the therapist is thus accepting the patients "for themselves" without judgment. Where real confrontation might be needed, in the neutral and empathic sense of recognizing, describing, and responding to the patients' communications, a passive therapist, however benign he or she might feel, is not offering support to the group in any way. On the contrary, such passivity represents an active abandonment of the group and the therapist's responsibility to it.

Other techniques often believed to offer support involve increased activity by the therapist, but not toward the goal of facilitating the group members' abilities to express feelings or ideas that concern them. Such techniques use a great deal of structure, including setting topics for discussion or limiting the areas of discussion to educational, problem-solving, or reality-related issues. Although such techniques can often produce more verbal material in the group, there is a real question as to whether this is more for the group's benefit or for that of the therapist, who may be measuring his or her effectiveness by the amount of talking that occurs or by the sense that the patients are "learning" something.

For example, in a group that was persistently reluctant to talk because of fears of aggressive impulses within and between group members, the therapist, feeling the resistance, had a strong urge to suggest external or superficial events as subjects the group might be able to discuss. It emerged in the supervisory group that this urge was related to countertransference feelings in the therapist which would have abated had the group been willing to cooperate and produce some material. Aside from wanting to avoid his own feelings of imcompetence, the therapist wished to demonstrate to the group that they could trust him because of his helpful and supportive approach. In fact, if he had gone along with his urge to circumvent the resistance and the group's fears, he might have given them even less reason to trust his ability to accept and deal with their aggression.

This is not to say that the group should not discuss superficial topics, or that such a technique might not have gotten someone to speak. If a *group member* suggests such a topic, the therapist's support consists of accepting the communication and attempting to help the group to recognize the meaning it might have about their feelings at the moment. However, if a group's predominant communication is one of paralysis and fear, the supportive function of the therapist lies in recognizing and labeling the feelings that may be oppressing the group members. Whether the group overcomes such a resistance will depend on the members' belief in the therapist's ability to accept and contain their aggression, not on a reinforcement of their wish to avoid such feelings.

A unique kind of attentiveness is required of the inpatient group therapist. Roth (see Chapter 14) has aptly described the almost overwhelming complexity of the multiple identifications the therapist must permit in order to maintain an empathic link with each member of the group and with the group as a whole. This necessitates a constant shifting of attention between the observable data and the cognitive and emotional associations of the therapist to this data, with the observing ego of the therapist monitoring and making decisions regarding appropriate interventions.

It is not surprising that the demands of this process, coupled with the demands of the patients in the group, can become overwhelming to the group therapist. It is here that the supervisory-observer group can serve invaluable functions: it offers the reassuring reminder that there are many ways of approaching a problem and undercuts the therapist's concern with having done the "wrong" thing; it creates an atmosphere in which emotional reactions to patients can be shared with an eye toward understanding their impact rather than suppressing or rationalizing them; because it is made up peers who either have been, or will be, leading the group or other groups themselves, it can be a source of support to the beleaguered group therapist (as in the case in which the therapist, after an extraordinarily difficult group session, walked into the supervisory group that had observed the session expecting to be criticized for mishandling the group and instead received a round of applause).

SUMMARY

The short-term inpatient psychiatric unit is a unique setting in which very specific variables place a number of demands on the group therapist. Lack of awareness of the impact of these demands can lead to the suppression or rationalization of countertransference reactions to individual patients and to the group process. Confrontation and support are techniques that are invaluable elements of inpatient group therapy but are extremely susceptible to interference from countertransference reactions. If technical decisions do not spring from empathy and neutrality, the therapeutic intent of the intervention may be subverted. It is particularly important to ask whether a choice of technique reflects a countertransference attitude that has been rationalized as therapeutic. The test of such interventions is whether they are based on an empathic response to the patients' communications and whether the group remains "held" within its boundaries. With hospitalized patients, this criterion is often measured very literally by their willingness or ability to remain in the room for the entire group session.

The proper atmosphere is as important for the group therapist as for the group members. For this reason, the focus of the supervisory-observer group should also be on the expression and understanding of feelings occurring in the group. Just as we implicitly value group psychotherapy and believe in its benefits by making it a part of patients' hospital experience, we should consistently apply the principles that make it work to other aspects of the hospital milieu. Since countertransference reactions are a permanent part of life on an inpatient unit, it is essential that the opportunity to share and discuss these reactions among colleagues be a permanent and valued part of the life of the inpatient group therapist.

REFERENCES

Friedman, H. (1969), Some problems of inpatient management with borderline patients. *Amer. J. Psychiat.*, 126:299–304

Greenson, R. (1974), Loving, hating, and indifference towards the patient. *Internat. Rev. Psycho-Anal.*, 1:259–266.

Grinberg, L. (1979), Projective counteridentification and countertransference. In: *Countertransference*, ed. L. Epstein & A. Feiner. New York: Aronson, pp. 169–193.

———Sor, D., & de Bianchedi, E. (1977), *Introduction to the Work of Bion.* New York: Aronson.

Gustafson, J. (1979), The large group meeting in a brief-stay in-patient psychiatric service: Toward the definition of a working model. In: *Group Therapy 1979*, ed. L. Wolberg & M. Aronson. New York: Stratton Intercontinental, pp. 117–128.

Harty, M. (1979), Countertransference patterns in the psychiatric treatment team. *Bull. Menn. Clin.*, 43:105–122.

Horwitz, L. (1977), Group psychotherapy of the borderline patient. In: *Borderline Personality Disorders*, ed. P. Hartocollis. New York: International Universities Press, pp. 399–422.

Kernberg, O. F. (1975), *Borderline Conditions and Pathological Narcissism.* New York: Aronson.

Kibel, H. (1978), The rationale for the use of group psychotherapy for borderline patients on a short-term unit. *Internat. J. Group Psychother.*, 28:339–358

Modell, A. (1963), Primitive object relationships and the predispositon to schizophrenia. *Internat. J. Psycho-Anal.*, 44:282–292.

Racker, H. (1968), *Transference and Countertransference.* New York: International Universities Press.

Roth, B. (1980), Understanding the development of a homogeneous, identity-impaired group through countertransference phenomena. *Internat. J. Group Psychother.*, 30:405–426.

Searles, H. (1979), Feelings of guilt in the psychoanalyst. In: *Countertransference and Related Subjects.* New York: International Universities Press, pp. 28–35.
Volkan, V. (1976), *Primitive Internalized Object Relationships.* New York: International Universities Press.

16

The Unwanted and Unwanting Patient: Problems in Group Psychotherapy of the Narcissistic Patient

BEATRICE LIEBENBERG, M.S.W.

In May 1908 Sigmund Freud referred a patient to Carl Gustav Jung with the promise that he would reclaim the patient in October. The two men discuss the patient tangentially in an exchange of letters (McGuire, 1974).

May 14. A very brief letter from Jung with an apology: "I have Gross with me. He is taking up an incredible amount of time. It seems to be a definite obsessional neurosis."

May 19. Freud replies. "Now to Gross! I can imagine how much of your time he must be taking. I originally thought you would only take him on for the withdrawal period [from opium] and that I would start analytical treatment in the autumn. It is shamefully egotistic of me, but I must admit that it is better for me this way; for I am obliged to sell my time and my supply of energy is not quite what it used to be."

May 25. Jung to "Dear Professor Freud": "You must be wondering why I am so slack in writing these days. I have let everything drop and have spent all my available time, day and night, on Gross, pushing on with his analysis. . . . Whenever I got stuck, he analysed me. In this way my own psychic health has benefited. . . . He is an extraordinarily decent fellow with whom you can hit it off at once provided you can get your own complexes out of the way. . . ." Then, near the end of the letter: "I finished the analysis yesterday."

May 29. From Freud: "I must say I am amazed at how fast you young men work—such a task in only two weeks, it would have taken me longer."

June 19. From Jung: "until now the Gross affair has consumed me in the fullest sense of the word. I have sacrificed days and nights to him. . . . Little by little I came to the melancholy realization that although the infantile complexes could all be described and understood, and although the patient had momentary insights into them, they were nevertheless overwhelmingly powerful, being permanently fixated and drawing their affects from inexhaustible depths. With a tremendous effort on both sides to achieve insight and empathy we were able to stop the leak for a moment; the next moment it opened up again. All these moments of profound empathy left not a trace behind them; . . . so that notwithstanding all the time and all the analysis he reacts to today's events like a 6-year-old boy. . . .

"I am afraid you will already have read from my words the diagnosis I long refused to believe: Dem. Praec. . . . He is now living under the delusion that I have cured him and has already written me a letter overflowing with gratitude. . . . For me this experience is one of the harshest in my life. . . . Should Gross turn to you later, please don't mention my diagnosis: I hadn't the heart to tell him."

June 21. Freud replies: "I have a feeling I should thank you most vigorously—and so I do—for your treatment of Otto Gross. The task should have fallen to me but my egoism—or perhaps I should say my self-defense mechanism—rebelled against it."

June 26. From Jung: "I wish Gross could go back to you, . . . not that I want to inflict a Gross episode on you too, but simply for the sake of comparison."

When I review the patients with severe narcissistic pathology in my groups, many of them must be seen as analytic failures not unlike Otto Gross. In analysis they showed poor reality testing. They heard interpretations as criticism. They became more disorganized on the couch. They were diagnosed as borderline cases and deemed unanalyzable.

Neurotic patients develop an object-related transference that is considered analyzable. Where object transferences are absent the patients are thought of as unanalyzable, unmanageable, interminable (Roth, 1982). Borderline patients do not develop object transferences. Instead they erect narcissistic defenses that are particularly resistant to treatment. Weigert (1970) suggests that "narcissistic defenses, particularly those of a negative malignant kind, offer the greatest resistance to psychoanalytic therapy" (p. 119).

The countertransference so vividly revealed in the Freud-Jung exchange regarding Gross has its counterpart in the group therapist's response to the narcissistic group patient. Roth discusses countertransference phenomena with borderline and narcissistic patients. The initial manic stage is followed by one of depression and hopelessness (Roth, 1980).

A colleague talked with me about a crisis in his group. He had a thriving, cohesive group until he added a narcissistic woman. Now he feared the demise of his group. His patient had already left one therapy group; this was her second. Although initially she bubbled with vitality and sparked the entire group, she then became demanding, greedy, and contemptuous. She monopolized each session and enlisted two male members as an outside support group. She accused the therapist of jealousy, and he reacted by being jealous. The therapist began to feel the way the patient perceived him; the "escalating cycle was set in motion" (Horwitz, 1983).

He confessed that she owed him a considerable amount of money, which only added to his resentment. It was another indication that he had let himself become involved in the patient's transference. He abandoned all attempts at objectivity: "I want the guys in group to drum her out." Shortly after, he reported that she had left the group. "I know I should feel defeated," he said, "but I feel wonderful. What a relief."

Although there is a tendency to derogate our therapeutic failures as patients who are too manipulative, passive-aggressive, or narcissistic (Schafer, 1983); the experience of my colleague is an indicator of the potency of the patient.

What makes the work with the narcissistic patient different from our work with other patients? One can delineate three major areas: listening, empathy, and ambivalence.

LISTENING

Sympathetic listeners are extremely helpful for borderline and narcissistic patients in group. Therapists must be alert, however, to what can become ritualized support that avoids areas of conflict (Lichtenberg, 1981). Therapists are unable to monitor such activity when they stop listening.

Meg, a petite and pretty woman in her mid-forties, had been in analysis for three years. This was followed by marital therapy with the same analyst. Earlier, she had had two short bouts of psychotherapy with therapists whose names she could not recall. She had tried various drugs under the supervision of a psychopharmacologist for tension and depression. She complained that the drugs gave her chest pains and a fast pulse.

She had weekly appointments with her internist, her gynecologist, the psychopharmacologist, a gastroenterologist, an immunologist, and a nutritionist who was studying her flora. She deplored the lack of coordination among her doctors. She was angry that they did not sit down together to discuss her case and that she had to wait for all of them to return her phone calls. She felt helplessly dependent on them but perversely triumphant when she was sent on to yet another specialist. Ganzarain similarly describes a patient who devalues her therapist and thus feels triumphant (Ganzarain, 1983).

She gave an amorphous description of her mother, a remote and exacting woman dedicated to the church. "Daddy" was dismissed as "poor sweet thing." Her husband was portrayed as bungling and vaguely penitential. She had never been sexually interested in him and viewed their marriage as an act of malice directed against her.

In the group she played the role of compassionate listener. Her red flag was waving but I was looking elsewhere. She began by asking members about their health insurance. Her husband's policy did not cover social workers. "It's so unfair," she said, "that a person like Mrs. L., who has been doing this for years and years, should not be included. They told me that they couldn't run the risk of covering someone without the training a doctor gets."

I did see the flag then. And yet again when she turned to each member to ask insightful questions and was delighted when one member guessed her to be a psychotherapist.

Meg continued her assault on me somewhat later when she reported that her internist said she needed more competent help with her emotional problems. He thought she was getting worse and that until she got her feelings out her physical condition would not improve. I could feel my hackles rise. "He asked where we were with my therapy, whether we were talking about my relationship with my mother. I said we never got around to talking about those things." I felt as if she had entered into a demonic pact to undermine me in the group. My memory is that I stayed silent.

Meg recommended that I read current self-help books on depression and marriage, but for the most part I was impersonalized. There was no one for whom she expressed real concern. Her doctors, her minister, her previous analyst, the group, and I were all interchangeable. My feeling of irrelevance was her own unconscious denial of personal relevance. It was as if we were the same person, as if she could not perceive me as separately able to help her (Searles, 1984).

She was my bete noire and yet she had a wayward charm. There were flashes of humor and pathos, and I would willingly suspend my foreboding that we were on course for disaster. There were gains. She was able to leave on a vacation with her husband without her customary trepidation, looked tan and vibrant on her return, and announced that they had made love while away and she had actually felt aroused.

The very next session Meg was rambling disconnectedly about her stomach pains. She questioned whether she was getting anywhere, whether it was the right group for her. She talked about a friend's therapist who allowed group members to scream and pound and throw things. She announced to the group that she had signed up for a weekend growth marathon. I did not bless this venture.

She declared herself a changed person following the marathon. For the first time she could get her feelings out. She had talked about her mother in front of all those people and she sobbed while the trainer held her. "It's not enough to talk like we do here," Meg said. "You need someone to hold you close and to just cry it out. We don't have that."

I was unable to cut through the bathos. The group joined her. Members began to assail the boundaries I had established, just talking, not meeting on the outside where they could be so much closer. "We never get enough time." I felt unjustly pushed out to the periphery of the group.

It was all reminiscent of Volkan's description (1976) of his patient: "Behind the narcissistic armor was a 'hungry infant' busy collecting narcissistic supplies" (p. 248). All the pathology was now masked as personal growth. The truths she had gleaned from the trainer made her feel authentic and real. The old narcissistic defenses were mobilized.

Encouraged by her trainer, Meg enrolled in the advanced pro-

gram. Self-mesmerized, she spilled her ideas for changing the world.[1]
I tried to remember that the grandiose self is maintained unconsciously, but it was all downhill from there. I felt angry, devalued. It
was an absolute nadir in the group. Meg left the group the following
week.

An outside report is a clear indication of what the patient would
like to establish at the present moment. I did not hear it. Meg
prepared for a rapprochement with her mother in the arms of her
male trainer. I lost sight completely of the role I fulfilled for her and
the role she fulfilled for the group. The group protected her fantasy.
Each individual in the group contributed to the tension because they
all harbored hidden wishes for a sexual relationship, as well as a
dependent one, and they feared my opposition.

When the group appears to be enclosed in an impenetrable
barricade the therapist must listen for what is being avoided. The
feelings of helplessness and loneliness in the group were not addressed by me. I was so intent on Meg's dynamics that I failed to focus
on the group as a whole, which would have illuminated Meg's
response as well (Wong, 1983).

Two years later Meg came to see me. Her husband had been
transferred and they were moving. She said nothing had changed.
She was disappointed in her doctors, disappointed in her relationship
with her husband. It could have been our initial interview. On leaving
she said, "You know, sometimes I wish you had made me talk about
these things. We never got around in group to talking about *me*."
Listening requires the participant-observer to stay therapeutically
objective. Only then can he be empathic.

EMPATHY

The therapist's empathic responses are crucial in establishing
patient empathy. Stone and Whitman (1980) observe that "participation in the group enterprise provides an interactional perspective
which may be as powerful as a personal historical perspective in
providing a basis for empathic understanding (p. 112). The narcissistic patient longs for empathy in the group, but fears it as well.
Warm acceptance by the group will frequently result in lateness or

---

[1]Freud (McGuire, 1974) in his letter of July 1, 1907, notes that Gross "wallows in
superlatives. Everybody is a 'blazer of trails', a 'herald of the new.'"

absence the following week. In the group, members have the opportunity to "examine the interactive precursors of narcissistic injury" (Stone and Whitman, 1980, p. 112).

Empathizing, Schafer (1983) points out, stirs up conscious hope when defensively none is wanted: "Being the object of empathizing can be disturbingly over-stimulating especially when, consciously or unconsciously, the analysand invests it with erotic significance, homosexual or castrating significance" (p. 49). Stone and Whitman describe the members' fear of merger and loss of self. When the therapist allows temporary identification with this fear it can be processed and used empathically.

The pain in experiencing human warmth, interest, or concern is illustrated in Rod's interaction with group members. Rod begins to talk, even before he sits down, about the pressure he is under at work, that he cannot afford the time to listen to other people's problems, which have no interest for him. "I didn't want to come today." The men question him about his campaign efforts on behalf of a local candidate and he responds, still with anger, that he should be back in his office. Gradually he reveals that he is concerned about his inability to spend more time with his children and his wife.

Members listen to him sympathetically, and he becomes sad. He wants the group to tell him that he is important to them. The men, in particular, applaud him for coming. He says at the end of the session that he is also glad he came. He feels so much better. But he is not sure he will be able to make it next week.

In another group Susan announces that she has to fly to Atlanta. She is terrified of airplanes and dates her fear to a harrowing flight during a thunderstorm when she was a child. Her earliest memory, however, is waiting with her older brother at the airport for her parents to arrive. She watched as her mother came toward her, pushing her father in a wheelchair. His face was partially paralyzed; he was not the father she remembered. Her mother wept as she greeted her. From then on Susan considered herself alone. Her father required the mother's constant care, and Susan was left to her brother.

Her ties to the group were tenuous, and she would frequently mishear what people said. In this particular session the group was responsive. Various members talked about their own white-knuckle flights, exploring their mutual fears. The discussion proved longer than the impending flight, but they stayed warmly supportive.

Susan heard their anecdotes as unrelated to her, proof of their insensitivity, their unwillingness to "give to her" when she had been so giving to all of them. Susan's barrage of criticism was a defense against feeling vulnerable and dependent. She would not believe that people could really care about her, and her fear was the ultimate fear of fragmentation of the self.

In both these examples the patients counteract the threat of empathy. It is the therapist's task to enable the patient and the group to understand this fear of what is most desired. Members react against the rejection of their empathic feelings. The therapist may also forgo his analytic stance. Jung (McGuire, 1974) refers to Gross as "a bitter experience." In his letter of June 4, 1909, he writes, "To none of my patients have I extended so much friendship and from none have I reaped so much sorrow."

AMBIVALENCE

The neurotic patient recalls old transference-linked memories and can then integrate them into the rest of his life (Stanton, 1984). With the borderline patient it is a question not of the recovery of unconscious material but of his becoming aware of and integrating separate and emotionally independent ego states (Schulz, 1984).

Gradually, often obliquely, the narcissistic patient reveals the events in his life, past and present. Much remains tentative and fragmentary. Considerable repetition is needed before the patient begins to see a pattern. Schulz (1984) points out that integration is not achieved at once or with finality. Splitting and all-or-none stances alternate with increasing ambivalence.

Stephanie is a patient who illustrates the tortuous path to integration. Stephanie had a history of unilateral congenital glaucoma which had been corrected by surgery when she was an infant, but her eyes were noticeably asymmetric. She had described herself as a graceless, short-sighted child always aware of the embarrassment her thick glasses caused her mother. During large family celebrations she was permitted to escape to the movies.

For several weeks Stephanie immobilized the group with her threats to leave. Finally Frank told her that she had taken enough time without any benefit to her or to the group. "You really don't want to listen to anybody else," he said.

She glanced at the clock. We were one minute away from ending.

She got up and screamed that she had taken as much shit from Frank as she intended to take and flounced out.

She called me the following week to tell me that she would not be coming back to group that night or ever. I told her that she was too important to the group to stop so precipitously. She said, "Fuck the group," that she was sick of taking Frank's shit and that she was being set up once again by me. We had now used up my ten-minute interval between patients and I asked her to call me before my next hour.

The next call included more scabrous comments about Frank and a few chilling glimpses into my own character. Feeling pretty frazzled by then, I said with some astringency that she had to come tonight. She would have my help in saying goodbye. Despite the panic in her voice I kept from wobbling.

Members were relieved to see her. She looked strained, but the semaphoric waving of the scarf she held expressed belligerence and disdain. "She set me up," she said, explaining that she had been forced to come to say goodbye. "There was no way I was coming back."

There was an uneasy disquietude. Members were subdued. Someone asked if this was to be her last session. She gave an incoherent explanation about how good her life was now and that she could not get much further here.

Frank said he was sorry if he had pushed her out. He saw a lot of change in her since they had entered the group together, but he refused to believe everything was wonderful. Besides, he would be sorry to lose her. Various members spoke just as directly. I could feel her oscillations but stayed silent.

Finally Rod reminded her of the session in which he had wanted the group to tell him they were glad he came. "Is that what you want? Do you want us to beg you to stay?"

She dodged the question by inveighing against me, saying that she was not getting the kind of help she needed. More meandering followed, and then, surprisingly, she admitted that she wanted the group's attention, to be begged to stay. "The scene last week didn't bother me because you gave me attention."

Members expressed no jubilation. "It's not enough that you want to stay," someone said. "It has to be a real commitment. No more threats." They were like a group of latency children playing softball, where half the game is argument, forcing a player to abide by the rules and play fair. There was considerable back-and-forth until she agreed. With that, the group turned to discuss another matter.

The group situation evoked early experiences similar to family celebrations. Unlike the original family, this family wanted her to stay. And they afforded me a respite and held me to objectivity. Ganzarain comments that other members give the therapist a respite to regain and keep objectivity (Ganzarain, 1983).

The group forced her to see them as separate from her natural family, at least momentarily. Considerable work is necessary for patients to recognize that their inner worlds are dominated by archaic needs and that they do not take others into account as separate autonomous persons (Stone and Gustafson, 1982).

Often the patient provokes anger from both the group and the therapist as reassurance against an unconscious fear that she may harm them. Stephanie had acted on her ambivalence. She wanted to stay, wanted attention, but rather than be confirmed in her belief that others would be endangered by her she had to protect herself through flight.

In a long stream of words Stephanie viewed that session as having moved her toward some inner destination. "It's a fear of the intimacy and my own identity. I felt guilty that I was pushing you all away. I put out feelers and then I back off. I'm 38 years old and I feel like an infant. The part of me that feels like an infant is how afraid I am of expressing all of this neediness stuff."

It is a year and a half later and we have survived Stephanie's sarcasm and scatological language and her biting attacks. She is freer now to express her jealousy of the other women in the group, rivals for her father's attention, which in the transference she experienced with me. She is able to explore oedipal fears without first seeking my protection or evoking punishment from the group. She can talk about feeling lonely and abandoned by her father. Other women join her in halcyon memories of reading Nancy Drew mysteries and of all the other girl heroines who had their fathers to themselves, their mothers having gracefully died or receded. Stephanie acknowledges that her parents have their own relationship.

As the integration becomes established there is a sense of sadness and remorse at having missed something in the past. "There is a sense of estrangement including the perception that the therapist has changed, and a diminution of affective transference intensity" (Schulz, 1984).

DISCUSSION

When the therapist is able to acknowledge his own narcissistic investment in the group he is freer to listen and to decipher the unconscious meaning of the narcissistic patient's discourse. He pays particular attention to how the group listens and responds to that patient. Members who experience discomfort with that patient's remarks may interrupt with totally unrelated comments. Yet all the disparate stories and associations have a common theme. The therapist has the complex task of listening to each individual and to the group as a whole and framing an interpretation that will enable the patient to begin to understand the underlying dynamic source.

We become attuned to the meaning of empathy for each patient. The patient who receives empathy may fear merger and loss of self, that he will turn into "a puddle of ghee." The therapist may feel unable to maintain his separateness from merger-oriented regressive borderline patients. The regressive pull of the group makes it difficult for him to empathize with the individual or the group as a whole (Stone and Whitman, 1980). Jung (McGuire, 1974) writes, "For me this experience is one of the hardest in my life, for in Gross I discovered many aspects of my own nature, so that he often seemed like my twin brother" (June 19, 1908).

The patient who proffers empathy will react keenly when it is rejected. The empathic therapist may also feel rejected. When empathic failure results in anger or withdrawal, the therapist makes members aware of the process in group interaction. They begin to understand their needs and wishes and the ambivalence such needs engender.

There is no laser for narcissism. It is a zigzag process. We begin by listening to the patient and sifting what we hear, understanding the hazards of empathy, working through the narcissistic transferences, identifying the characterological defenses, and working toward the resolution of oedipal anxieties.

And if we survive that remorseless hammering and begin to see a change in the patient's self-representation that is more than just another coat of varnish, we can only agree with Freud (McGuire, 1974) when he writes to Jung: "Deeply as I sympathize with Otto Gr., I cannot underestimate the importance of your having been obliged to analyse him. You could never have learned so much from another case . . ." (June 21, 1908).

REFERENCES

Ganzarain, R. (1983), Working through in analytic group psychotherapy. *Internat. J. Group Psychother.*, 33:281–295.

Horwitz, L. (1983), Projective identification in dyads and groups. *Internat. J. Group Psychother.*, 33:259–279.

Lichtenberg, J. (1981), The empathic mode of perception and alternative vantage points for psychoanalytic work. *Psychoanal. Inq.*, 1:329–355.

McGuire, W., ed. (1974), *The Freud/Jung Letters.* Princeton: Princeton University Press.

Roth, B. (1980), Understanding the development of a homogeneous, identity-impaired group through countertransference phenomena. *Internat. J. Group Psychother.*, 30:405–426.

———(1982), Six types of borderline and narcissistic patients: An initial typology. *Internat. J. Group Psychother.*, 32:49–56.

Schafer, R. (1983), *The Analytic Attitude.* New York: Basic Books.

Schulz, C. (1984), The struggle toward ambivalence. *Psychiat.*, 47:28–36.

Searles, H. (1984), Transference-responses in borderline patients. *Psychiat.*, 47:37–49.

Stanton, A. (1984), Some implications of the complexities of ego-functioning and of self-representation for psychotherapy with psychotic patients. *Psychiat.*, 47:11–18.

Stone, W., & Gustafson, J. (1982), Technique in group psychotherapy of narcissistic and borderline patients. *Internat. J. Group Psychother.*, 32:29–47.

———Whitman, R. (1980), Observations on empathy in group psychotherapy. In: *Group and Family Therapy.* New York: Brunner/Mazel, pp. 102–117.

Volkan, V. (1976), *Primitive Internalized Object Relations.* New York: International Universities Press.

Weigert, E. (1970), *The Courage To Love.* New Haven, CT: Yale University Press.

Wong, N. (1983), Fundamental psychoanalytic concepts: Past and present understanding of their applicability to group psychotherapy. *Internat. J. Group Psychother.*, 33:171–191.

NAME INDEX

323

SUBJECT INDEX